Constructing Community

Constructing Community

MORAL PLURALISM
AND TRAGIC CONFLICTS

J. Donald Moon

PRINCETON UNIVERSITY PRESS

PRINCETON, NEW JERSEY

Library of Congress Cataloging-in-Publication Data

Moon, J. Donald.
Constructing community: moral pluralism
and tragic conflicts / J. Donald Moon
p. cm.
Includes bibliographical references and index.
ISBN 0-691-08642-7
1. Liberalism. 2. Pluralism (Social Sciences)
3. Community. 4. Ethics. I. Title.
HM276.M56 1993
320.5′1—dc20   93-12930

HM276
.M56
1993

FOR AMY

_____

Contents

Preface

THIS BOOK IS AN EXPLICATION and a vindication of political liberalism, which I will argue provides the best way to structure public life in a multicultural, morally pluralist society. In keeping with its central message, it is written in a voice that risks impersonality in striving for a certain objectivity and impartiality. For political liberalism shares with other forms of liberalism a commitment to an ideal of respect for persons, and a vision of political and moral community in which the principles that govern our relationships with others are principles that all who are party to those relationships can fully and freely accept. This view gives rise to an understanding of public life as a limited sphere, one in which we are united with others by genuine and deep ties of justice and mutual regard. But in our public lives we appear to others not in the fullness of our selves and our lives, but as human beings and as fellow citizens. These roles are important, even fundamental, but they are only partial, for they capture only certain aspects of our identities, and in some ways they may even obscure or disguise other parts of our lives.

Political liberalism, unlike at least some other versions of liberalism, strives to be deeply attuned to its own inadequacies and to the necessarily partial character of any account of how we should structure our relationships to others or understand our own identities. It seeks to remain open to the ways in which its own constructions may exclude some voices even as a result of its effort to be inclusive. It acknowledges that the principles and structures it advances may have consequences that stand in deep tension to the values with which it begins. And it recognizes that there is an important and essential connection between our private lives and our public commitments, that the voice striving for impartiality and objectivity is the voice of an engaged and limited self. It is because I am both engaged and limited that I reach out to others. But I do so in the idiom of political liberalism, in a voice of attempted objectivity and impartiality, because I have seen how the yearning for closeness and connection, for a certain kind of community, can deny the integrity of the other. Love can be a powerful force for controlling and defining another, all the more so because its undeniable altruism can blind us to the way in which it is also interested. Liberalism has often been criticized for its concern with justice and universality, which, the critics have argued, leads it to denigrate the values of community, love, and commitment. One of the deepest convictions on which this book is based is that we can realize those values most fully only when we aim at justice and universality.

There are many who have helped me as I have struggled with the ideas in this book. Wesleyan University has supported me in many ways. Its generous sabbatical policy enabled me to take a year off, in which I was able to do most of the writing, and without which it would never have been done. The staff of the Wesleyan library has been unfailingly helpful and attentive and has made some of the most frustrating aspects of scholarly work go more smoothly than I would have thought possible. My work has also been supported by my students, who were often the first to hear some of the ideas developed here, and whose questions and puzzles helped me see the issues more clearly. The moral and intellectual seriousness of the students I have taught here, their curiosity, their independence of mind, make teaching personally rewarding and intellectually stimulating. Several of the chapters of the book grew out of talks and papers I have given on many different occasions, including meetings of the American Political Science Association and seminars at various universities, including the University of California at Santa Cruz, the University of Minnesota, Princeton, and Yale. I am grateful to the commentators and members of the audiences whose questions and criticisms helped me clarify my ideas and correct some of my mistakes. Chapters four and six are substantially revised versions of papers previously published in *Political Theory* and in *Democracy and the Welfare State* edited by Amy Gutmann; in each case they were much improved by the comments and editorial suggestions I received.

I owe more personal debts to many friends and colleagues. The late Mulford Q. Sibley first introduced me to political theory and taught me the sensibility that I associate with political liberalism, though he would find much to disagree with in these pages. Fred Greenstein introduced me to the profession and has been unstinting in his encouragement and support; no one has ever had a better mentor. My colleague, Victor Gourevitch, has been a constant source of ideas and stimulation since I came to Wesleyan. I have also learned a great deal from my long conversations with Alexander Moon, whose critical and thoughtful observations have helped me enormously.

Ann Wald has been a wonderful editor; she not only gave the manuscript a careful reading, but she also forgave my failure to meet deadlines with style and grace. She also asked George Kateb and Jeremy Waldron to be the readers for this book when it was first submitted, for which I am grateful, as I found their suggestions to be invaluable. Bro Adams and Alex Dupuy have read parts of the manuscript and have spent hours of time talking with me about these (and many other) ideas. Nancy Schwartz and Stephen White read the entire manuscript and made innumerable suggestions for improvement. Both Brian Fay and Peter Euben read the entire book twice, in addition to commenting on particular sections several times, often at short notice. I am particularly grateful for Brian's close and generous reading and rereading of the text, and his many suggestions for rephrasing and rewriting. The long hours I have spent with Peter, who disagrees with almost everything I have to say, have not only taught me a great deal about political theory but also about myself and about friendship.

I have learned much of what I have tried to express in this book from Amy Bloom, both from living with her and from her writings. Her fiction reveals lives of enormous richness, complexity, and ambiguity, and has helped me to see, more than intellectually, how limiting and inadequate any theoretical account of our lives must be. She has helped me to see ways in which we are many-sided, and how we can remain open to others without losing sight of ourselves or the ability to make judgments. I dedicate this book to her.

Constructing Community

Introduction: Political Liberalism and Plurality

MODERNITY, IT MIGHT BE SAID, has produced three distinctive forms of political and social order, fascism, state socialism or communism, and democratic capitalism, but only the last has proven to be durable. While it is obviously premature to declare the "end of history," liberalism—the political theory underlying democratic capitalism—appears to have gained a certain ideological hegemony in the industrialized world today. Although there are only twenty or thirty countries that can claim to be liberal-democratic regimes, liberalism has few serious ideological competitors. Ironically, the triumph of liberalism in practical politics is not matched by its success in the world of ideas. Many see liberalism as yet another member of a dreary series of oppressive ideologies. One of the most frequent charges brought against it is that it is incapable of accommodating "difference," that it imposes a sterile and despotic uniformity on its subjects, an injury compounded by insult, by its claim to embody the ideals of freedom and equality.

We hear this criticism from many quarters. Some focus on the claims of those who fare poorly on the market, who suffer poverty and indignity. Some speak for women, and others voice the demands of cultural and ethnic minorities, invoking the claims of multiculturalism against what they see as the privileging of a particular set of traditions and values. These critiques strike at the heart of liberalism, and in many cases are inspired by its values and by its successes. But they also strike home, for liberal politics has often been a politics of exclusion, in spite of its aspirations—and pretensions—to inclusion. More often than not its exclusions are rooted in an all too human failure to live up to its own standards. But sometimes these accusations cut more deeply, for many versions of liberal theory are guilty as charged. But the liberal tradition, I will argue, contains the resources necessary to answer these critiques. Although many versions of liberalism construct a political and social world that excludes certain perspectives, certain voices, *political liberalism* is inclusive. Political liberalism is committed to a politics from which no one is excluded, a politics in which the principles governing human relationships are fully and freely accepted by everyone who is a party to these relationships.

The recognition of difference is by no means unique to political liberalism. All political life, as Plato pointed out long ago, rests upon differences. No one is self-sufficient; no one is capable of meeting the range of needs necessary to survival, not to mention flourishing. And so we are born, live, and die in groups in which different tasks are performed by different people, among whom there is an "interchange of giving . . . and taking" (Plato, *Republic* 369c). Even if we were otherwise identical, engaging in different activities would lead us to have different experiences and perceptions, and so to appreciate and sometimes to value different things. Plurality is intrinsic to the human condition—though it may be significantly circumscribed among those who spend their lives in small, isolated groups which, because of their size, provide little scope for specialized activities.

Plurality is at once a boon and a problem for us. It is a boon for obvious reasons: people with different perspectives, skills, temperaments, inclinations, and values will respond to situations differently. They will see different options and try different strategies, thus leading to social learning and innovation. And when individuals' interests and skills are congruent with their roles, the "interchange of giving and taking" can proceed more smoothly than it would if we were all the same. Interacting with a variety of character-types, we can experience a many-sidedness in our lives, finding occasion to express parts of our selves that would otherwise remain hidden. And, at least for many, the kaleidoscope of human types offers a pleasing spectacle.

But plurality may lead people to reach different and incompatible judgments, giving rise to conflicts that can threaten survival itself. Some, of course, would embrace such conflicts, welcoming struggle as an opportunity for men (rarely, if ever, do they include women) to demonstrate their courage and will: to determine who will prevail over those who are so weak that they choose subjugation or even slavery in order to live.[1] But there is much that is false in this picture—not the least being the image of self-sufficiency it projects. For if some prevail over others, they do so not as individuals but as members of a group, and within that group they face the issue of plurality. To dominate others, they must be able to cooperate with each other. Even the masters need common understandings and principles to which they can appeal to regulate their own "interchange of giving and taking." Justice, as Augustine argued, is necessary even for a band of thieves.

---

[1] I refer here to a popular, though now discredited, interpretation of Nietzsche, which focuses on such themes as his celebration of "noble" morality and his parable of the lambs and the great birds of prey (1967, esp. 44–46).

The picture of order emerging out of the triumph of the few is also misleading, because it simultaneously insists upon using the idiom of domination and struggle yet tacitly seeks to legitimize the masters' rule on the grounds of their nobility or excellence. But if nobility entitles them to rulership, then their relationship to subordinate groups is not, strictly speaking, simply one of domination, but of authority. The weak are obligated, not simply constrained, to obey. It may well be, of course, that they must be compelled because their baseness or stupidity makes them incapable of recognizing the truth of the masters' claims. It may also be necessary to control the rage they experience at their own subordination and, even more, their secret acknowledgment of their own inferiority. The crucial point, however, is that the ground has shifted from the question, "who prevails?", to a question of truth: *do* superior courage and strength entitle one to rule?

Truth can be a great seduction, for it promises to solve the problem of plurality by annulling the differences in our judgments. Gandhi insisted that authentic and genuinely effective political practice was "*Satyagraha*," from the Sanskrit words *Satya*, meaning "truth," and *graha*, meaning to grasp or hold firmly. *Satyagraha*, then, is firmness in truth, a politics oriented not to overcoming one's opponent, but to overcoming the conflict situation itself by the parties' coming to an agreement that realizes truth, or *Satya*. The crucial premises of Gandhi's philosophy are, first, that there is an underlying harmony of interests and needs among all people and, second, that we can discover it by acting according to the principles of Satyagraha. It is significant that Gandhi's autobiography is entitled *The Story of My Experiments with Truth*.[2]

If our interests are to harmonize, we must come to hold only certain ends, to have only particular character traits, beliefs, and aspirations, and to reject others. Proper and permissible ends and traits need not be identical for everyone, but they must be delimited in such a way as to be complementary, allowing for the creation of a unified whole. Thus, the ideal of truth leads as if ineluctably to the idea of a politics of virtue, arranging the "interchange of giving and taking" in such a way that only the correct or proper range of human types will be produced. Our education and experiences must be designed to form us with the skills and character, the values and ideals, that will enable us to play our parts in a harmoniously ordered whole.

A politics of virtue has been one of political theory's most enduring visions. In this view, our aim as political actors should not be to provide

---

[2] For an excellent account of Gandhi's theory of nonviolence, see Bondurant (1965).

people with what they want but to give their "desires a different direction
... by persuading and compelling citizens to adopt courses [of action]
that would improve them," making "the citizens themselves as good as
possible" (Plato, *Gorgias* 513e). The idea that our political lives should
be structured to realize a specific ideal of human well-being and/or excellence appears in many different guises, a commonality uniting such otherwise diverse thinkers as Aristotle and Hobbes, or John Stuart Mill and
Marx. For some, the political association itself is charged with the duty of
educating citizens, deliberately repressing vices and passions that undercut social unity. Others envision a limited role for political activity precisely to encourage citizens to develop such virtues as self-reliance and
independence. Still others imagine a form of social life in which the conditions creating estrangement and opposition have been overcome, a life in
which the free self-realization of each person enhances the self-realization
of others, thereby eliminating the need for authority to make, and for
coercion to enforce, social norms.

The ideal of a politics of virtue is not confined to the airy realms of
political philosophy. To offer but one example, in a recent case upholding
a Georgia law prohibiting sodomy, Justice White argued for the Court
that the community could properly enforce its belief that "sodomy is immoral and unacceptable" for the law "is constantly based on notions of
morality."[3] And how, we might ask, could it be otherwise? How could we
ignore what we know to be true about the human good or ideals of human excellence in framing the laws and practices of our society? Where
else can we turn in order to discover a meaningful and coherent system,
one that can enable us to reach correct judgments on the issues that divide us?

These rhetorical questions are one-sided, denying the essential bound-
edness of each person—bounds that are also gaps between people. The
drive for unity and coherence they express can be deeply problematic.
Consider, for example, Rousseau's claim that, in a well-regulated society,
"when the prince has said to [a citizen], 'it is expedient for the State that
you should die,' he ought to die." Rousseau goes on to say that "it is only
under this condition that [the citizen] has lived in safety up to that point,
and [that] his life is [not] a favor of nature, but a conditional gift of the
State" (1978:64), so the citizen has no basis to make a claim against the
collectivity on his or her own behalf. In a similar vein, T. H. Green argues
that the criminal "himself recognises [his punishment] as just, as his due

---

[3] *Bowers v. Hardwick*, 92 L Ed 2d, 149.

or desert." Although his sense of justice "has not been strong enough to regulate his actions, [he] sees in the punishment its natural expression" (1967:186).

But can we hope for such unity, such coherence? It is difficult to see how mutuality could exist between the judge and the criminal. The criminal's pain will often overwhelm his or her reason, his or her ability to view the situation from the point of view of the judge. On the other hand, the judge and those carrying out the violence the judge orders will not experience the criminal's pain. For them, the pain will be secondary, and they will focus on the legal or moral principles justifying their actions. Because of the essential separateness of persons, and of our experiences, "There will always be a tragic limit to the common meaning that can be achieved" (Cover 1986:1629).

Of course, if we could get the protagonists in this drama outside of their customary positions, so that they could see the situation from the perspective of the other, they might be able to recognize the validity of the opposed perspective. Sometimes law students and other law enforcement officials are put through a simulated arrest and incarceration as part of their training, to give them a sense of what an accused person experiences. And sometimes people who have been convicted of a crime acknowledge the justice of their suffering. But they are likely to do so only when the law itself is acceptable in principle to the person who has violated it. As Rousseau put it, "It is only in order not to be the victim of a murderer that a person consents to die if he becomes one" (1978:64).

But plurality can take a more radical form, reflecting significant differences in the fundamental moral commitments and beliefs of different individuals. In this condition of moral pluralism, the drive for unity and coherence, the effort to impose a particular moral ideal, will itself be a source of violence and suffering, undermining rather than enhancing mutuality. Sometimes this violence will be massive and widespread, as it was in the religious wars of the sixteenth and seventeenth centuries and in the Stalinist effort to construct a socialist society in our own time. Sometimes it will be more subtle, though no less pervasive and brutal in its own way, resting as much or more on informal social sanctions than overt coercion, as it does in the repression of homosexuality.

Liberalism has a complex relationship to moral pluralism. With its commitments to tolerance and freedom, it seeks to provide social space, that is, liberty, for individuals and groups to pursue their own ideals, restricting the scope of political decision as much as possible to matters that must be decided through collective, authoritative processes. But historically liberalism has also offered a unified vision of the good life, and so it also partakes of a politics of virtue, aiming to organize society to achieve such overarching moral goods as autonomy and individuality. And it too can become a party to political violence and imposition—for example, when regimes seek to impose rules of property and contract on societies accustomed to communal forms of organization, thereby destroying a cherished way of life.

In this book I will present and defend what I will call political liberalism,[4] which differs from other varieties of liberalism in rejecting the idea that society should be politically ordered in such a way as to realize a particular vision of the appropriate ends of human life. Political liberalism is a response to moral pluralism. It does not break with the ideal of truth, but it seeks to build moral and political community only on those truths that can be and are shared by all its members. Political liberalism differs from other forms of liberalism because it takes political community itself as an aim, and not the realization of a particular vision of human flourishing or human excellence. Many liberals take autonomy, the protection of rights, or the satisfaction of individual wants, as the objectives or values that the practices and institutions of society ought to realize. Political liberalism also differs from other versions of liberal theory in that it does not claim a universal validity founded on enduring features of the human condition. On the other hand, it does not endorse moral relativism. It is best understood as a strategy for constituting political order under conditions of moral pluralism, a strategy that seeks to "bracket" the differences among individuals and groups in the search for common values and principles on the basis of which their "interchange of giving and taking" can be regulated in a way that is fully acceptable to each.

Explaining the strategy of political liberalism is the task of this work, but perhaps the best way of approaching it is to think of political liberalism as a generalization of the broad approach Locke took in arguing for religious toleration three hundred years ago. Rather than using political authority to enforce and promote religious truth, Locke advocated limiting the scope of political authority to what he called "civil interests," which could, he believed, be regulated by rules that would be at least generally acceptable to people of any religious persuasion. To make this strategy work, however, all citizens must acknowledge a duty of toleration: "No private person has any right in any manner to prejudice an-

---

[4] In using this term I follow the example of Rawls in his more recent writings.

other person in his civil enjoyments because he is of another church or religion" (1955:24).[5]

In taking this approach Locke in effect broke with a long tradition of political theorizing, central to which is the idea that the purpose of the political association is to direct and organize social life to promote the human good. Different theorists advance different understandings of the human good because they hold different conceptions of the self, and these conceptions ground the values on which a political vision is based, explaining why a society realizing this vision will enable its members to enjoy lives that are worthy and fulfilling. Any vision of political life will incorporate some understanding of the self, including an account of basic human capacities and needs (which may, of course, be seen as historically and socially conditioned). Most political theories are based upon a rather "full" conception of the person, grounding a more or less complete ideal of human well-being and excellence, and prescribe a form of social life that will enable that ideal to be achieved.

Because political liberalism seeks to provide space for moral diversity, it does not offer a comprehensive view of the human good or a particular ideal of human excellence. In order to provide justifiable rules governing the public aspects of our lives, and to define the scope of liberty within which individuals can pursue their different visions, political liberalism must be committed to a limited, but widely shared, set of values and principles. These common values will be incomplete: a full moral life will necessarily have to incorporate other aims besides those of political liberalism. The common values will be based only on a "thin" conception of the self, one that abstracts a set of common elements from the contrasting views of the person held by different members of a society. As I will show below, the concept of oneself as an agent is central to the strategy of political liberalism, serving to ground many of the principles and practices of political liberalism.

Many of the criticisms of political liberalism are based upon a misunderstanding of its "thin" conception of the self. Because they conceive of political liberalism on the model of other political theories, critics reject the liberal self on the grounds that it cannot account for the whole of our moral lives. They fail to realize that it is not intended to do so, that it is purposely a partial and incomplete understanding of the self, designed to ground only certain aspects of our lives.

[5] This sketch is amplified in chapter seven below. For an excellent discussion of Locke's argument, one that is critical of the idea that it can be extended in the way I suggest, see McClure (1990).

9

Although it is only partial, the thin self of political liberalism is grounded in important aspects of modern life. In particular, it reflects the (relatively) high level of mobility in modern society, and the fact that many, perhaps most, of our interactions are with strangers or, at least, with people to whom we reveal ourselves selectively because their direct knowledge of us is highly limited. These experiences are so pervasive in modern society that the sense of oneself as an agent is not only an aspect of most people's identities (which is certainly not unique to modernity) but is likely to be of central importance to them as well.[6]

Although its aspiration is to discover values and principles acceptable to all, political liberalism recognizes that this may be an unrealizable ideal. Even if we could find principles and values that all could accept and that were sufficient for determining the scope of individual liberty and the ways in which our public life could be structured, their very partiality would mean that some people would experience their own ways of living as unfairly disadvantaged in a society organized in this way. The decision to use the liberal strategy is itself a moral choice, one that may exclude certain perspectives, certain experiences, certain ends and moral ideals. Thus, its aims are doubly limited: not only does it eschew the objective of giving unity and coherence to all aspects of our lives, but it recognizes that even within its own sphere there will be oppositions that it cannot overcome. It offers, then, a tragic view of political life and its possibilities, resting on the recognition of the inevitability of conflict and the experience of imposition on the part of those whose ideals are denied.

Not every conflict or experience of imposition is tragic. Although any resort to coercion involves a denial of mutuality, not every use of force contradicts the aspirations of political liberalism itself. It is only when the liberal strategy suppresses voices to which political liberalism itself seeks to remain open that we encounter its tragic dimension in its full form. It is unfortunate, though not tragic, if we find it necessary to use force against those who deliberately attack us; to suppress people engaged in "wilding"—deliberate, random attacks on others—is not tragic. A more troubling case involves conflicts between radically opposed, holistic moral outlooks, in which one side claims a privileged access to truth and so refuses to engage in a search for ways of living together peacefully. Conflicts involving certain kinds of religious beliefs may be of this nature, and they are obviously deeply troubling. Unlike the wilders, we can rec-

---

[6] Durkheim (1984) is the classic source for the argument that people come to see themselves as "individuals" as a result of the structural features of modern societies with an advanced division of labor.

ognize that our opponents are motivated by a certain kind of moral vision, even if we cannot recognize the good they so ardently seek, and seek to impose on us.

But there is a third kind of conflict that is even more troubling for political liberalism, for it forces us to recognize a certain inner contradiction. In these cases, we have deeply opposed, irreconcilable values, but the protagonists acknowledge the moral personality of the other and are willing to seek principles and rules that all can accept. Here political liberalism must acknowledge its own limits, for these are cases in which some voices must be suppressed or at least seriously disadvantaged, in spite of its commitment to be open to all points of view. In this book, I use the example of the conflict over abortion to illustrate this kind of case, but other examples might include certain conflicts over environmental policy and animal rights. One of the most poignant may be the use of state power to compel parents to provide medical treatment for their children, when that treatment violates the parents' religious beliefs. In such cases, our wish to protect the child's rights (and the goods that these rights protect) directly contradicts the goods that constitute the way of life of these citizens.[7] The main focus of this work, however, will be on situations in which the principles and institutions that appear to be necessary for the liberal strategy, and that are intended to be inclusive, function in such a way as to burden or even exclude some citizens, based on their possession of property or skills, their gender, or their cultural identities. These cases are taken up in chapters six through eight.

If political liberalism abandons the aspirations to the kind of unified moral truth characteristic of traditional theory (including much liberal theory), it does not join in the currently fashionable attack on the universalist emancipatory programs of the past, an attack that denies the validity or even the possibility of a universalist standpoint. What has been put forward as a universalist standpoint, according to these critiques, is in fact a disguised particularism—the parochial interests of a particular group, representing itself as the whole (often identified as that of white, upper- or middle-class males). This kind of argument, unmasking the false pretensions of a theory or group, has traditionally been used to project a new version of the truth, of what would constitute genuine universality. What is new—and disturbing—in some currently fashionable arguments is the denial of the possibility of genuine universality or commonality at all. This is disturbing because it represents the human condi-

---

[7] Frohock (1992) offers an excellent discussion and examination of many cases of this sort.

tion as one in which we are condemned to face each other over an un-bridgeable gulf of mutual incomprehension and hostility. In this vision—or should I say nightmare?—there is no possibility of resolving our differences in a way that we can each regard as valid by finding a standpoint of justice or truth binding on each of us, because there is no such standpoint.

Political liberalism acknowledges that there will be tragic moments in the political life of any society, moments in which its strategy for creating political community fails, in which conflicts can only be resolved through the imposition of the will of one party on another. But it denies that these moments are as pervasive as the foregoing picture suggests. If our differences make a politics of virtue impossible, our commonalities make a world of justice a reasonable ideal. These commonalities will be based on shared conceptions of fundamental needs, interests, and capacities, common understandings of the self and its situation. But because they are held by a wide range of perspectives, they will necessarily be "thin," completely inadequate to account for much of our moral and social lives. To the extent that they make it possible for a political community to be erected only on those truths that can be and are shared by all its members, a community that permits diverse ways of life to flourish, the thin selves of political liberalism enable us to lead rich lives.

Moral Pluralism and Political Theory

THE "STANDARD FORM" of a political theory can be said to be "Aristotelian," using this term in a broad sense. That is, the theorist begins with a conception of human nature, including an account of basic or essential human needs and capacities, such as the ability to reason, fundamental motivations, sociality, and emotional makeup, and a description of central human experiences, such as birth and death. On the basis of this conception, the theorist offers a vision of human flourishing or the human good—an account of the conditions that contribute to the fulfillment of beings who have these traits. This account will also contain a theory of the virtues, of the traits that contribute to a person's ability to realize the good, and thus it will project an ideal of human excellence. The theory can then be used to prescribe the kinds of practices and institutions that are required if these conditions are to be realized, given the motivations and capacities that the theory posits.

This is obviously a highly schematic model, one that does not capture important features of political and moral theories, such as their rhetorical structure or their implications for epistemology and metaphysics. Nonetheless, it can be used to explicate significant dimensions of many theories, including those of thinkers such as Hobbes, who are in other respects deeply critical of Aristotle. At the risk of caricature, we could say that Hobbes's account begins with a picture of the individual as an instrumentally rational being who is motivated to satisfy his or her desires or passions, proceeds to offer us an account of the human good or felicity as the "Continualle successe in obtaining those things which a man from time to time desireth" (1909:29) and, accordingly, an understanding of death as the supreme evil. Given his account of human nature, Hobbes argues that we can avoid the greatest evil and attain the maximal satisfaction of our desires only in a political order in which there is an absolute, undivided center of sovereign authority.

Hobbes, as is well known, would have his theory taught in the universities, whose graduates would in turn teach it to the common people, so that they would come to know "their duties" and accept the authority of the ruler (1909:395–96). The success of this theory—or any theory developed on this model—depends upon its ability to persuade its audience as to the truth of its conception of human nature and the associated vision of the human good and human excellence. As Nussbaum argues, the "Aristotelian conception believes that the task of political arrangement cannot be understood or well performed without a rather full theory of the human good and of what it is to function humanly" (1990a:208).[1] Societies that are characterized by moral pluralism, societies in which there are significant differences among individuals and groups in their fundamental moral commitments and beliefs, pose a deep challenge not only to this view of theory but to the very idea of just or legitimate political arrangements. In the absence of a widely shared conception of the good, based upon an understanding of what it is to be a human being, we would lack a standpoint from which conflicting interests and aspirations could be adjudicated, and specific policies and institutions justified. In this view, value pluralism is a threat to the very possibility of legitimate political authority.

Moral pluralism is also inimical to an important political value, what I will call political or moral community—a society in which social interactions and relationships are governed by principles, or speaking more generally, "considerations" that are freely accepted by the parties to the relationship. The idea of a political or moral community as I have just expressed it is not entirely clear. One of the main purposes of this book is to spell out what it means, why we should endorse it, and what implications it has for the ordering of our collective lives. But even understood broadly, the idea of political community would appear to exclude moral pluralism. Historically, those political thinkers who have generally been associated with ideals of "community" have seen diversity as a threat that must be carefully controlled. Rousseau, for example, envisioned a society in which differences among citizens were minimized by a restricted division of labor, small size, limited external trade, and an absence of class divisions, reenforced by institutions such as a civil religion and the censorship that encouraged and even enforced common beliefs and sensibilities. Rousseau, like the classical republicans generally, held that certain differences could not be eliminated, and so he denied citizenship to women. The very commonality necessary to any notion of community, it might be thought, augurs against diversity, at least of the sort involving fundamental moral and evaluative commitments.

In this chapter I will examine moral pluralism more closely and con-

---

[1] It should be noted that what I call the "standard form" of a political theory shares Nussbaum's concern with human "functioning" as a basis for moral and political judgment and evaluation, but my use of the term "Aristotelian" in this context is different from Nussbaum's.

sider a variety of responses that have been offered to it. In the next two sections I will consider two ways in which the issue of pluralism might be "dissolved," so to speak. The first is characteristic of many societies and involves what I will call "hierarchical encapsulation," a structure in which different groups are confined to particular places in the social structure. The second views pluralism as a matter of "separate spheres" and not as conflicting moral worlds. Neither of these moves, however, is adequate, at least for the world in which we live. I will then present a fuller account of the meaning and sources of moral pluralism, and conclude by considering the argument that moral pluralism can be overcome by developing a "correct" account of essential human capacities and functioning, showing that this hope cannot rescue us from our predicament.

Varieties of Pluralism: Hierarchical Encapsulation

Arguably, all human societies are pluralist, if only because everyone's experiences and identities are in some ways distinctive. Even Durkheim recognized that there would be individual consciousness in societies characterized by what he called "mechanical solidarity" (Durkheim 1984: 145). Many if not most societies include groups that are culturally, religiously, or ethnically distinctive. In what we might call "traditional pluralism," the boundaries and character of these groups are defined by practices and belief systems that are long-standing, their forms of political authority are at least in part traditional, and most members of these groups are born into a group identity.

Traditional pluralism includes moral pluralism when it encompasses religious differences (as it almost always does). Characteristically, traditional pluralism is managed through hierarchical encapsulation as the dominant group excludes all others from political participation. Sometimes a subject group will play a specialized role in politics, one that they are given precisely because of their status as "outsiders," but one that also renders them ineligible to compete for higher or more significant forms of power. Hierarchical encapsulation may also be combined with indirect rule, in which direct authority over particular groups is exercised by a notable within the group who, whatever his[2] traditional authority might have been, has come to owe his power mainly to his relationship to the

---

[2] I use the term "his" advisedly, since with few exceptions these roles were exclusively occupied by men.

ruling stratum. In such cases, subordinate groups are subject to their own laws and customs, which may be enforced in their own courts or in courts administered by the rulers. In spite of this limited autonomy, they are nonetheless subservient to the dominant stratum.

It is theoretically possible that this kind of society could be a moral community, if the beliefs and self-understandings of its various members were such that they all accepted the legitimacy of these rankings and exclusions.[3] But the possibility is only of speculative interest, since hierarchical encapsulation no longer constitutes a viable response to the problem of moral pluralism. To be legitimate, traditional hierarchies require a widespread acceptance of inequality and of the belief that certain groups are "naturally" suited to perform particular social roles such as ruling, domestic service, or common labor.[4] The "disenchantment of nature" that Weber so poignantly described has fatally undermined the worldviews that sustained such attitudes. Rationalizations of inequality can no longer depend upon ascriptions of "natural functions" to categories of people in a world where nature itself can no longer be seen in functional terms.

It might be argued that moral pluralism can constitute a serious problem for political community only when there is fairly widespread acceptance of fundamental human equality. Indeed, it might be thought that equality is built into the concept of moral community itself. The idea that people should freely accept the norms to which they are subject might be taken to rule out any form of hierarchy, particularly those founded on differences of wisdom or other virtues which subordinates—precisely because of their deficiencies—are unable to grasp or recognize. Plato, for example, did not think that most people could fully understand why philosophers should rule, and he resorted to "noble lies" to persuade them to accept a truth they could not directly grasp. For people to freely accept something, it might be suggested, requires that they have genuine alternatives, and that there be some public process of criticism and discussion through which their acceptance could be manifested and confirmed. Thus, no undemocratic society could be a moral community.

---

[3] Although I do not want to exclude the possibility of hierarchical societies being moral communities, I do not want to suggest that they generally are or were in the past. See Scott (1990) for a rich and compelling account of the opposition engendered by traditional hierarchies of caste, slavery, and serfdom.

[4] For a general discussion of social hierarchy and an interpretation of a particular case, see Dumont (1980).

I do not, however, wish to privilege a particular conception of freedom by interpreting the concept of "moral community" to rule out the possibility of, say, Plato's *Republic* or a traditional society based on hierarchical encapsulation being moral communities. These kinds of societies have always constituted the paradigmatic cases of "community" or *gemeinschaft*; to rule them out would be to use the term in a stipulative way that would invite confusion. More significantly, I do not wish to adopt a particular meaning of the key phrase, "freely accept." What it means to freely accept something is itself a highly disputed and contentious issue, and much political theory in the past has foundered by dogmatically assuming a particular interpretation. Thus, at least provisionally, I wish to understand the idea of a moral community in a very general way, one that is not committed to a particular view of freedom or consent, or that requires its members to be equal.

Varieties of Pluralism: Separate Spheres

There is a second sense in which all societies might be described as "pluralist," recently made prominent by Michael Walzer's *Spheres of Justice*. All societies include different "spheres of life"—clusters of practices or institutions organized according to particular values and norms. As we move from one sphere to another, we move from one set of role expectations to another; as we move from school to family, from work to political party, from temple to informal friendship circle, the values and norms that govern our behavior change. There is a certain amount of "compartmentalization" in all societies. Along the boundaries of the spheres we may find ourselves subject to conflicting expectations, and there may be difficult problems in determining where the boundaries are, or should be drawn. But in central cases the meanings are more or less clear and determine appropriate behavior, including the legitimate uses and distributions of the "goods" that are produced in each sphere.

Walzer has argued that justice in a society marked by a pluralism of spheres requires that the proper boundaries be maintained. The goods of each sphere must be distributed in accordance with their social meanings, and no one should be able to convert a superior position in one sphere into privileges in another. Illicit conversions, such as using wealth to acquire political power, violate the integrity, the social meaning of the goods in question, and constitute a form of tyranny.

The pluralism of spheres is quite distinct from moral pluralism; indeed, at least as an idealization, this model excludes moral pluralism[5] since it presupposes that the meanings of each sphere are shared by those who participate in it. Because these "spheres" encompass different aspects of any person's life—Walzer mentions (inter alia) membership, money, leisure, education, love, and politics—their meanings would have to be (almost) universally shared; otherwise, there would be no common meanings defining the spheres. No doubt, there might be some differences among individuals in the priority they assign to different aspects of their lives; some might emphasize the goods produced within the sphere of commodities while others devote themselves to the demanding tasks of love and kinship or the struggle for recognition. But there is no space in this conception for fundamental differences regarding the meanings and identities of the spheres themselves.

For example, Walzer distinguishes between the spheres of "money and commodities" and that of "security and needs." The former encompasses activities directed toward the production and exchange of goods and services "beyond what is communally provided, that individual men and women find useful or pleasing" (1983:103). The latter, by contrast, includes goods and services that are socially recognized as needs, and that therefore must be communally provided, for the "social contract is an agreement to reach decisions together about what goods are necessary to our common life, and then to provide those goods for one another" (65). Because "longevity is a socially recognized need" (87) in our society, Walzer argues that medical care must be communally provided and therefore removed from the sphere of money and commodities. Doctors should be "effectively conscripted" because they "serve for the sake of social need and not, or not simply, for their own sakes." There is "no reason to respect the doctor's market freedom" (89–90).

Although Walzer's argument is attractive in many ways, it is easy to see how deeply it conflicts with other understandings of the meaning and value of health care. Quite apart from the views of health care providers (who may not relish a life in which they are forced to become employees of a national health service), ordinary citizens may wish to be free to purchase health services that they find "useful and pleasing," even if they are not socially recognized as needs. Consider, for example, services

---

[5] Except, of course, in those spheres (such as religion in contemporary liberal societies) in which the social meaning of the sphere itself permits a diversity of particular forms of expression. See Walzer 1983, chap. 10.

such as contraception, abortion, cosmetic surgery, and unapproved treatments for cancer or AIDS. In all these areas we have seen deep conflict about whether such treatment should be available to people, let alone whether it represents a need that should be met through communal provision. Removing medical care from the sphere of money and commodities can effectively make it impossible for people to obtain such services. In a world in which everyone had the same understanding of the values served by health care (say, longevity), such a decision might not be experienced as oppressive. But it could well be oppressive in a morally pluralist world, where the values served by medical care were not universally shared.

Nor is this an isolated case. Walzer, for example, would exclude education from the sphere of money and commodities (though he would allow a limited role for private schools), on the grounds that an essential purpose of schools is the training of citizens (219). Others would place even greater restrictions on the sphere of money and commodities; Margaret Radin, for example, advocates rent control on the ground that part of the meaning of housing is bound up with a particular sense of personal identity and community which would be threatened unless the interests of those with established homes were protected (1986:362–66).[6] And Radin (1987) and others invoke similar arguments to show that sex and surrogate motherhood should be excluded from the sphere of commodities. In Radin's view, these decisions must be based on an account of human flourishing, and she argues that people should not be free to produce and exchange goods if doing so will adversely affect well-being. But in a morally pluralist world, in which people do not share the same understanding of the human good, such exclusions will be deeply resented by those who are denied the opportunity to advance their ends by entering into voluntary relationships with others. When such differences arise, when moral pluralism as distinct from a plurality of spheres develops in society, we cannot achieve justice by maintaining borders between spheres, for the borders—indeed, the very definition—of the spheres is precisely what is in question.

[6] Nor, she argues, should landlords be compensated for the reduction in the value of their property resulting from the imposition of rent control, "for reasons analogous to why it is inappropriate to compensate 'expropriated' slaveholders" (1986:367), since housing—like human beings—should not have been commodified in the first place. There is this difference, though; without the slaveowner, there would still be a human being, but without the commercial landlord, there might not have been the housing.

SOURCES OF PLURALISM

Even if moral pluralism characterizes some societies, might it not be illusory, reflecting mistaken judgments about the good, which could be overcome through instruction? The appropriate response to moral disagreement, according to this suggestion, would be to discover the "correct" moral position. That there is a single, unitary "truth" on which sincere and rational people can and will converge is a powerful and in many ways appealing idea. One version of it has been brilliantly characterized by Martha Nussbaum in her *Fragility of Goodness*, a view she sees exemplified in Plato's middle dialogues (particularly the *Republic* and *Symposium*). Nussbaum's Plato[7] insists that we must distinguish between what people take to be valuable and what is intrinsically valuable. We do that by using our reason to attain "the undistracted viewpoint of perfection," which enables us to assess goods not in terms of their role in satisfying our needs, but in terms of their intrinsic, objective quality (1986:156). As our sights are raised from the mundane, particular life in which we are sunk, we come to see that individual things have value only to the extent that they share or participate in what is objectively of intrinsic worth. Thus, in the *Symposium* Diotima leads the young person to maturity by helping him to see that the love he feels for another is directed toward his beauty, a beauty shared with others, and from there she leads the young lover to an appreciation of beauty itself. Eventually, he comes to lose his attachment to particular others, having discovered the true source of their value (179). Thus, in Plato's conception of moral knowledge, the only source of moral pluralism is error. Conflict, incommensurability of values, and particular attachments can all be transcended with the correct understanding of the true source and nature of value.

This conception of moral objectivity arises naturally from what we might call the "skyhook" model of argumentation, of which (Nussbaum's) Plato is only one example.[8] According to this model, the request to justify a particular principle or moral judgment is answered by providing a more general, higher-level principle from which the first follows.

---

[7] Nussbaum's interpretation of Plato (like anyone's interpretation) is subject to dispute, and my argument does not depend upon its interpretative adequacy. For an account of the *Republic* which sees it as acknowledging the "doubleness" of political life, see Euben 1990a, chap. 8.

[8] I owe this metaphor to the late Mulford Q. Sibley, who used it frequently in his lectures.

This principle, in turn, is justified in the same way, in terms of a third, even more abstract and higher-level principle. And so it goes, until we reach the "skyhook," some (set of) ultimate principle(s) which provides unity and coherence to our moral views. Our ultimate appeal might be to the idea of the Good, or to categorical imperatives that are dictates of pure practical reason, or to the presuppositions of some ideal setting for discursively settling conflicting claims to truth. But if these principles are to be adequate, they must be absolute, universal, and invariant.

It is easy to see the appeal of this model of argumentation and the associated view of theory. It offers to provide an objective structure to moral knowledge, and thereby promises to avoid the problem of subjectivism with its threat of nihilism. And by blazing sharply the distinction between what is allowable and what is not, it promises to provide a check against self-deception and backsliding—constant temptations in murky ethical worlds, where the genuine difficulty of distinguishing between shades of gray provides an opening for all kinds of rationalizations. Finally, at least in its "Platonic" form, it promises a kind of security. Once we apprehend the good, and recognize that particular objects have value only to the extent that they instantiate or participate in the good, we can transfer our allegiances from the unstable and ephemeral things of this world to their true sources of value.[9]

But this understanding of moral objectivity is fatally undermined by the existence of particular attachments and incommensurable values in our moral lives.[10] One particularly ripe source of moral conflict is the significance people attach to particular others and objects, and the emotional and passional energies they invest in them. In a trivial sense, all particularistic values might be considered to be a form of moral pluralism or at least difference, since they involve valuing different objects, but they do not necessarily give rise to the kinds of conflict that will undermine moral community. Plato's image of a polity in which all politically active members are stripped of the sensibilities and attachments that provide the bases for particularistic values is by no means the only viable model of political community. Indeed, particularistic ties can strengthen commu-

---

[9] I do not mean this as a caricature, as though this security can be purchased cheaply. To maintain one's faith in, and commitment to, a life oriented toward the Good, even in the face of deep suffering and deprivation, is enormously difficult, Socrates's equanimity in the *Phaedo* notwithstanding. The issues involved here are insightfully discussed in Winch (1965–66) and Fingarette (1978).

[10] My critique of this unitary conception of value follows Nussbaum's argument closely.

21

nity when they lead to an identification and attachment of the individual to the group.

A second source of moral pluralism is the existence of incommensurable values as integral components of the good life, values that may come into deep conflict with each other. The demands of friendship, for example, can conflict with those of political activity. The components of the good life are "capable, in circumstances not of the agent's own making, of generating conflicting requirements that can themselves impair the good of the agent's life" (Nussbaum 1986:7).

Incommensurable values and particular attachments are closely related ideas. Valuing particular objects and others is itself a form of incommensurability. When I value a friend, for example, I do not value her only for the concatenation of valuable qualities she possesses nor would I esteem her less if I were to meet someone who had an even more worthy set of properties—who was more intelligent, more thoughtful, more caring, funnier, or whatever. I value her for the person she is, quite apart from her wonderful qualities, and for the relationship we have, for the history we have shared or created together.[11] The Platonic position—and in this respect it is akin to much contemporary moral theory, particularly utilitarianism—commits an intellectualist error in viewing moral life in essentially cognitive terms, as a matter of basing actions on the correct moral principles, principles that can be intellectually apprehended, to the neglect of the particular attachments, shared histories, and emotional ties that constitute an essential part of the significance of our lives.

But particular attachments and incommensurability do not necessarily lead to moral pluralism, in the sense of fundamental differences in moral commitments among different individuals and groups. Aristotle, for example, recognizes the multidimensional character of our moral lives, but he does not appear to recognize, let alone endorse, moral pluralism. Indeed, his politics is premised upon a vision of a political community united in its concern with virtue and the human good. Although he insists that the city is made up of a plurality of individuals and families, and opposes the radical unity that Plato would achieve by abolishing family and property (for the ruling group), he does not see plurality as leading to irresolvable conflict among groups with opposed values. Aristotle is deeply concerned with political conflict, but his focus is almost entirely on conflict along economic or class lines. To the extent that he deals with

---

[11] Nussbaum discusses this point in several places; for a particularly succinct exposition, see her 1990b:117–19.

moral conflict, his concern tends to be with the opposition between those who are virtuous and those who are not.[12]

Moral pluralism does not simply involve the existence of what we might call "contingently" incompatible values—values that may come into conflict with each other depending upon circumstances. Rather, it arises when different people resolve these conflicts in systematically different ways, or when they come to hold ends or principles that are inherently incompatible. Moral pluralism exists when people hold opposed moral principles or incompatible conceptions of the human good or ideals of excellence, or when their particular identities and attachments lead to systematic differences on matters of policy.

An example of moral pluralism rooted in incompatible conceptions of the human good is offered by Charles Taylor, who describes four different visions of the ends of life. The first is a life of integrity, in which one commits oneself to acting only in accordance with one's own convictions, and to resisting all pressures to conform to "social demands." A second ideal is a life dedicated to *ahgape*, in which one aims "to associate oneself with, to become in a sense a channel of, God's love for men." Third, one may dedicate oneself to liberation, to bringing about revolutionary changes that will make it possible for human beings to direct their own lives and decide "for themselves the conditions of their own existence." Finally, one might seek to live a life of (secular) reason, which requires "the courage of austerity"—"the ability to adopt an objective stance to things" and eschew all illusions, all interpretations of the world that not stand up to "the cold light of science" (Taylor 1985:234–35).

Each of these ideals is a genuine good, but each excludes the others. The lives of (secular) reason or of liberation, as Taylor describes them, are deeply incompatible with the Christian ideal of agape. While there may be ways in which one could, to some degree, balance some of these ideals against the others, and to combine them in various ways, such balancing destroys the value that can only be realized through the dedicated pursuit of a particular ideal. There is a kind of grandeur, a kind of excellence, that is possible only with a certain kind of narrowness, a certain one-sided-

---

[12] Equalization of property will do little, Aristotle argues, "to prevent the citizens from quarrelling" since "the avarice of mankind is insatiable." What is therefore needed is "to train the nobler sorts of natures not to desire more, and to prevent the lower from getting more; that is to say, they must be kept down" (*Pol* 1267a37–41; 1267b1–9). To avoid destabilizing conflict between rich and poor, Aristotle would have the noble repress the base, substituting virtue for economics as the principal locus of conflict in the political community.

ness. A world in which no one chose to pursue an ideal in its pure form would not be as rich a world as ours, even though it might be a more comfortable, and perhaps even a more just world. Further, even if we suppose that the truth lies in a balancing of different values, of different conceptions of the good, there are many different combinations that can be rationally defended. There is no single pattern of "trade-offs" which can defeat all others in the tribunal of reason.

In a similar vein, Isaiah Berlin has argued that the deep "originality of Machiavelli" was his discovery—a discovery he himself did not appreciate—that "not all ultimate values are necessarily compatible with one another—that there might be a conceptual . . . and not merely a material obstacle to the notion of the single ultimate solution which, if it were only realised, would establish the perfect society" (1972:71). In Berlin's view Machiavelli accomplished this by his juxtaposition of two moralities, the Christian vision of a life of virtue and a pagan vision of "a good, successful, social existence" (71), two visions that exclude each other but that are "equally ultimate, equally sacred" (74).[13]

Moral pluralism, then, results from the presence of incompatible but equally ultimate systems of values, each of which commands a significant following in a society. It can also result from the existence of different patterns of particularistic attachment and identity. Ties of family, love, friendship, and attachments to land and home can give rise to moral pluralism when they lead to distinct group identities and significant cultural differences within a society. Efforts on the part of groups to give public expression to their distinctive identities, to organize their affairs in terms of their particular traditions and values, and to protect their integrity and existence over time by controlling education and residential or occupational patterns are among the most important and intractable sources of political conflict in the world today.

In any concrete setting, these two sources of moral pluralism—conflicting value systems and particularist identities—will inevitably be inextricably intertwined. In chapter four, for example, I discuss the different understandings of the value and meaning of life which underlie the conflict over abortion in American society today. Many of these differences

---

[13] Berlin's analysis may be faulted, inasmuch as he doesn't demonstrate the equal sacredness of these visions. His point, however, is that—while we may choose between them—both are visions of genuine moral value, and there is no third position to which we can appeal in adjudicating the conflict between them. Note that it is essential to Berlin's argument that both systems are of "genuine" value; not only is his position not a skeptical one, it is incompatible with skepticism.

involve understandings of gender and family which, at least in principle, are independent of particularistic attachments and identities. But because of the fact that these value systems have historically been carried by different social and ethnic groups, the conflict over abortion also divides people to some extent along lines of cultural and ethnic identities as well. To the extent that heterogeneous considerations overlap and reinforce differences, the conflicts induced by moral pluralism can become quite intractable.

It would, however, be a mistake to exaggerate the extent to which moral pluralism leads to conflict. In the first place, shared values are no guarantee of peaceful coexistence; people who value the same objects can, when those objects are scarce, come into conflict over their distribution. In Hobbes's theory, for example, it is precisely because people in the state of nature share a desire for "gain, safety, and reputation" that they are led to invade one another, and the state of nature becomes a state of war. When people have different aspirations, they may not only have fewer reasons to quarrel because they have less to quarrel over, but these differences may provide a basis for cooperative interchange. Trade, for example, is mutually beneficial, and (as a practical matter) is possible just because the parties do not have identical preferences.

Second, no matter how extensive the differences, there will always be significant commonalities. Moral pluralism, and the conflicts it engenders, will always occur in a context of some shared beliefs, values, and sentiments. These commonalities may be minimal when two societies that had previously had no relationship come into contact with each other; in a limiting case, all that they may share are the traits of a common humanity. But—a point I will develop at greater length throughout this book— these traits are by no means insignificant. Whatever hope there is of constituting political community in the face of moral pluralism rests on their existence.

But it will rarely be the case that the commonalities will only be those of a common humanity, for most conflicts occur in the context of more or less settled communities, where groups have encountered each other over time and share a framework of meaning within which their conflicts arise. Even conflicts that appear to involve the "clash of absolutes" (Tribe 1990), such as the struggle over abortion in the United States today, rest upon shared understandings and interests. Reporting on her study of a conflict over the establishment of an abortion clinic in Fargo, North Dakota, Ginsburg found that "at the practical level of daily life . . . the concerns shared by pro-life and pro-choice activists alike were apparent,"

25

both to her as an observer and to the actors themselves (1989:218). Both sides in this struggle were committed to "helping women with unplanned pregnancies" and wrestled with the "experiential dissonance between motherhood and wage labor" (219), which has come to be central to the lives of American women today, and which rests upon a host of shared experiences and values, deeply rooted in common American traditions.

Overcoming Pluralism:
The Appeal To Essential Human Capacities

If the conflicts engendered by moral pluralism are conducted against a background of shared beliefs and values—at a minimum those which are implicit in our common humanity—might we not appeal to those commonalities to find a basis for adjudicating these disputes? Perhaps the effort to employ the Aristotelian strategy has proven inadequate because it has been based on too narrow a view of human nature, one that is itself implicated in the controversies of a morally pluralist society; perhaps the strategy would be successful if it employed a suitably abstract or generalized conception of human nature. An account of essential human capacities, framed in sufficiently general terms to encompass cultural and historical variety, could be used to develop an account of human flourishing and, given the specific circumstances of a particular setting, to prescribe the kinds of institutions and policies necessary to realize the human good. Naturally, we should not expect to be able to reduce moral and political life to a precise science; but what we can hope for is a framework within which conflicts could be resolved and political community attained.[14] And this framework would be an essentially Aristotelian one, in the sense that it would specify a conception of human flourishing and evaluate political and social practices in terms of their contribution to the realization of that ideal.

Many theorists have offered sophisticated Aristotelian approaches to contemporary moral and political argument, ones that are self-consciously framed in such a way as to incorporate the wide cultural and historical variability in ways of life. Nussbaum has offered one of the most persuasive accounts along these lines, one that is based on "certain features of

---

[14] It has become a cliché to quote Aristotle's remark in the *Nicomachean Ethics*, that we should "look for precision in each class of things just so far as the nature of the subject admits," and so our objective in ethics and politics must be "to indicate the truth roughly and in outline" (1094b).

our common humanity," that grounds what she calls the "thick, vague theory of the good."[15] Nussbaum's list of common features includes: our mortality; our being embodied creatures with specific needs, possibilities, and vulnerabilities; our experience of pleasure and pain; the fact that we "reach out for understanding"; our capability to direct our lives in some measure; our helplessness in a prolonged period of infancy; our being "by nature social animals"; and our capacity for humor (1988b:48–49). Nussbaum is deeply sensitive to the cultural variations that affect the ways in which these common conditions are experienced in different times and in different societies, and insists that there is no pregiven, culturally free experience to which we can appeal to support some particular account of human life and the human good. But the existence of a significant overlap in the circumstances that human beings face in all societies provides a basis for articulating a universal account of the human good. With respect to each of these areas of experience, we would have to ask what would constitute "good functioning" with respect to it? In answering this question, we would be determining what constitutes virtue or excellence in each area (1988a:178).[16] Our answers, it should be stressed, will be defeasible in light of further experience, study, and reflection.

The purposes of this exercise is to define important limits to pluralism, based on our common human experiences. But a glance at the list of common experiences, and the indeterminacy of the notion of good "functioning," suggests that the limits are very broad. These limits can be narrowed by noting that there are two "architectonic functions," practical reason and affiliation, "which organize and arrange all of the others" (1990a:226). "Practical reason" serves to "link" all the virtues specific to particular areas of human experience. It is "at the core of all the functions" that are "definitive of who we are" as persons, for a life that is not in some ways directed by reason would not count as a human life (1988a:182; 1992:222–23). Further, distinctively human activities are "done with and to others"; when we plan our lives, we do so in a social context; we plan "with and to others" (1990a:227).

The centrality of practical reason rules out certain ways of life, such as "a life totally given over to bodily pleasure without reason" (1988a:182). It also imposes certain constraints on public policy, requiring legislators to provide scope for citizens to exercise reason; food, for example, should

[15] Nussbaum 1988b:48 and 1992:214. She has developed her theory in a series of papers; I have drawn mainly on her 1988a, 1988b, 1990a, 1992, and Nussbaum and Sen (1988).

[16] For a succinct statement of human functionings, see Nussbaum 1992:222–23.

not simply be distributed to people, but they should be enabled to "regulate their nutrition by their own reason" (1988a:183). More generally, this conception requires institutions and policies that will provide "for the adequate realization of these and other fully human capacities in the citizens" (1990a:227).

An obvious difficulty with this argument is that the term "reason" is notoriously open-textured. If we interpret it broadly, then it will do little to narrow the bounds of moral disagreement. Hedonists, for example, do not advocate that bodily pleasure be pursued without any thought or consideration of consequences or alternatives. And few political thinkers have advocated a political order in which citizens have no scope for thought and choice in how they act or in what they consume. But if we interpret "reason" narrowly, so that it comprises not merely a capacity to draw and act upon logical inferences but includes a substantive doctrine regarding the ends we should pursue, then the claim that it is "definitive of who we are" becomes deeply problematic—at least if the "we" is intended to comprise all humanity.

In general, each of the human functionings that Nussbaum describes is subject to differences in interpretation and so contestation. Because there are so many significant dimensions of human functioning, even people who share the same understandings of the individual dimensions may differ on the "weights" or significance to be attached to each in their accounts of a minimal, let alone a good, human life. The "thick, vague theory of the good" appears to be too indeterminate to settle the conflicts that moral pluralism can give rise to, let alone provide a basis for political community. To the extent that agreement can be reached on a more precise theory of the good, this objection can be overcome. But what reason is there to suppose that we can move from a vague theory of the good to one that is sufficiently precise to offer the guidance we require?

AUTONOMY AND PLURALISM: LIBERAL ARISTOTELIANISM

The lack of determinacy in plausible conceptions of human flourishing is exacerbated when a conception of human nature is advanced in which a capacity for autonomy has pride of place, as it does for many contemporary theorists, including Nussbaum (see her 1990a:234–37; 1992:224–25). Amartya Sen has advanced a conception of social theory in which human "functioning" and "capabilities" play crucial roles. Sen is critical of theories such as Rawls's, which focus on the just distribution of certain "resources" or "primary goods,"[17] because people differ significantly in their ability to translate such goods into capabilities. At the most basic level, people have different rates of basal metabolism, and so need different amounts of food if they are to avoid starvation or malnutrition (Sen 1990a:116; see also 1980:217–20; 1990b:49–54). Thus, what is important is not the resources we possess, but what we can do with them in terms of realizing our various ends, and so our focus should be on the capacities or the "freedoms people actually have" (1990b:52). Furthermore, Sen argues that we should not focus only on the conditions that people actually experience, because an essential part of well-being involves what Sen calls "agency freedom," that is, "what the person is free to do and achieve in pursuit of whatever goals or values he or she regards as important." In this conception, the value of freedom is not tied to the achievement "of something in particular" for "agency freedom is freedom to achieve whatever the person, as a responsible agent, decides he or she should achieve" (1985:203–204). This understanding of persons as agents goes beyond Aristotle's conception of agency and the importance of choice, which is tied primarily to the individual's choosing the right or virtuous action. As Nussbaum argues, this may involve the exercise of practical wisdom in balancing conflicting values and claims, but it does not extend to the choice of the ends themselves. And, as Sen recognizes, when we allow scope for the "different conceptions of the good that different people may have," we will be faced with the problem of moral pluralism (1990a:120–21).

Sen's endorsement of "agency freedom" echoes a common theme in modern, particularly liberal political thought, in which individuality and autonomy are held to be fundamental to human flourishing and/or vital forms of human excellence. The most famous, no doubt, is John Stuart Mill's paean to "individuality," which he describes as "one of the principal ingredients of human happiness," central to developing "the qualities which are the distinctive endowment of a human being" (1951:153–55). More recently, Joseph Raz has developed an account of the "morality of freedom" based on the premise that "personal autonomy" is "an essential element of the good life," and he argues convincingly that "valuing autonomy commits one to . . . value pluralism" (1986:424–25, 398). Following the "standard model" described above, Raz argues that "Govern-

---

[17] In Rawls's theory, the primary goods are certain "basic liberties" and opportunities, the "powers and prerogatives of offices, income and wealth," and "the social bases of self-respect" (see Rawls 1982:162; 1971:62–63). Rawls's account of primary goods is discussed in chapter three, below.

ments are subject to autonomy-based duties to provide the conditions of autonomy for people who lack them," and goes some way to specifying what this role entails (415).[18]

It would not be difficult to multiply examples of essentially "Aristotelian" arguments that terminate, not in a harmonious, integrated political order united around a shared understanding of the human good, but in a significant degree of moral pluralism—qualified, of course, by the acceptance of the value of autonomy itself. No doubt there are many sources for this understanding of human functioning, but one of the most important is Locke's emphasis on the "inwardness" or "subjectivity" of the person, which figures prominently in his argument for religious toleration. One of Locke's key arguments is that "All the life and power of true religion consist in the inward and full persuasion of the mind; and faith is not faith without believing" (1955:18). This stress on subjectivity, on "the inward and full persuasion of the mind," is akin to some classical and early Christian ideas, particularly the Christianity of the gospels where conformity to the law is devalued in relation to purity of intention and love for God. But in Locke, as Plamenatz has argued, it is developed in a new and distinctly modern form, as an argument for liberty of conscience, for "the right to hold and profess what principles we choose, and to live in accordance with them" (1963:1.49). If what is of value is the authentic confession of faith, then people morally and logically could not agree to vest authority over their affirmation of faith in any external party, including the "civil magistrate" (which could, of course, be the people as a whole). They could not do so morally, for that would be to alienate something that they have come to see as essentially human about themselves, namely, their capacity to reach their own decisions about their religious life. And they could not do so logically, for any faith that they would accept on the authority of another would not, by definition, be their own faith: "faith is not faith without believing."

This conception of the individual was an important part of the liberal justification for limiting the sphere of legitimate political authority: "The whole jurisdiction of the magistrate . . . neither can nor ought in any manner to be extended to the salvation of souls" (Locke 1955:17). Unlike the argument of the *Second Treatise*, the argument of the *Letter* does not invoke (or require) a hypothetical social contract, nor the positing of the "individual" as in any sense "prior" to society. Indeed, we only come to be individuals (in the sense of subjects who possess and identify ourselves

---

[18] Galston (1991) also offers an essentialist account stressing autonomy and the organization of political and social life to realize it.

in part in terms of our "inner" lives) because we live in a certain kind of society. But for people who have come to see themselves in this way, liberty of conscience, and the closely related idea of moral autonomy, are values of immense importance, especially for determining the structure and scope of political authority.

One of the ways in which "modern" conceptions of subjectivity and inwardness differ from classical or early Christian notions is that they involve a view of the self as a *particular* person, and a celebration, so to speak, of that particularity. The self is not conceived merely as an instance of a divine or cosmic spirit, a self whose particular qualities are accidental or inessential, and whose realization or good consists in the harmonization or union of the self with the divine or cosmic whole. Premodern notions of the self support (or have an affinity to) a conception of freedom as "self-perfection,"[19] according to which one becomes free to the extent that one is properly oriented in one's actions and character to the divine or cosmic order. For Plato, the Stoics, and many early Christians, the truth could make us free just because freedom is "internal," a matter of the proper or "just" relation of the soul to ultimate reality.

Most theorists who focus on autonomy break with this image by denying that the achievement of unity with something universal exhausts what is essential to a person. For them, a person's good depends upon his or her particular qualities and needs, and especially upon how one has come to see oneself, that is, upon one's "identity." Thus, they advocate a kind of freedom which Plamenatz calls "self-realization," which involves both "asserting one's 'identity,' [and] seeking to discover or achieve it." The person "who strives to realize himself seeks to become what he aspires to be or to achieve something that proves his worth to himself and to others."[20]

The scope of self-realization—the specific goals that one may pursue— is necessarily restricted by the recognition one owes to others, and by the claims that the community as a whole can make upon us (including obligations to provide people with opportunities for self-realization). But these constraints are compatible with a wide range of differences in ways of living. Nonetheless, all these ways of living will be shared ways of living—for at the very least we seek recognition from others for who we

---

[19] I take this term from Adler (1958); Berlin (1969:134) disparagingly refers to this idea of freedom as "self-abnegation," a term that obscures the moral ideal it represents.

[20] Plamenatz 1975:332. The term "self-realization" has been used with a great variety of meanings; this use is quite different from Berlin's (1969) where it denotes a form of "freedom" that is, by contrast to Plamenatz's, deeply illiberal.

are and what we do. But self-realization may involve breaking with established or traditional ways and finding (or founding) new communities to create and share new ways of life. Self-realization may thus involve a significant element of what we might call self-determination or self-creation. One does not, of course, create oneself out of nothing, or radically determine every aspect of one's identity or being. On the contrary, in determining oneself one consciously affirms and extends some aspects of one's identity in adopting certain projects and rejecting others. But in making these choices, one necessarily takes most aspects of oneself and one's situation for granted. Over time, perhaps, one might come to shape a number of important features of one's life. But this process of self-determination is as much a process of self-discovery as self-creation. Freedom consists as much in one's being able to affirm who one is as in shaping and directing who one becomes. This ideal, then, presupposes an understanding of persons as social and historical creatures with particular capacities and possibilities that they can discover and develop. Who we are and who we become depend upon our particular histories and the situations in which we have found ourselves.

The ideal of self-realization goes well beyond freedom of conscience or moral autonomy, for the aspirations and capacities one seeks to realize may not (and often will not) be moral imperatives. Self-realization may not be a matter of finding salvation, or standing on conscience, but instead may involve self-expression or the cultivation of one's own individuality. It may involve the formation of a plan of life—to the extent that one forms such things—involving the choice of vocation, friendships and marriage, residence, patterns of consumption, leisure activities, and so forth. It may also involve forming and living in accordance with a personal ideal of excellence. Thus, what is involved in self-realization ranges from the mere cultivation of personal idiosyncrasy to the deepest questions regarding the meaning and purpose of life.

A conception of moral autonomy and of self-realization can be found in most theories that conceive of the self as having, as part of its essential powers, the capacity for choice and self-direction, and that see the exercise of these capacities as an essential part of human flourishing. But these notions are not abstract conceptions that exist only in the imaginations of theorists, nor do they give rise to moral pluralism simply because they are propounded in political theories. These conceptions are widely shared at least within American and Western European societies and underlie the commitment of these societies to "individualism" broadly understood. People come to see themselves in these terms only as a result of living in a certain kind of society and culture, which has emerged from a particular set of historical processes. The acceptance of these values has important implications for the ordering of our political lives, because individuality gives rise to a plurality of possible ways of life within a society. For if people are autonomous, and if they value self-realization, then different groups of individuals will[21] make different choices about their basic aims and attachments. Of course, to the extent that the members of a society share this essentially liberal view of human nature and accept the value of autonomy, the resulting moral pluralism would tend to be seen as desirable, at least if the conflicts it engendered could be managed by principles based on the shared value of autonomy. In a society in which all were liberals, we could say that there would be "first-order" moral pluralism, because different people would pursue different ideals and goods, but there would be no "second-order" pluralism, as all would accept the centrality of the values of autonomy and self-realization.

However, there is no reason to suppose that the "liberal" conception of human nature would prove any less controversial than other views. Even if the liberal commitment to autonomy would provide a basis for political community in the face of moral pluralism, it would prove inadequate in a society where this commitment was itself in doubt.

PLURALISM AND THE POSSIBILITY OF COMMUNITY

The arguments I have been making for the possibility of moral pluralism do *not* appeal to any kind of skepticism about our ability to make rational judgments about the ends and purposes of our lives. I am not arguing that we do not or cannot know what is truly valuable, but rather that we know that (at least some of) the things that *are* truly valuable exclude each other. This does not mean that a choice among these values must be arbitrary (which would involve a kind of skepticism at a higher level). For an individual may have good reasons for making a particular choice, for committing himself or herself to some way of life at the expense of others. As long as the conditions of our lives are variable, as long as the considerations that can be urged in favor of one course over another are indeterminate, or subject to further criticism, as long as our choices have to be true to our deeply felt emotional commitments as well as to our judgments, different people will properly and rationally make different choices.[22]

---

[21] This is not a conceptual necessity, of course, but as a practical matter, different choices will be made reflecting different experiences and life situations.

[22] The issue of skepticism is addressed more fully in chapter four below.

Moral pluralism is rooted in our particular attachments and identities, in our emotional and passional natures, in the incommensurability of values, and in the values of autonomy and individuality. Where these values are held and are effective in social practices, we can expect that they will encourage the development of differences among people in other moral commitments as well. They will do this in part because a society that holds these values will tend to eschew certain mechanisms of social control that reinforce uniformity, ranging from legal censorship and established religious institutions to certain child-rearing practices. And to the extent that people are free to choose their own commitments and ways of life, their own vocations and religious beliefs, their own partners for marriage or life-commitment, to form their own political beliefs and allegiances, and to travel and move freely, they are apt to make different choices expressing different moral commitments and beliefs. Because these values are adopted in part in response to moral pluralism, we can see that moral pluralism will tend to be self-sustaining. And, as Berlin has argued, attempts to impose some "correct" choice, some "final solution," will necessarily be resented as domination rather than celebrated as liberation:

> One belief, more than any other, is responsible for the slaughter of individuals on the altars of the great historical ideals—justice or progress or the happiness of future generations, or the sacred mission or emancipation of a nation or race or class, or even liberty itself, which demands the sacrifice of individuals for the freedom of society. This is the belief that somewhere, in the past or in the future, in divine revelation or in the mind of an individual thinker, in the pronouncements of history or science, or in the simple heart of an uncorrupted good man, there is a final solution. This ancient faith rests on the conviction that all the positive values in which men have believed must, in the end, be compatible, and perhaps even entail one another. (1969:167)

Berlin's observation points to the most fundamental reason why the Aristotelian strategy is inadequate. The problem is not simply the difficulty of securing agreement on the specific set of capabilities involved in a conception of human flourishing, nor of making them sufficiently determinate that they can serve even as a framework for normative judgment. The real problem is the very way in which the Aristotelian strategy structures the issue of political judgment itself. If the point of a policy or institution is to cultivate the qualities that conduce to human flourishing, as the Aristotelian strategy holds, and if there are different views of what constitutes human flourishing, then politics becomes a contest among those different views. Either the differences must be overcome through the participants coming to a deeper understanding of the human good, or one side must lose. Unfortunately, given the reasons for doubting that agreement is possible even in principle, particularly for those who accept choice and self-determination as important human capacities, this strategy is an invitation to a conflict in which there are likely to be winners and losers. What we require is a strategy—the strategy of political liberalism—that offers an alternative formulation of the problem of political community. For political liberalism offers us a way of reaching agreement on policies and institutions without requiring us to agree on the ends they will serve. Of course, to the extent that people can reach agreement on a particular conception of human flourishing, they can employ that conception to shape their collective lives as well. Political liberalism and the Aristotelian strategy (when the conception of human well-being includes significant scope for autonomy) may not be so much opposed as complementary.

Moral pluralism is by no means a universal problem for social order, or for the creation of a moral community. Even if some sources of pluralism are virtually universal, the degree of difference they create may be small, and may be easily contained, perhaps by hierarchical encapsulation or the judicious drawing of spheres in the manner suggested by Walzer. Moral pluralism becomes a problem only when fundamental differences emerge regarding the values and institutions that might once have secured the normative integration of society, and when it involves groups with enough power to resist repression or encapsulation. These conditions describe many societies today, not only in the West but in all parts of the world. The migration of peoples has thrown formerly separate cultural and ethnic groups together, and a variety of economic and social changes has undermined both the integrative values and the structures of hierarchical encapsulation that formerly limited or contained moral pluralism. Moreover, as many thoughtful observers have pointed out, the idea of a "domestic" society more or less separate from other countries and cultures, free to order its own affairs, is increasingly anachronistic. More and more, there are critical issues—regarding the environment, economic affairs, migration, scientific research, and military security—that can only be addressed at an international level, where we must learn to mediate among the very different cultures and ways of life of different peoples. In the contemporary world we face the often difficult—and sometimes tragic—tasks of living with moral pluralism and managing moral conflict.

Appealing to Nature

LIMITED POLITICS

ONE BROAD CLASS of responses to the problem of moral pluralism—which we can (roughly) identify as liberal—attempts to create as much scope as possible for the differences among individuals and groups to be expressed. For liberals, toleration of difference is a crucial premise or starting point. Another broad set of theories, often arising in reaction to the first group, is what might be called "moral-transformative" theories. Rather than attempting to accommodate the differences among groups, moral transformers would reorder social relationships in such a way that these differences are either transcended or no longer cause conflict and division. Locke's writings can be taken as exemplary of the first group, and Rousseau's and Marx's of the second.[1] Both of these approaches seek to achieve moral or political community, but seek a form of community that does not rest upon a fixed, invariant conception of the human good. In this chapter I will set out the main parameters of the liberal response, turning to moral-transformative theories in the next chapter.

The basic answer that liberal political theory gives to the question of pluralism is to limit the authority of the state to a distinct "public" sphere in which a person's activities necessarily impinge directly upon others. Within that sphere, relations must be governed by principles that everyone can accept; beyond it, people are free to direct their lives as they wish. The state should not seek to "be the architect of the social order" (Anderson 1983:15). On the contrary, most aspects of social life, including the

---

[1] In offering this classification, I would like to stress that it plays a purely heuristic role in my argument. I do not wish to make historical claims about the specific intentions of particular theorists, but to appropriate their ideas and arguments for my purposes. I conceive of political theories as efforts to diagnose and resolve problems that arise in managing our common affairs. The concepts and ideas that we use for this purpose can only be drawn from the preexisting stock of intellectual materials, which often requires that they be refashioned to address new questions. My main interest is not to engage in interpretative disputes regarding historically situated political theories—though I do not think those unimportant—but to draw on a rich body of ideas to address questions that face us as we seek to understand and to create a common life.

economy, religious activity, education, and culture, should be determined through voluntary associations and organizations. In a political community whose scope is limited in this way, "space" is created within which people can follow diverse values and interests. By limiting the areas that are to be decided authoritatively for the society as a whole, we can create a moral community within which a plurality of sometimes conflicting values and ways of life are followed.

Liberals seek to limit the scope of authority in order to permit groups to live in accordance with different moral visions. These limits go beyond those intended to prevent social and political barbarism. Berlin has cogently articulated this second sort of limit:

> No society is free unless it is governed at any rate by two interrelated principles: first, that no power, but only rights, can be regarded as absolute, so that all men, whatever power governs them, have an absolute right to refuse to behave inhumanly; and, second, that there are frontiers, not artificially drawn, within which men should be inviolable, these frontiers being defined in terms of rules so long and widely accepted that their observance has entered into the very conception of what it is to be a normal human being, and, therefore, also of what it is to act inhumanly or insanely; rules of which it would be absurd to say, for example, that they could be abrogated by some formal procedure on the part of some court or sovereign body (1969:166).

Berlin identifies these rules as those that are broken when a person is declared guilty without trial, or punished under a retroactive law, when children are ordered to denounce their parents, friends to betray one another, soldiers to use methods of barbarism, when people are tortured or murdered or minorities massacred because they irritate a majority or a tyrant (166). The limits at issue here are not peculiar to, or definitive of, liberalism; they are limits that nonliberals can endorse. To be sure, as Shklar has insisted, avoiding cruelty is fundamental to liberal political thought, but one need not be a liberal to eschew cruelty.[2] Distinctively liberal limits are intended not simply to prevent barbarism but to create a moral space within which individuals and groups can freely pursue their

---

[2] Shklar and others have argued that nonliberal political programs can only be realized by violating, or at least running a serious risk of violating, these limits. To the extent that the actual alternative we face is "between cruel military and moral repression and violence, and a self-restraining tolerance that fences in the powerful to protect the freedom and safety of every citizen" (Shklar 1984:5), the distinction between specifically liberal limits on authority and the limits needed to restrain barbarism is only of theoretical interest.

ends and ideals without having to seek approval from others, or suffer serious legal liabilities for their choices.

Liberals envision a public arena conforming to universally acceptable and accepted principles, embracing and protecting a private sphere within which people are free to pursue diverse visions of the good life. Unfortunately, it is a vision that cannot be fully realized: any method of specifying these principles necessarily carries with it a set of exclusions that undermines the claim to universality. In the rest of this chapter I will review several liberal theories, bringing out the ways in which they fail to fulfill their promise. My purpose is not to reject the liberal strategy but to prepare the ground for a more adequate formulation, one that is sensitive to its own limitations.

Specifying Limits: Classical Contractarian Models

Different theories articulate the limits essential to liberalism in different ways and thus provide fuller and more specific accounts of how political life ought to be arranged in a liberal, pluralist society. Such theories set out the specific principles that define the limits of authority (including the grounds for overriding these limits), specify the institutions required to realize these principles, and spell out the duties these principles impose on citizens. Utilitarianism and contractarianism are two of the more important traditions of liberal theorizing.

Specifying a set of political principles that are precise enough to be the basis for political order, and that could be accepted by people who hold quite different values, may appear to be an impossible task. Pluralism requires limits on the scope of political authority, but might it not preclude agreement on these limits? Wouldn't people who hold different conceptions of the ends of life wish to draw these limits in different places? As MacIntyre has argued, "social dissensus" precludes the kind of moral reasoning that could lead to agreement on the scope and direction of public life (1988:590–91; 1981). To address this difficulty is the task of what I will call "contractarian" theories. In these theories, the principles of political association or, more generally, the principles governing the "basic structure of society,"[3] are supposed to represent the consensus of

---

[3] The term is Rawls's, referring to "the way in which the major social institutions distribute fundamental rights and duties and determine the division of advantages from social cooperation" (Rawls 1971:7).

the members of society that would emerge in a situation in which no one can exercise authority or coercion over others, that is, a situation in which people are free and equal.

Different theorists offer different representations of the contractual situation or process. The earliest formulations saw it as a social contract creating society out of a state of nature, while more recent theorists view it as a thought experiment of one sort or another. One theorist, for example, models it as a discussion among space travelers as they are about to colonize a new, uninhabited world; others, more prosaically, formulate it in terms of bargaining theory or as a "device of representation" intended to describe the circumstances under which agreements would not be distorted by "contingent advantages and accidental influences."[4] However it is conceived, the social contract is necessarily an idealization since any actual process of discussion and agreement could be distorted by imbalances of power, ignorance, inattention, irrationality, and the like. We can always ask whether any actual consensus is "genuine," whether the reported agreement was in fact fairly and freely obtained. Thus, contractarian theories attempt to provide an idealization of social processes of discussion and agreement against which any actual social consensus can be tested.

In constructing these idealizations, and in using them to generate reasonably specific political principles, contractarian thinkers generally employ what I previously called the "standard model" of political theory. That is, they invoke some conception of the person, some image of the self or selves who are parties to the agreement. These images typically consist of a set of fundamental assumptions regarding human nature, particularly assumptions about motivation, capacities, and rationality. Using these assumptions, the theorist attempts more or less formally to show that parties in the ideal contractual setting would acknowledge certain principles of justice to govern their interactions in society. The theorist then attempts to spell out the implications of these principles. Central to virtually all these theories is a conception of humans as agents, as "doers" who in important ways are capable of shaping their own lives and directing their actions according to their own purposes.

Although there are important differences among contractarian thinkers, a common pattern of argument begins with a conception of human agency which is used to justify a system of rights or principles of justice, which are then used to define and to govern the "public" sphere. This

---

[4] See Ackerman (1980), Gauthier (1986), and Rawls (1985:236), respectively.

sphere includes those activities that are subject to authoritative decision, the sphere in which all individuals can be required to conform to a common set of norms. By defining these principles (and so this sphere) only by reference to human reason and agency, the theorist seeks to show how political authority can arise and function in a pluralist society. On the one hand, political authority enforces only those rules that all possible human agents would necessarily accept; on the other, it preserves space for different individuals and groups to pursue their own distinctive ends. In this conception, the state or political authority should be "neutral" among the different systems of values, and the various groups and individuals, who make up the society, since it will enforce only those values or ends—those based on human agency—that are universally shared.

Unfortunately, the contractarian project is unsuccessful. Although there is much to learn from this effort, I will show that it rests upon conceptions of human nature and an ideal of neutrality that cannot be sustained. In the rest of this section I will consider contractarian accounts of human nature, and later I will take up the question of neutrality.

Contractarian theories are sometimes quite informal, dispensing with much of the contractarian apparatus itself and appealing directly to some idea of human nature. Nozick, for example, develops his theory of the minimal state and his critique of redistributive policies, including the welfare state and socialist visions of society, on the basis of a theory of human rights which is not only poorly specified but for which he offers very little justification. Rights, he insists, should be seen as constraints on how one can treat others, and our having rights is (somehow) based on the capacity not only for shaping one's life but also for giving meaning to one's life (1974:48–51). Nozick's remarks are suggestive, but do little to explain either why we should think of ourselves as bearers of rights or what these rights might be.

Because the idea of agency has come to seem so natural, many liberals have thought that it can be used to answer the questions that Nozick's account begs. They contend that human agency can provide a conceptually powerful basis for an elaborate system of human rights. We might call them "agency rights," for they recognize and provide scope for the exercise of our capacities for agency. In a particularly perspicuous account, Herbert Morris has argued that what is distinctive about persons is that we are "capable where animals are not of making, of creating, among other things, ourselves" (1976:42). This capacity for self-creation underlies practices central to our moral lives—including the value we place on achievements, our use of praise and blame, and our experience of resentment when wronged. Given this understanding of what it is to be a person, to treat someone as a person is to act toward him or her in terms of that person's capacity for agency. At a minimum, this means that we must respond to persons *in terms of their choices*, for to do otherwise is to treat them not as persons but as things. Thus, we must provide them with reasons for acting and not try to influence their behavior through the use of force or manipulation: "We treat a human being as a person provided, first, we permit the person to make the choices that will determine what happens to him and, second, when our responses to the person are responses respecting the person's choices"(48–49). Morris goes on to argue that we have a right to be treated as a person, which is "natural, inalienable, and absolute" (49). It is natural because it is "connected with a feature of men that sets men apart from other natural phenomena"— "the capacity to reason and to choose on the basis of reasons" (50). It is inalienable because no meaning can be given to the idea of transferring the right to another: the right to have one's choices respected is inherently self-referential; nor could it be waived, because your giving me permission to treat you as an object would not make it permissible for me to treat you that way (53). Finally, it is absolute because even when it is morally necessary to override the right, the person is still wronged, is still treated unjustly.

The right to be treated as a person requires that there exist a system of "rules that prohibit violence and deception," a system that "provides benefits for all persons" consisting of a sphere within which each "is immune from interference by others with what each person values," including "life and bodily security." It also involves burdens, consisting "in the exercise of self-restraint by individuals over inclinations that would, if satisfied, directly interfere or create a substantial risk of interference with others in proscribed ways." Thus, the "rules establish a mutuality of benefit and burden" where "benefits and burdens are equally distributed" (33–34).

Morris offers a powerful argument linking the idea of agency with a theory of human rights, but he has little to say about why we should single out agency as the critical dimension governing our moral relationships with others. He claims that this feature distinguishes us from the rest of nature, but why should we respond to other humans in terms of what makes us different from other things? Why not in terms of what makes us similar—say, our liability to suffering or our neediness? Even if agency is distinctive to humans, why should we suppose that it is (or ought to be) of significance to everyone, that everyone wants (or ought to want) to be, and to be treated as, a "person" in this sense? In the first place, many people are sometimes, and a few are virtually always, incapable of exercising the powers of agency—children, the ill, the mentally disturbed or incompetent, people suffering from certain disabilities such as Alzheimer's. Second, we often value ourselves and others not in terms of their capacity to direct their lives according to their own purposes, but in terms of other abilities, such as the capacity to act faithfully in the socially prescribed roles and relationships in which we stand to others. If faithful action is of less importance in our own way of life than it was in past generations, it is still important in other cultures and societies. I would not wish to deny that agency is an important—indeed, a fundamental—human characteristic, one that must be recognized and expressed in any viable moral or political theory. But Morris's argument rests on the selection of this quality as the sole basis at least for our political lives, and this requires a stronger argument than we have been provided.

I have dwelt at length upon Morris's argument in part because I wish to use his analysis of the connection between agency and rights later (in chapter five), but principally because it strikingly exemplifies the problem of false essentialism, which can be found in all versions of classical contractarian theories.[5] Beginning with an account of human nature, these thinkers seek to demonstrate that there are certain norms that everyone has sufficient reason to accept, and which therefore are binding on everyone. Because their accounts of human nature do capture important aspects of our being, there is always a certain plausibility to their analyses. But what their theories do not—and cannot—do is to show that the aspects of human nature they select have the priority they assign to them. In Morris's case, for example, he would have to show not only that humans can usefully be described in terms of rational agency but that this description overrides other possible descriptions. Until that is done, his account of agency rights has at best only a prima facie character and is subject to being overridden by normative or evaluative considerations resting on other dimensions of the human condition.

Because moral beliefs are not "free floating" attitudes or emotional responses, but are part of a more general understanding of ourselves and the world, moral disagreement always involves other issues as well. Sometimes these issues will be straightforwardly "factual"; we might judge someone's actions differently because we disagree about exactly

---

[5] Morris's argument does not, strictly speaking, employ the contractual metaphor or apparatus, but it is closely allied to such arguments.

what he did. More often, our disagreements will involve important conceptual and theoretical issues as well, as when we disagree about the merits of a public policy because we have different views about its consequences. When a society is characterized by significant moral pluralism, these differences will be profound, involving the very concepts and terms through which we understand ourselves and the world. Competing systems of value are accompanied by competing conceptualizations and descriptions as well. Classical contractarian theories, by privileging a certain account of human nature, beg the very questions at issue.

This can be seen in a striking way in the work of David Gauthier, who sets out "to generate morality as a set of rational principles for choice," showing "why an individual, reasoning from non-moral premises, would accept the constraints of morality on his choices" (1986:5). In Gauthier's explicitly contractarian account, a "person is conceived as an independent centre of activity, endeavouring to direct his capacities and resources to the fulfillment of his interests" (9). This does not mean that humans are by nature rational egoists. Gauthier allows that we may value any number of different things, including the welfare of others, but the crucial point is that we are only motivated to advance our own values, whatever they happen to be. Rather than being egoists, Gauthier assumes that people are "non-tuistic" in that "each person takes no interest in the interests of those with whom he is interacting" (1988:213).

There is considerable controversy about whether Gauthier succeeds in his project,[6] but what is crucial for my purposes is its irrelevance for my concern with moral pluralism. In morally pluralist societies, the problem is not to persuade rational actors that they should accept moral constraints on the pursuit of their interests, but to mediate among opposing moral conceptions, opposing views of what morality (broadly conceived) demands of us. The energy invested by some philosophers in developing a rational justification for morality appears to be quite disproportionate to the social significance of this issue. There is, of course, a great deal of moral conflict everywhere. Consider the sometimes violent confrontations at abortion clinics in the United States, the vituperative attacks on advocates of euthanasia in Germany today, or the efforts by Hindu fundamentalists to seize a mosque in Avodhaya, India.[7] But it is hard to find

---

[6] See, for example, the articles in *Social Philosophy and Policy* 5, no. 2 (Spring 1988) and *Ethics* 97, no. 4 (July 1987), and Barry (1989) for critical discussions (both issues are wholly devoted to Gauthier).

[7] Abortion is discussed in chapter three, below. See Singer (1991) for a chilling account of the conflict over euthanasia in Germany today.

conflicts pitting advocates of "morality" against those who reject moral considerations altogether.[8]

The conception of morality as a constraint on the pursuit of one's interests is inadequate to resolve conflicts that arise from moral pluralism. Rather than being independent of our moral commitments, the values we hold are in part determined by these commitments. Consider, for example, the different visions of the ends of life that Taylor presents.[9] The revolutionary dedicated to human liberation or the Christian dedicated to agape adopt their ideals in part because of their "tuistic" concern for the well-being of others, because they identify themselves as part of a broader, indeed universal, human community. Gauthier's image of humans as rational agents intent upon advancing their own interests, who must be restrained by moral rules, obviously distorts the issues separating these two positions. Both would decisively reject his conception of human nature, which makes nonsense of their ideals of life. Nor could we resolve the conflict between the revolutionary and the Christian by constructing a system of morality that would prove superior to the "presocial" baseline of a state of nature in which people take no regard of others and view social relationships in purely instrumental terms. No doubt, conflicts between altruists will be similar in certain ways to the kind of conflict that Gauthier's model is constructed to handle since in both cases individuals pursue incompatible objectives that may be mutually frustrating. But the substantive outcomes will be very different, since people who are concerned with the well-being of others will accept rules that "non-tuists" would reject. Gauthier recognizes this point, acknowledging in particular that his model does not make "appropriate provision for the raising of children, given the affective demands involved" (1988:217), and that this requires relaxing the assumption of "non-tuism" for this case. This is by no means a trivial concession, as it involves the very possibility of social life itself. But the critical point is that in morally pluralist societies the assumption of "non-tuism" will fail to characterize the participants in moral conflicts over a wide range of issues. Although we have much to learn from the contractarians, a different approach is needed if we are to handle moral conflict.[10]

[8] Perhaps common criminality is an exception. It is significant that those who speak out on the side of criminals generally do not defend criminal conduct as such, but point to the ways in which criminals themselves have been victimized.

[9] See chapter two, above.

[10] My criticism of Gauthier has focused on his implicit conception of human nature. Alternatively, one might argue that his model places arbitrary constraints of the "preferences" that are considered in formulating moral rules. For such a critique, see Gaus (1990:348–51).

SPECIFYING LIMITS: THIN SELVES AND THE LIBERAL STRATEGY

The failure of what I have been calling "classical contractarian" models suggests the need for a new approach to constituting political community in the face of moral pluralism. Rather than deducing a political morality from some "ontology," some conception of human nature and reason, this approach conceives of liberalism as a *strategy* for creating a morally just political order. In this view, liberal political theories are, above all, theories about *politics*, about the ways in which public power can and should be organized, and the ends to which it should be directed. These theories are examples of what I call "political liberalism," a version of which I shall present and defend in chapter five. Like classical contractarian theories, political liberalism must posit some conception of the self, but that conception should not be taken as an adequate representation of the whole person. Rather, the conception of the self is self-consciously offered as an abstraction from the rich complexities of actual human lives, designed to respond to the specific problems of creating a political community.[11]

Critical to our circumstances is the fact that our societies incorporate large numbers of people, distributed over territories of significant size and divided into a plurality of groups that differ in important ways—including their moral and religious commitments. Liberal constructions of the self should, in the first instance, be thought of as models designed to capture the relationships that are possible under such conditions, and to indicate the forms of political association that will enable people to enjoy diverse and rich ways of life. Because these images of the self are partial, they are thin. But their very thinness is what, in a sense, makes rich lives possible.

The liberal strategy necessarily involves a method of conceiving of people in a way that abstracts from the full complexity of their lives to specify some elements of commonality, some model of the self, which can

---

[11] I use the term "strategy" here with some hesitation, since I do not wish to suggest in any way that this interpretation of liberal theory views it as taking a manipulative stance, or as being unconcerned with truth. Unfortunately, some liberals have spoken that way, responding to criticisms of the truth of liberal theories by holding that key concepts were not intended to correctly describe social life, but were used strategically to produce certain effects in their audience. Such an interpretation contradicts the deep liberal aspirations to a society that is fully and freely accepted by its members. For an example, see Herzog (1987). (I might note that this is a polemical piece and does not appear to reflect Herzog's considered views; see, e.g., his 1989.)

enable them to find a basis for political association. It is only on the basis of such abstractions that a set of moral principles can be found to which everyone in the society can subscribe, so that the society can be a moral community.

It is important to see that these abstractions do not necessarily constitute a shared "basis" of the different understandings of the self, or different conceptions of the good, that are available in that society. The elements that can figure in the model(s) of the person that underlie a liberal polity must be widely shared, but they do not need to play the same role in the moral lives of everyone or every group in the society, nor must these elements be accepted by everyone for the same reasons. The account of the commonalities on which we should base our public life are not offered as a "social ontology"; they should not be seen as theories of human nature or as specifying the "essential" aspects of human beings. The only requirement is that the various groups in the society be able to recognize some significant aspect of their own self-understandings in the public or common model, so that they can see the point and value of the principles to which this model gives rise.

I would not wish to argue that political theorists have conceived of their work in these terms, though Hume's famous discussion of justice as an "artificial" virtue could certainly be seen in this way. Nonetheless, there are elements of this "strategic conception" even in theories such as Bentham's, which is commonly seen as a particularly reductive model of human nature, one in which people are conceived as instrumentally rational want-satisfiers. For Bentham (at least in this popular interpretation), the individual is assumed to aim at the maximization of "pleasure," understood to be a measurable kind of sensation. More recent (and more plausible) versions replace Bentham's hedonism with preference orderings, in which a wide array of goals may be found. But whatever the version, it can be argued that the point of this characterization is to find a sufficiently general—and so reduced—notion of the self that it can embrace people with widely varying aspirations and values, and thereby serve as a basis for ordering public life. Thus, in a revealing passage Bentham begins by asking "is it never, then, from any other considerations than those of utility, that we derive our notions of right and wrong?" And he continues:

> I do not know: I do not care. Whether a moral sentiment can be originally conceived from any other source than a view of utility is one question: whether upon examination and reflection it can, in point of fact, be actually persisted in and justified on any other ground, by a person reflecting within

himself, is another: whether in point of right it can properly be justified on any other ground, by a person *addressing himself to the community*, is a third. The two first are questions of speculation: it matters not, comparatively speaking, how they are decided. The last is a question of practice: the decision of it is of as much importance as that of any can be. (1948:142; italics added)

In other words, the decisive argument for the principle of utility is to be found *not* in the speculative account of human nature with which Bentham begins the *Introduction*, but in the (supposed) fact that this principle is the only one that can be accepted by everyone in the community, in spite of their differences in interests and moral outlooks.

If this "pragmatic turn" is only a minor theme in what we might call "classical" liberal theories, it is the point of departure for many contemporary theorists. One of the richest and most systematic accounts of the self in this tradition is Rawls's recent work. While Rawls's earlier (1971) account of justice was much closer to the tradition of classical contractarianism, his Dewey Lectures (1980) offer an analysis in terms of what he calls "model-conceptions." These are deliberate abstractions designed not to account for the entire range of our social and moral experience, but to capture "our deeper understanding of ourselves and our aspirations" in order to "articulate a public conception of justice that all [in our society] can live with" (519).

Rawls uses these "model-conceptions" to develop what he calls a "political conception of justice," one that is "rooted in the basic intuitive ideas found in the public culture of a constitutional democracy" (1985: 246), particularly the conception of "society as a fair system of cooperation between free and equal persons" (231). Rawls does not claim that this conception of the person and society describes essential features of human nature. But it is not arbitrary, nor does it represent a mere modus vivendi between competing groups. Rather it "is a moral conception: it has conceptions of person and society, and concepts of right and fairness, as well as principles of justice with their complement of the virtues through which those principles are embodied in human character and regulate political and social life" (247). The conception of the person from which Rawls's account begins includes the idea that we have "a capacity for a sense of justice and a capacity for a conception of the good" (233), and that we are free not only in being able to develop and revise our conception of the good (240–42) but also that we are "self-originating sources of valid claims" (242) and are "capable of taking responsibility for [our] ends" (243). Although different people will hold these concepts for different reasons, each will see the conception of justice that is based on them as morally binding, and not merely a matter of a strategic compromise based upon considerations of prudence.[12]

The conceptions of the self offered by different theorists vary in important ways, but all of them are "thin," quite incapable of capturing many of the most important truths about our lives. But the crucial point is that such a model should not be seen as a complete philosophical anthropology, one intended to encompass the essential aspects of human life. Rather its task is to articulate a representation of the self that is sufficiently general to embrace a plurality of moral communities, but that is sufficiently determinate to provide principles that everyone can accept as defining a just basis for cooperation. Only a "thin" self, one that abstracts from the particular ends that people hold, will be appropriate, for only such a conception can command agreement and permit a plurality of rich lives.

This point might be clarified by considering the deep and searching objections that Michael Sandel has raised against the conception of the self underlying Rawls's account of justice.[13] Sandel argues that Rawls's form of "liberalism supposes that we can, indeed must, understand ourselves as independent" in the sense that we "stand to our circumstances always at a certain distance, conditioned to be sure, but part of us always antecedent to any conditions" (1982:10–11). In particular, according to Sandel, this version of liberalism rests on an essentially "voluntarist" conception of human agency, so that the identity of the self "is given independently of the things [it possesses], independently, that is, of [its] interests and ends and its relations with others" (55). The relationship of the self to its ends is voluntaristic in that one chooses one's ends as a voluntary act. They are not in any way *constitutive* of one's identity.

---

[12] A *purely* political conception of justice, one beginning only from an empirically existing plurality of communities, could have considerable moral force. Peace, as Augustine remarked, is a value for everyone (or almost everyone—Augustine never had to worry about fascists). But it is ultimately unsatisfactory unless some moral basis can be provided for the initial condition of pluralism. It may also be unstable (to the extent that public conceptions of justice are efficacious in affecting behavior) in the face of a shifting balance of power among the groups (witness Lebanon in the 1970s and 1980s).

[13] A particular conception of the self developed to explain the possibility of, and appropriate principles for, the political system may be objectionable not because it is "thin," but because it fails to support the principles of justice which the theorist offers. For example, Sandel argues that Rawls's notion of the self does not provide an adequate grounding for the difference principle. I do not consider that issue here, for my interest is only in the general critique he offers of the liberal project.

But this conception, Sandel argues, is inadequate because it is "incapable of making sense of what choice and deliberation could possibly consist in" (161). If one's aims are just those things that one happens to choose, on what basis could one make such choices? On the voluntarist account, Sandel argues, choice is reduced to either one's being determined by already existing desires or to an exercise of pure caprice. It is only by developing a fuller notion of the self, one that takes "the bounds of the self as open and conceive[s] of the identity of the subject as the product rather than the premise of agency," that we can capture our experience as moral beings. In this connection, the "relevant agency" is "not voluntarist but cognitive; the self [comes] by its ends not by choice but by reflection, as knowing (or inquiring) subject to object of (self-)understanding" (152).

It is not difficult to see that a purely voluntarist conception of the self would be fatally defective as a *complete* account of human agency. But the voluntarist self is a deliberately thin conception of the self, constructed to explain only a *part* of our moral lives. A radically voluntarist model is not the only model that the liberal project could use, but even it may be capable of constituting the basis of a political order in a pluralist society, as long as the complete or full conceptions of the self that are widely shared within the society include voluntarist elements.

It is plausible to suppose that a complete conception of the self would combine both cognitive and voluntarist aspects. We can agree that the self is necessarily "encumbered," in the sense that one does not merely will but also discovers one's ends. However, the very process of self-discovery can free one from the "givenness" of any particular ends. Self-understanding can provide a critical distance on one's ends, so that they are not, or do not continue to be, one's ends unless one acknowledges—that is, wills—them. To pretend that one has not chosen them is to act in bad faith. But at the same time, one does not simply choose one's purposes as a whole. Rather one chooses particular projects and principles on the basis of reflection and experience. And when one considers a particular question, or when one reflects on a particular aim, one does so against the background of a series of aims, affections, commitments, loyalties, and capacities that are given. When I reflect upon my vocational aims, for example, I take my familial commitments as given. I cannot, at the risk of madness, call every aspect of my being into question at once. But neither can I disclaim responsibility for my aims, for they are not imposed upon me, even if my freedom in choosing them is not unlimited, and even if there is an important element of contingency in them looked at as a whole.[14]

If members of the society hold conceptions of the self which conform to this very general model, that is, which contain both voluntarist and cognitive aspects, then it may be possible to ground the general kind of argument that Rawls makes by abstracting from what Sandel calls the cognitive elements of the self for the purpose of defining the principles of political life. The liberal project requires that the complete or full view of the self contain voluntarist elements; but these need not be the only elements. Liberals can admit that the self is not "independent in the sense that [its] identity is never tied to [its] aims and attachments" (Sandel 1982:179). One's identity may be tied to one's aims and attachments, but it must not be *exhausted by* these aims. For the liberal, a person's identity does not simply consist in being an agent with the capacity to choose, but also in the choices that one has made, and in what has happened to one. What is crucial, and what makes one (relatively) independent, is that one can reflect upon his or her history and, as a result of that reflection, come to alter one's aims and attachments. Of course, such alterations must be continuous in the sense that one must be able to explain why one made (or affirmed) certain changes. These continuities and explanations will inevitably make essential reference to aspects of one's being that are not chosen. This dependence of what we choose on what is (at least presently) not chosen is a condition of being free, for our freedom is that of rational beings and is not mere capriciousness.

But our freedom also consists in the fact that we cannot tell ahead of time what particular features of everyone's identities will be seen to be alterable or unalterable. This is a key insight of political liberalism. Because we can call into question our goals and projects, and thereby alter ourselves, political liberalism holds that we should not take a particular system of aims or purposes, a particular conception of human excellence

---

[14] Contrary to what is often claimed, autonomy does not require that one be able to renounce or even conceive of oneself as renouncing all of one's attachments, values, and commitments as a whole, but only that one be able to abstract oneself from any particular aspect of one's identity, so that one's identity is something that reflects one's affirmations. The claim that people are capable of autonomy does not involve either the mistaken social-psychological view that we make ourselves, or the mistaken moral view that freedom and responsibility are only possible where they are unqualified or absolute (from which it would follow that they are never possible at all). My interpretation blocks the kind of inauthenticity where someone denies responsibility for some part of his or her character by claiming that he or she could not control it, and calls upon the individual who is tempted to absolve him or herself from responsibility either to change or to affirm the feature in question.

and the human good, and use it as the basis for an ideal social and political order. Rather we must abstract from the particular identities we have discovered and chosen and base our political lives on an admittedly narrow understanding of ourselves in terms of our capacity for agency. To do otherwise is unnecessarily to restrict the ways of life open to members of the community. Such restrictions not only exclude those who do not share the particular ideal in question, but it also limits the moral autonomy of everyone.

Discovering Commonalities: Rawls and Larmore

That political liberalism bases the political association on a thin conception of the self, then, is an integral part of the liberal strategy for constituting a moral community under the conditions of moral pluralism. But can this strategy work? Can it find sufficient commonalities to constitute a common life in the face of moral dissensus?

Rawls's answer to this question invokes the idea of an "overlapping consensus," a set of shared understandings that happens to exist in modern, democratic societies. However, Joseph Raz, like many others, has argued that Rawls's "route seems barren in pluralistic societies" because the "degree of existing diversity is just too great" (1990:45). Even worse, Raz contends, Rawls's version of the liberal strategy is incoherent. If we have good reasons to adopt a particular theory of justice, then "those reasons show (or make) this the true theory of justice" (15). And if the theory is true, it must be grounded in comprehensive moral views and cannot simply reflect a contingently existing consensus, even one that makes "social unity and stability" possible, unless these goals are of such importance as to constitute the foundation of justice.[15] In short, "There can be no justice without truth" (15). And, Raz argues, the most perspicuous way of understanding Rawls's theory of justice is to see it as embedded in a "true moral theory" that values "people's freely developing their

---

[15] Raz's critique frequently attributes to Rawls the view that social stability and unity are goals that are so important that they can be taken to be the foundation of a theory of justice. Raz (correctly) criticizes this view, partly on the grounds that agreement on principles of justice plays no more than "a partial, perhaps even a merely subsidiary, role in securing unity and stability" (31). But this is to misunderstand Rawls's concern, which is to achieve a "well-ordered society," one that is "effectively regulated by a public conception of justice" (1971:5). Rawls's notion of social unity, then, is normative, referring to unity based on a shared conception of justice and not merely a shared interest in political stability.

own understanding of the meaning of life" and their "living in accord with their own freely developed conception of the good" (25)—that is, a theory in which autonomy is central. The commitment to autonomy requires that we respect the views and choices of others, even when they are mistaken, and so commits us to seeking a "doctrine of justice" that will be acceptable to others. It is on this basis that we should be willing to modify our own views of justice in order to reach such agreement.

Gerald Doppelt has made a related criticism of Rawls, arguing that his recent work is best understood as resting upon a "Kantian conception of persons." In this conception, the exercise of the capacities for self-determination and for recognizing and respecting others constitutes "an essential part of the moral identity of persons" because "it provides the basis on which any conception of the good, including their own, has value and reflects the value of its agent" (1988:421). The Kantian ideal, then, is a "meta-value," a condition of other things having value, rather than a good to be directly pursued. Thus, any system of justice must provide scope—both in terms of liberty and the availability of resources—for the exercise of autonomy. According to Doppelt, if we do not construe Rawls's theory in this way, but understand it simply as a device to deal with moral diversity, it will be incoherent. Understood as a strategy to accommodate pluralism, the theory reflects the impossibility of reaching a rationally justified agreement on a particular account of the human good. But unless that diversity itself is, in some sense, valuable or justified, the absence of agreement "concerning the good may be taken to justify a *skepticism* concerning the very values or conceptions of the good protected by Rawlsian justice, and thus a skepticism embracing the value of justice itself" (422, emphasis in original). Moreover, the capacity of liberal justice to achieve social unity and stability would be endangered because of the possible conflict "between the supposedly shared fundamental ideal of Kantian personhood and the particular conceptions of the good individuals end up choosing" (423). This conflict between public and private identities can only be overcome if we conceive of the "good of Kantian personhood" as linking both public and private realms, conditioning and limiting "the particular conceptions of the good and forms of human agency which are valued in Rawlsian society" (423).

The suspicion that liberalism rests upon (a self-defeating) skepticism has been voiced many times, and it is easy to understand why conceiving of liberalism as a "political strategy" would reinforce such suspicion. But it is deeply mistaken to see the "political" conception of justice as one that rests on "shallow foundations" (in Raz's words), and that does not make a claim to be, in some sense, "true." As Rawls argues, "it would be fatal to the point of a political conception [of justice] to see it as skeptical about, or indifferent to, truth, much less in conflict with it" (1987:12). Rawls's political conception of justice is supposed to rest not on shallow foundations but on "multiple foundations": "We hope to make it possible for all to accept the political conception [of justice] as true, or as reasonable, from the standpoint of their own comprehensive view [of morality], whatever that might be" (13). The liberal theory of justice, then, might be seen as a set of "theorems" that can be derived from different sets of axioms.[16]

Nor should we suppose that moral pluralism will lead to skepticism unless it is embedded in a comprehensive moral view such as Kant's, in which "self-determination" is recognized as "a universal pre-condition or ground of all value, that in virtue of which any particular conception of the good or way of life has value" (Doppelt 1988:420). As I argued in chapter two, there is an important distinction between value pluralism and skepticism; the former rests on a denial of monistic theories, according to which all values can be rationally ordered, but that very denial presupposes the truth or genuineness of our various and incommensurate goods and aims. Thus, moral pluralism is itself committed to truth and is thereby antithetical to skepticism.[17]

---

[16] Raz charges that Rawls adopts "a posture of epistemic abstinence" in that "he refrains from claiming that his doctrine of justice is true" (1990:9), but this is misleading. Rawls denies that a *particular account* of the truth of this doctrine is itself part of the doctrine. For example, Rawls is unwilling to "say that reaching [a] reflective agreement [on justice] is itself grounds for regarding this conception as true" (1987:15), not because he is agnostic about the truth of his theory of justice, but because he is unwilling to endorse the consensus theory of truth presupposed by this judgment. Similarly, when Rawls writes that his conception of justice "presents itself not . . . as true, but one that can serve as a basis of informed and willing political agreement," that is because the "*aim* of justice as fairness as a political conception is practical, and not metaphysical or epistemological" (1985:230, emphasis added); that is to say, once again, that the theory does not include an account of its truth, for the purpose of putting the theory forward is to provide a basis for a moral community rather than simply advancing our theoretical understanding of justice.

[17] Of course, embracing a conception of persons in which autonomy is an essential ideal may lead us to see moral pluralism as a cause for celebration rather than, perhaps, a misfortune, a source of conflict and instability. In that sense, accepting autonomy or self-determination, interpreted either as a "meta-value" in the sense that Doppelt suggests, or as an aspect of human flourishing in the manner of Raz, may reinforce pluralism. For further discussion of the issue of truth in moral argument, see chapter five, below.

Nonetheless, Raz and Doppelt do point to a crucial problem for any account of justice that sees it as resting on "multiple foundations," in the sense of an overlapping consensus among distinct, comprehensive theories. This is the problem of priority. Adherents of different theories are unlikely to place the same priority on the values and principles that make up the "overlapping consensus" because these principles and values will occupy different positions in different comprehensive theories. In the event of conflicts among various principles and values, then, adherents of conflicting comprehensive views will support different "trade-offs" or assert opposed priorities.[18] Moreover, the common values and principles are likely to be quite abstract (cf. Rawls 1987:15n), and using them to make concrete judgments may lead to conflict as the adherents of distinct comprehensive doctrines insist upon their own interpretations of these principles. And these conflicts may manifest themselves within the moral consciousness of each individual, in the form of the conflict between public and private identities which Doppelt discusses.

Rawls expresses the hope that the common values will "normally outweigh" particular values that conflict with them and suggests that over time the liberal conception of justice may come to be incorporated in its own terms into comprehensive moral doctrines, including those that did not previously espouse tolerant views (see 1987:15–23). This is not an unreasonable hope; as Rawls points out, it appears to describe the emergence of religious toleration in Western societies. Moreover, the internal conflict between public and private identities that Doppelt fears is, at least in many contexts, a source of dynamism and innovation in our personal and social lives. It is an instance of the moral and social differentiation of modern societies, of our need to act on different values and expectations in different spheres or roles. Such differentiation has always been resisted by those who yearn for a social order in which one can fully express oneself in all of one's activities, and who resent what they see and experience as alienation or fragmentation. But managing such conflicts is not always difficult; in many ways it can be liberating, providing the opportu-

---

[18] Raz sees this objection as "decisive," since a political theory based on an overlapping consensus "can neither assure us that conflicts [among values] do not arise nor adjudicate them when they do arise" (1990:23). However, in a pluralistic society we will face such undecidable conflicts among the opposed comprehensive theories; since political liberalism promises to settle at least some of these, it is better than the existing alternatives. Moreover, many comprehensive views contain a plurality of values among which there are no clear rules of priority, and different, but equally qualified, individuals may reach different judgments.

nity to develop and to express different possibilities or parts of oneself. But there may be times when these conflicts are irresolvable, tearing individuals and communities apart.

Rawls's theory is designed to provide an impartial framework within which these conflicts can be resolved, but in some cases what is in dispute is the framework itself. Rawls argues that the principles of justice are those principles that would be chosen by rational individuals in what he calls "the original position"—a setting in which they encounter one another as free and equal persons whose judgments are not biased by the desire to advance their own particular aims, since they are assumed not to have any knowledge of their own particular qualities, including their specific aims and abilities. Their choice of principles of justice, then, should be in some sense "neutral" among the final aims that people may hold. Although they are ignorant of their particular ends, they seek to assure themselves as great a quantity of "primary goods" as possible, because that will enable them to advance whatever ends they happen to hold. Thus, they will choose principles of justice that will fairly distribute primary goods, which Rawls defines as the generalized media of income and wealth, the powers and prerogatives of office, and the social bases of self-respect (Rawls 1982:162). These principles would then be used to design the basic institutions of society.

This analysis is based, as I pointed out above, on a thin conception of the person which is "rooted in the basic intuitive ideas found in the public culture of a constitutional democracy" (Rawls 1985:246), particularly the conception of "society as a fair system of cooperation between free and equal persons" (231). Participants in the original position, however, do not choose or reflect upon this self-understanding: they do not question their understanding of "society as a fair system of cooperation between free and equal persons," their view of themselves as having "a capacity for a sense of justice and a capacity for a conception of the good," nor do they discuss the essentially instrumental or engineering conception of designing social institutions in accordance with principles of justice. These parameters determine critical aspects of the resulting conception of justice, including the list of primary goods. Each of these components of Rawls's theory is at least potentially exclusionary; far from providing an impartial perspective on our conflicts, this framework can work to silence or, at least, to disadvantage certain voices.

The partial character of Rawls's framework results from the existence of other conceptions of the person and of society in our culture besides those he invokes. Doppelt mentions "bourgeois," patriarchal, and religious views, arguing that "these rival ideals shape the structure of our desires, expectations, institutions, practices, and conditions of life in ways which result in destructive zero-sum struggles among individuals and groups for scarce dignity, recognition, respect, achievement, and status" (448). Unfortunately, there is no way of addressing these conflicts within Rawls's system because he *presupposes* a particular understanding of the self, an understanding that is implicated in these very struggles.[19] I do not necessarily wish to endorse Doppelt's account of social conflict in America today, but his general critique of the structure of Rawls's analysis points to serious problems in Rawls's version of the liberal strategy. These can be seen by considering, first, Rawls's analysis of primary goods and, second, his conception of the problem of institutional design.

The concept of primary goods plays a critical role in Rawls's theory, in part because they are required to make the choice of principles of justice in the original position determinate. Because the contractors are assumed to be ignorant of their ultimate aims, Rawls must posit intermediate ends in order to give them a basis for choosing principles of justice. But primary goods also figure in Rawls's (Humean) account of the circumstances of justice, which "obtain whenever mutually disinterested persons put forward conflicting claims to the division of social advantages under conditions of moderate scarcity" (1971:128). The primary goods constitute the "social advantages" that are to be justly distributed, and the only "kinds of claims which it is appropriate for citizens to make when questions of justice arise" are claims to primary goods (1982:161). Further, Rawls's conception of the problem of justice rests on the assumption that what we care about in our social institutions is the way in which they assign these goods to positions, and the way in which they assign persons to positions. In Rawls's scheme, basic liberties and opportunities are to be distributed equally to all; the remaining primary goods are to be assigned to positions in such a way as to maximize the amount received by those in the least advantaged position, and people are to be assigned to positions in accordance with the principle of "fair equality of opportunity."

In order to construct a list (let alone an index)[20] of primary goods there

---

[19] An adequate social theory, in Doppelt's view, must be "transformative," in that it must reflect upon these competing ideals and redefine or reinterpret them in such a way as to overcome these conflicts. I take up the analysis of transformative theories in the next chapter.

[20] An index is necessary if we are to talk about having "more" or "less" of them, though its construction obviously raises grave difficulties, some of which are discussed in Rawls (1982).

must be a significant commonality to our ends, in that they all would require the same kinds of resources for their realization or achievement. The source of this commonality of our aims, in Rawls's theory, is his concept of the person, which holds that we have "two highest-order interests," to realize and exercise our capacity for justice and our capacity to form and pursue a conception of the good. In addition, Rawls's persons have an interest in advancing their "determinate conceptions of the good," but this is subordinate to the first two interests (1982:165). The primary goods, then, are just those goods that are necessary or instrumental to the realization of these interests. It is crucial to note that "what are to count as primary goods is not decided by asking what general means are essential for achieving the final ends which a comprehensive empirical or historical survey might show that people usually or normally have in common." Whatever ends people actually adopt, and whatever means may be required for those ends, the primary goods are determined "in the light of a conception of the person given in advance" (1982:166–67).

This means that the scope of conflict is limited by the conception of the person on the basis of which Rawls constructs his theory of justice; certain kinds of issues and claims will not be given a hearing, certain voices will be excluded on the grounds that they do not express legitimate claims. Those excluded include people for whom the "capacity to form and pursue a conception of the good" is not subordinate to their "determinate conceptions of the good," that is, those for whom the capacity for agency may be overridden by their particular moral beliefs or religious views. And this exclusion does not *reflect* a rational consensus of citizens but is a *presupposition* of the processes through which a rational consensus is formed. This will not be a problem, of course, if moral pluralism is sufficiently limited that such voices do not exist. But if Rawls's concept of the person is not universally shared in a society, then his theory of justice cannot serve as the basis for a moral community. Those whose voices are excluded will experience this as an imposition and thus as unjust.

In addition to excluding certain voices, the Rawlsian use of primary goods runs the risk of seriously disadvantaging some groups in the pursuit of their ideals, even when those ideals are broadly consistent with his political conception of justice. Because different comprehensive views will require different resources, and different relative quantities of the same resources, any particular index will advantage some and disadvantage others, viewed from the perspective of their comprehensive views. Rawls dismisses this concern, arguing that the definition of primary goods is not supposed to be "fair to comprehensive conceptions of the good associated with such doctrines, by striking a fair balance among them"; on the contrary, "they are fair to free and equal citizens as persons affirming such conceptions" (1988:276). Because the index of primary goods is drawn up only in terms of our status as citizens, as free and equal persons, we can endorse it as fair even if it does "not approximate very accurately to what many people most want and value as judged by their comprehensive views" (260).

This response may be adequate for the basic rights and opportunities included in the index, which are to be distributed equally. Basic rights are necessary for the satisfaction of the interest Rawls takes all citizens to have, namely, the exercise of the two moral powers of justice and the good. But this response is not plausible for the other primary goods, which are only necessary for the pursuit of particular ends. If our ends diverge significantly, then we will not require "roughly the same primary goods, that is, the same basic rights, liberties, and opportunities, as well as the same all-purpose means such as income and wealth, all of which are secured by the same social bases of self-respect" (257). In that case, we may be unable to construct a suitable index of primary goods to use in justly settling these conflicts.

There is one type of good that is likely to cause particular difficulties—the good of self-respect. Self-respect is obviously not something that "society" directly distributes to its members, but there is a close connection between social practices and individuals' achieving self-respect. For self-respect involves holding the belief that one lives up to certain standards that define what it is to be a person of worth, a person entitled to respect. To some extent, these standards will be rooted in a person's (or a group's) comprehensive moral view, such as one's religious commitments. But to an important extent these standards will necessarily be part of the institutions and practices of the society, defining the expectations to which different people are subject, and to which they must "measure up" if they are to be seen as persons of worth and honor. Rawls is acutely aware of this issue, which is why he includes the "social bases of self-respect" on his list of the primary goods, often calling self-respect "the most important primary good" (1971:440).[21] In Rawls's view, "self-respect is secured by the public affirmation of the status of equal citizenship for all," together with a rich associational life in which the accomplishments and endeavors of different individuals can be affirmed by others (544–45).

---

[21] My use of the term "self-respect" is somewhat different from Rawls's; I take his usage to be closer to the meaning of "self-esteem," and he often uses these terms interchangeably. I discuss this distinction in chapter six, below.

Equal citizenship and a rich associational life are vital, but there are other contexts in which individuals are subjected to standards and expectations, contexts in which their self-respect may be reinforced or threatened. In many cases, such as the family or the workplace, these standards will have to be politically recognized and enforced, which may lead to conflict among the adherents of different comprehensive moral views as to how they should be formulated. For example, people who have different views about the place of marriage among the ends of life will hold different beliefs about the conditions under which divorce is acceptable. Even if everyone accepts the public conception of justice, it is by no means clear that this conception will be adequate to settle such disputes, since in these areas there is no clear way of separating the public, shared conception of justice, and the private, diverse conceptions of our ends and ideals.[22]

Because there is an internal connection between the standards and expectations of institutions and individual self-respect, social institutions and practices should not be seen merely as instruments to be employed to achieve certain purposes, for they will often be expressive of our moral and personal identities. Unfortunately, Rawls's essentially instrumental conception of institutional design, in which institutions are assessed in terms of their conformity to the two principles of justice, does not make adequate allowance for this fact, which makes his theory inadequate to deal with conflicts in which private values are inseparable from public (or publicly regulated) institutions in a morally pluralist society.

The difficulties attendant upon Rawls's effort to ground the liberal strategy on a "Kantian" view of the person suggest that we try a somewhat different approach, one that appeals to an even "thinner" view of the self. Charles Larmore, appealing only to a limited conception of rationality and the value of equal respect, offers a general defense of liberal political morality on the grounds that it represents a "modus vivendi" among incompatible moral ideals, making it possible for us to create a just and stable political order in the face of a plurality of moral ideals and commitments. The key to this political morality is the "neutrality of the state" (1987:43), which requires that the state "not seek to promote any particular conception of the good life because of its presumed *intrinsic* superiority—that is, because it is supposedly a *truer* conception" (43). Of course, the consequences of political action may have a differential effect on some goals or ways of life compared to others, but this is compatible with neutrality so long as the policies in question were not adopted *in*

---

[22] See the last section of this chapter and chapter six for a discussion of this problem.

order to promote those goals. Further, the state can be used to promote values that can be justified on neutral grounds—grounds that do not invoke controversial values or judgments. Thus, the state can pursue economic "efficiency" (because everyone supposedly accepts this goal) but not religious conformity (on which there are profound differences in the society).

In some ways, the terms "modus vivendi" and "neutrality" do not do justice to Larmore's argument, for they suggest that he conceives liberal political morality as a matter of prudence or even calculated self-interest. This suggestion is completely mistaken: in Larmore's view, it is morally incumbent upon us to organize our public lives on the basis of neutrality and to show tolerance toward others whose commitments and attachments differ from our own. This obligation is rooted ultimately in "the wish to show everyone *equal respect*" (61), something we owe to others "by virtue of their capacity for working out a coherent view of the world and . . . of the good life" (65).

Equal respect, Larmore suggests, is rooted in the very notion of justification itself. When someone calls upon us to justify an action or situation, he or she recognizes that we have "a perspective on the world" in terms of which we think our "action makes sense." By calling for justification, our interlocutor expresses a "willingness to discuss it rationally" with us; and because we are "obligated to treat another as he is treating us," I have an obligation to respond to the demand to engage in rational conversation, to attempt to convince the other of the justifiability of my action (64–65).

Rational discourse in the face of disagreement—including disagreement over the conditions or "norms of rational conversation" (55) itself—requires that the participants seek to discover "*neutral ground*, with the hope either of resolving the dispute or bypassing it" (53). If we cannot find shared premises, we would have no possibility of engaging in rational discussion, as opposed to attempts to manipulate or dominate each other. If we are to have a political order that is justifiable to all who are subject to it, it can only be based upon shared principles or values. Because everyone will be able to accept them, they will be "neutral" among the conflicting moral ideals that exist in a pluralist society. Outside of political life we are free to pursue our own ideals and need not accept the priority of neutrality. In particular, the commitment to neutrality in the political sphere does not entail that we be committed to individual autonomy as a moral ideal. In public life I must be prepared to "bracket," as it were, disputed ideals and values, to "suspend" my adherence to them in the search' for neutral grounds. But there is no reason for me to take the same attitude toward them in private life by, for example, conceiving of myself as a person who autonomously chooses my ends, therefore putting a certain distance between my "self" and my "ends." I do not, then, have to accept the disputable views of the meaning and value of life that have been advanced by theorists such as Kant or Mill in order to accept a liberal political morality. In this way, Larmore strongly rejects the idea that "the political order express our personal ideal" or "our deepest moral commitments" (91).

Larmore contends that his justification of liberal political morality is "neutral" in the sense that it does not depend upon disputed moral ideals. His argument requires that one accept only a fairly weak notion of reciprocity, requiring that one respond to the demand for justification by offering reasons to another, and the recognition that rational discourse involves the search for shared premises from which to resolve disagreement. But what happens when we cannot discover enough commonality to resolve our differences? Larmore's answer is that we must restrict the activities of the state to those that can be justified by appealing only to shared values or principles. On issues (such as policies regulating the distribution of income) where some action must be taken, Larmore would allow neutrality to be compromised by admitting disputed ideals in order to reach a decision. But in doing so, he would insist, only the least controversial ideals should be employed, so that neutrality is maintained as much as possible.

Larmore's account of liberalism as a political strategy, and his articulation of it in terms of a "norm of rational dialogue," in which disputed ideals are "bracketed" in the search for common ground, are important ideas, which I will develop further in the next chapter. But he is too sanguine in his expectations for this strategy, in part because he exaggerates the "neutrality" of his justification of neutrality. The key part of his argument is his claim that, in the face of disagreement, we must limit the scope of political choice to those questions that can be resolved in terms of common values. To do otherwise would be to coercively impose one's views upon others, and so to violate the norm of equal respect, which requires that we justify ourselves to others through rational dialogue. But is such coercion never justified? Larmore himself does not believe so, referring contemptuously to "fanatics and would-be martyrs" who are prepared to disturb "civil peace" to advance their views. "A liberal political system," he insists, "need not feel obliged to reason with fanatics; it must simply take the necessary precautions to guard against them" (60).

It is not the tough-mindedness that is problematic here, but the self-righteousness, particularly in the context of an argument stressing respect for others. Larmore's fanatics, I suspect, do not experience the "norm of rational dialogue"—construed as requiring only shared values to serve as the basis for public policy—as neutral in the least. This conception drastically restricts the ends that can be served through public action to those that are common to all citizens. Some people will be required to subordinate their most cherished ideals and to accept other, secondary values to govern their social lives. Worse, they may feel that the "shared" values—just because they represent something of a "lowest common denominator"—are completely unsuitable for this task. Being largely instrumental goods, such as economic efficiency and opportunities to achieve status and power, their proper role is perverted when they are made the directive principles of social life. Far from providing a framework that is "fair" to all, and within which different individuals and groups can pursue their own moral visions, a society oriented toward these interests will systematically encourage some ways of life (for example, those in which acquisition and status-competition are central) at the expense of others. Of course, disrupting civil peace is coercive. But so, it might be argued, is restricting public action to those justified by "shared" premises or values. For the laws and the norms of the institutions we create are, it goes without saying, intended to be enforced, and when they systematically prevent some from achieving their most valued ends, they will be experienced as coercive.

I will argue later for the bracketing strategy Larmore recommends. But (unfortunately) it cannot be defended on the grounds that it is "neutral," for there is a sense in which the shared values it discovers may not be genuinely shared. The sense or meaning that a value has depends to a large extent upon the place it occupies in a whole system of beliefs and commitments. Larmore's strategy of discourse, by abstracting apparently common beliefs and principles from the systems in which they originally found their homes, may distort them in various ways by severing their links to the other aspects of these systems. Because the "same" values play different roles in different systems, the distortions may not be "equal" for the different groups involved, leading some to feel coerced by a procedure which, to others, appears to be the paradigm of fairness. Although Larmore recognizes the possibility of deep, irresolvable conflicts in moral life, I would suggest that they are much more pervasive than his account allows.

Beyond Thin Selves: The Impossibility of Neutrality

One of the major reasons why Larmore's project does not fully succeed is that it rests too heavily upon a commitment to neutrality. It is easy to see why neutrality appears to be crucial to the liberal strategy in general, and not just to Larmore's version. On the face of it, neutrality would seem to be implicit in the liberal strategy of basing the public sphere on a conception of the self that abstracts a set of common elements from the diverse array of particular ways of life to be found within the society. After all, the whole point of the liberal project is to discover a way in which people with different values may live under principles that they regard as just or legitimate, and the obvious way to do that is to limit the scope of political authority to unproblematic areas and to provide space within which citizens can pursue their own conceptions of the good. But this presupposes that the state will at least seek to be neutral among these conceptions, and not formulate policies that are intended to advance the ideals of some citizens or hinder those of others. It is not surprising, then, that many liberal theorists have attempted to give an account of liberalism that centers on neutrality. As Ackerman argues, the state ought not to pursue a policy whose justification requires the assertion that some "conception of the good is better than that asserted by [other citizens], or that, regardless of one's conception of the good, [any citizen] is intrinsically superior to one or more of his fellow citizens" (1980:11). The belief in neutrality is ultimately rooted in the faith that the liberal strategy can work completely, that our political and moral lives can be conducted in such a way that we never face tragic conflicts—situations in which, no matter what is done, some will experience the action as an imposition.

If the state were sharply separate from society, functioning only to uphold a set of rules guaranteeing peaceful intercourse within which people could pursue their individual aims, then the ideal of neutrality might have some plausibility. In such a world, the state would merely enjoin actions that interfered with the free exercise of its citizens' various attempts to live what they saw as the good life. This is the traditional liberal picture of the state as traffic cop, helping citizens travel safely to their different destinations, but not interfering with their decisions about where they are going. But that is not our world. There are many ways in which the constitutive aims and attachments of citizens may figure in public life and become the

63

subject of political action, but which do not conform to the "traffic cop" model.

In too many cases liberals have confined their accounts of the state to its distinctive activity of coercively sanctioning certain forms of behavior.[23] But the political association affects us in many other ways besides subjecting us to its commands. For example, political activities and institutions give expression to shared or normatively sanctioned conceptions and values, thereby reinforcing them in the society. Further, different ways of organizing the political sphere and different public policies have important implications for the kinds of structures that exist in "nonpolitical" areas, and on the structures of opportunities (and even what will be regarded as an opportunity) that people will face. These facets of political life cannot adequately be captured by a model of the state as traffic cop. In these areas there is scope for the political association to promote aims and attachments that go beyond those based on a "thin" conception of the self, and in which neutrality is at best an uncertain guide and, at worst, undesirable in itself. I will examine three such cases.

The Private Sphere: Family Law

One area in which the state cannot be neutral, but must structure opportunities in ways that will give some preference to one or another view of the good, is family law. This is an area that has been contentious in recent years, as laws have been altered to reflect widespread changes in social expectations, particularly regarding gender roles. More radical changes have also been advocated, including extending the institution of marriage (or marriage-like arrangements) to same sex couples.[24] Most states have passed laws that make "no fault" divorce possible, abolish the legal presumption that the mother should receive custody of minor children, and limit the award of alimony to a relatively short period of time. These

---

[23] I do not want to minimize the difficulties issues of neutrality raise even in the area of the criminal law. In a masterful, four-volume account of the "moral limits of the criminal law," Feinberg finds that he has to appeal to the value of "autonomy" in order to block carefully formulated arguments for criminalizing actions that do not cause specific harms to assignable persons, since in at least some cases it is hard to argue that the actions in question do not result in genuine evils. See, for example, his discussion of a hypothetical "gladiatorial show" and his analysis of the issues involved in preserving valued ways of life (1988:129 and 67). But, as Larmore and others have pointed out, "autonomy" is by no means a neutral value.

[24] See, for example, Sullivan (1989).

changes reflect the increasingly common view that a marriage should be satisfying to both partners, so that they should be able to dissolve it without having to demonstrate that someone has committed a specified fault or offense, such as cruel treatment or adultery. They further reflect the view that both men and women should be responsible for child-rearing and for supporting the family economically. Thus, by marrying, a man does not take on the responsibility to provide for his wife for the rest of her life, even if the marriage should end in divorce, because it has come to be expected that women have the same obligation as men to support themselves. The purpose of alimony, then, is not to provide income support for a dependent woman, but to permit her a period of time to effect a transition to an economically independent status.

These expectations are in many important ways dramatically different from the expectations that informed divorce and family law even a generation ago. And they are based upon important changes in the way in which large numbers of people in our society conceive of an appropriate and worthwhile way of life. In particular, the notion that gender should determine social role, so that women should—because they are women— have the principal responsibility for child care, has been rejected by large numbers of people in our society. Laws based on that expectation had previously seemed to be reasonable, but came to be seen as unjust, making it impossible or at least difficult for men and women to achieve many of the things that had come to be seen as conditions of self-realization. At the same time, however, these changes have been deeply resented, particularly by those women who identified with a more traditional view of a woman's role. For them, the new laws are threatening and, it appears, have been materially harmful. Because they must now struggle to retain custody of their children, it is said that they must often give up other claims they might be able to make to family assets or alimony awards, and because they often do not have the earning power that genuine independence requires, the change in the practice of awarding alimony has in many cases condemned them and their children to poverty.[25]

While it is possible to imagine laws that might be more "neutral" than the current laws,[26] it is hard to imagine how they could be completely neutral on these matters. How can we determine what the grounds for divorce should be without an understanding of the role that marriage

[25] On the consequences of these changes for women, see, for example, Weizman (1985) and Mason (1988).

[26] See Okin (1989a) for proposals designed to accommodate both traditional and nontraditional family patterns.

plays in life? How can we decide on the division of family assets, or on the basis for the award of alimony, without having some view about what men and women are expected to contribute to a marriage? And how could these questions be answered without reference to some idea of what a worthwhile life involves, some conception of human excellence, some idea of the human good? Nor, I might add, is it conceivable not to have laws regulating marriage. The option of civil marriage is vital, if individuals are to be free of ecclesiastical authority in these matters. And some regular process for settling disputes that arise regarding domestic matters is obviously required if we are to have a stable society in which private power is checked by public authority. In secular societies there must be family law; and in family law there must reside a specific, nonneutral conception of the good. In this area, neutrality is not a genuine possibility, and consequently some visions of a meaningful, worthwhile life will be disadvantaged, if not excluded altogether. Those who hold such visions, needless to say, will have reason to resent the resulting imposition of values they do not share.

CONSTITUTIVE ATTACHMENTS: NATIONALISM

A second area in which neutrality is impossible, even as an ideal, concerns the fundamental *political* attachments of citizens, including their sense of national identity. The sense of oneself as a member of a nation is a paradigm case of a constitutive attachment that is not only communal but inherently political. For what is distinctive about nationalism is the demand it expresses for at least some degree of *political* autonomy, so that the nation can organize and direct its common affairs and give expression to itself as a distinct human community alongside other nations.[27] Further, at least for many people, the nation is an essential part of their self-identity, something that gives significance and purpose to their lives, something for which they are (or think that they ought to be) prepared to die. The nation is an object of public veneration, celebrated in myth and ritual, and it commands an allegiance that often overrides even deeply held moral principles. As Weber said, it is one of the few inventions of modernity that can give meaning to death.

Liberalism and nationalism have not always had a happy relationship, for there is the potential in nationalism for deeply illiberal policies and

---

[27] This demand need not take the form of political sovereignty, but may be limited to issues such as culture or education.

actions. When nationalism takes the form of xenophobia, when it defines the "people" in terms that exclude law-abiding groups long resident in its territory, or when it conceives of an imperial mission for itself, it runs afoul of liberal values. Liberalism has always felt a strong attraction for internationalism or cosmopolitanism, an attraction that manifests itself in calls for international law and perpetual peace, in the advocacy of free trade and movement of people, in the often-derided effort to make human rights a consideration (if not a touchstone) in foreign policy, and in the development of international organizations (including especially the League of Nations and the United Nations).

On the other hand, liberalism is compatible with, and even supportive of, nationalism in many ways, above all in the idea of a right to national self-determination.[28] Further, the idea of the "nation" generates a certain pressure in the direction of moral equality, for it unites people horizontally and defines them as having a common identity, at least vis-à-vis outsiders.[29] And, of course, there are also full-blooded "national liberals," people whose liberalism is largely confined to the internal arrangements of their own societies, and who view the rest of the world in terms of the power-interests of their state.

Liberalism, then, poses no obstacles to and may even legitimate the organization of political societies along national lines. Of course, liberals cannot condone the state's requiring of all its citizens that they accept the nation as part of their own identity, or incorporate the nation's "good" as part of their own good. Loyalty oaths and the like (at least outside of positions directly concerned with state security) have no place in a liberal polity. Further, the nation must be understood to be "open": citizenship must not be withheld on such grounds as ethnicity and religion.[30] So long as the liberal state observes these constraints, it could legitimately promote a sense of national identity.

As long as the active participation of its citizens is not *required*, nationalist considerations may be a basis for policy-making in a number of areas. These could include domains in which the state's activity impinges

[28] Some liberals—notably J. S. Mill—have offered justifications of colonialism essentially along tutelary lines, the role of the colonial power being to act as "trustee" to the colony in helping it prepare for self-government. While such arguments may explain why a liberal regime coming into power should not immediately abandon its colonies, it is hard to see it as a justification for adding new ones.

[29] See Anderson 1983, chap. 4, for a suggestive discussion of this idea.

[30] See Kohn (1965), who distinguishes between open and closed nationalism. The latter admits only those who in some (often mythical) sense can trace descent from a common ancestor to membership in the political community. All versions of liberal theory insist upon inclusiveness: all who are subject to political authority must be equal as citizens.

on questions of culture (such as policies regarding education and the arts), and in the display of political symbols and the performance of political rituals. Unless the state could, for example, invoke the symbolism and provide occasion for practicing the rituals that give expression to the national identity, citizens would be deprived of the means necessary for realizing this aspect of their fundamental attachments. And while these policies or activities would not involve restrictions on individual freedom of conscience, in that no particular actions or professions of faith would be required, they do involve the state in promoting a particular set of values. Since it is quite possible that this kind of commitment to the nation may not be part of the identity of some citizens, these values may not be universally shared in the society. Thus, the state would not be neutral between, say, cosmopolitans and patriots, and cosmopolitans may suffer some discomfort in sitting out the rituals in which their neighbors participate. Even in a liberal polity, the promotion and expression of national identity will impinge on the lives of some of its citizens.

EQUALITY, MEMBERSHIP AND THE WELFARE STATE

Family law and nationalism are questions that are imposed on the liberal state by features of the societies in which such states exist. If my analysis of these examples is correct, they involve issues that cannot be settled in a strictly neutral manner. While some policies may be less neutral than others, the ideal of pure neutrality is chimerical. But even if neutrality on issues such as these were possible, there are reasons internal to the liberal ideal itself which preclude neutrality in other areas. I have argued that we should interpret the liberal project as beginning not with a theory of human nature, but with an understanding of persons as "individuals" which is widely shared in a particular society at a particular point in time. This understanding of ourselves as individuals poses the problem of pluralism as a moral and not merely a strategic issue, and underlies the liberal strategy of developing a basis for political association on a deliberately "thin" conception of the self.

This understanding of the self includes the idea of moral equality, or the equal worth of persons. In what we might call "classical liberalism," and in certain versions of libertarianism today, the idea of equal worth was largely exhausted by the idea of juridical equality—equality before the law, or equality of rights. Historically, and in (too) many contexts today, this was, and often still is, a radical demand. But at least since the nineteenth century, even when acknowledged and achieved, formal equality has been seen to be inadequate. In the first place, and most obviously, one may have a "right" without the means to exercise it—the right to counsel but being too poor to hire such help, to use a standard example.

But there is a deeper reason why formal equality is inadequate, and that has to do with the difference between what I have called a "thin" and a "complete" theory of the self. If classical liberalism was content with formal equality, it was to a large extent because the abstract, ahistorical conceptions of the person on which it was based were taken to be complete accounts of the self, as capturing what was essential to us as humans. If we conceive of people in such reduced terms as, for example, merely having a capacity for rationality and being moved by desires, then it is reasonable to understand equality simply as equality before the law—being equally subject to the requirements of reason which all persons supposedly possess. But if we recognize that people are not "individuals" apart from or outside of their social relationships, that they come to be individuals and to make claims for moral equality only in certain kinds of societies, then we must develop a richer understanding of the idea of equality itself. Equality of respect and human dignity can be realized in ongoing social relationships only for people who are *full members* of their society, who are able to share in what Richard Henry Tawney called "a common heritage of civilization." For it is not by virtue of our relationships as abstract individuals that we can be equals of one another, but by virtue of sharing in a way of life in which the conceptions of moral equality and individuality are central. Thus, moral equality requires membership, or what Marshall (1977:101) revealingly calls "equal social worth," and not merely negative liberty and formal equality. It follows that certain opportunities or "life chances" must be provided to all citizens if moral equality is to be realized.

Membership requires a great deal more of the state than does formal equality, for it means that every individual must be provided with those capacities and opportunities that are essential for full membership in society. The ideal of the nineteenth-century liberal state, one that provides a legal order that enshrines the principle of juridical equality and that scrupulously observes the sharp border between "state" and "society," has never really described any political reality. But in my account of liberalism, it could not even be an ideal. For the minimal state fails in a primary task of the liberal state, which is to provide the necessary means for everyone to attain full membership in society, since that is a condition of our understanding ourselves as morally equal persons. This task requires that the liberal state be a democratic welfare state. For what is distinctive

69

about the welfare state is not a commitment to a pure egalitarianism, or even a Rawlsian difference principle, but to the provision of a set of opportunities and services which make it possible for everyone to enjoy a common status of citizenship.

Exactly what citizenship or full membership requires (beyond equal civil and political rights) is, naturally, a contentious and contestable issue, and has constituted much of the focus of political argument and innovation for the past century. One of the most obvious requirements is universal education, freely available to a level considered "normal" for the society, and the provision of public education is always among the first social tasks that liberal governments undertake. Full membership also requires regulation of the market to reduce or ameliorate the socially adverse effects of essentially self-interested exchanges. And it requires the provision of a level of material well-being that is sufficient to enable people to live at least minimally "respectable" lives.

Often overlooked when lists like these are compiled is that the *way* in which these services are provided is as important as the services themselves. It is essential that these needs be met in a way that is compatible with the recipients' maintaining their dignity and status as full citizens. This involves acute dilemmas for a liberal society, because in such societies individuals (or, at least, families) are expected to be independent in the sense that they are expected to provide for their own needs through their own activities and resources. To the extent that welfare state programs involve the acknowledgment that an individual has failed to meet this expectation, they can undercut the objective of enabling people to achieve full membership. While they may provide some service that is vital to membership, they sometimes do so in a way that undermines the individual's independence and self-respect, which is an equally (or even more) vital aspect of membership.

It is not my purpose at this point to explore the ways in which the democratic welfare state has wrestled with these issues.[31] What I would like to argue here is that a state committed to providing a wide range of services, in a way that is consistent with the self-respect of their recipients, cannot possibly be "neutral" among different conceptions of the human good and different ideals of human excellence. For both the identification of the minimal needs that must be met, and the specification of the norms that must be observed in meeting them, require some conception of what it is to lead a worthwhile life. In many cases these judgments will not be particularly controversial, not because they are "neutral" but because

---

[31] See chapter six, below, and Moon (1988b).

they will be widely shared in the society. But in other cases they will be deeply divisive, and no "neutral" resolution will be possible.

That the welfare state cannot be neutral can be seen by considering the controversy surrounding the state's provision of medical care in America in recent years. In particular, the use of public funds to provide abortion and birth control has been bitterly resisted by those who see these activities as deeply immoral. Far from seeing state provision of these services to those who want them as neutral (because no one is required to accept them), they see it as promoting a particular set of values and a particular(ly immoral) view of the ends of life—one that subverts the "true" meaning of human sexuality. By making such services available as part of public programs designed to meet what we, as a society, have come to see as minimal requirements for full membership in our society, we give public expression and legitimation to this view of the human good. On the other hand, it is hard to see the denial of such services as "neutral" either. For those who see a woman's ability to control her own sexuality and reproduction as essential to her autonomy and self-realization, these are necessary medical services that must be included in the social minimum the state provides. To deny them is to deny that they are necessary to equality of social worth, to full membership in society.[32]

In a liberal society, where the state must secure the conditions for membership for everyone, at least so far as this is possible, the ideal of neutrality is not desirable. Membership cannot be understood, let alone achieved, apart from a particular conception of the capacities and resources citizens must have to be full citizens enjoying a status of equal respect with others. But the very effort to achieve this goal will create potentially tragic choices, as policies intended to promote equal membership for all will make it more difficult or even impossible for some to achieve their ends.

Conclusion

Liberal responses to moral pluralism seek to accommodate differences by limiting the scope of authoritative political decision, providing a large area of social life within which individuals and groups are free to pursue their own ideals and ends. I have examined two broad liberal approaches

---

[32] For an account of the abortion issue that focuses on the social meanings of abortion (or its prohibition) for women and conceptions of women's roles, see Luker (1984). See also chapter four, below.

to defining these limits. The first approach is essentialist; it draws these boundaries by specifying a set of rights and principles of justice based on a general theory of human nature. But this approach involves the same difficulties as the "Aristotelian" theories canvassed in chapter two. Conceptions of human nature that can command general agreement are so abstract and indeterminate that they cannot support clear, determinate normative principles—at least principles adequate to the task at hand. Specific conceptions of human nature, on the other hand, are not only controversial but appear arbitrary in their selection of traits on the basis of which the theorist would erect the normative structure of society. All liberal theories rest upon some conception of human agency; even if we agree that this is an essential human trait, it is not the only one, and there appears to be no way to establish its priority relative to other traits.

In light of these difficulties, a second approach reinterprets liberalism as a "political strategy" designed to solve the difficulties of creating a genuine polity in the presence of moral pluralism. This approach self-consciously embraces a "thin," but widely shared, conception of the self that can be used to ground a conception of justice. In spite of its richness and power, this approach suffers from some of the same difficulties as its "essentialist" cousin, difficulties that are rooted in its reliance on the metaphor of the social contract. In order to discover rules that can provide a just framework for social life, these theories specify a structure of decision or choice within which such rules can be formulated. But any such structure necessarily excludes certain possible perspectives, certain voices, certain forms of human experience, and it does so prior, as it were, to the process of social decision itself. In order to make agreement possible, certain perspectives are ruled out by the very way in which the choice situation is structured. In Larmore's revealing phrase, "A liberal political system need not feel obliged to reason with fanatics; it must simply take the necessary precautions against them" (1987:60). This may well be required, but resorting to these "necessary precautions" is also to abandon the hope for a moral community. Moreover, both contractarian and strategic approaches are wedded to a notion of neutrality that is unrealizable even as an ideal. There are many areas in which the liberal state must act, and it must do so in a way that invokes a particular conception of the good life or citizenship. In these cases, the liberal state cannot be—nor should it be—neutral. Thus, if the strategic interpretation of liberalism is to offer a solution to the problem of creating and sustaining a genuine political community under conditions of moral pluralism, it will have to be reformulated in such a way as to recognize its own limitations. To be viable, the liberal strategy must become less "contractarian," less a model of an ideal setting under which agreement on the principles of public order is reached. Rather than a contractarian vision of political life, the liberal strategy must be based on a model of social decision in which agreement on the norms governing society would reflect an open process of discourse—one that is designed not to exclude any perspectives, even while it acknowledges the impossibility of neutrality.

From Contract to Discourse

"DISCOURSE" AND "contractarian" strategies are obviously closely related. They both seek to ground political and other associations on the "free agreement" of participants, and they both, therefore, must offer some account of what is meant by "free agreement." Various theories have been proposed to answer these questions. The more ambitious have attempted to specify in a reasonably full way what substantive agreements we could expect to see reached if the conditions of free agreement were realized. Others, more modestly, offer only "a particular way of thinking about fair procedures for adjudicating normative claims" (White 1988:73). Contractarian theories attempt to specify the conditions of free agreement in a general way, applicable over a wide variety of settings, and to show what substantive outcomes will necessarily be reached in a free agreement. Unfortunately, any way of doing this—any list of conditions such as Rawls's original position, Gauthier's "initial bargaining position," not to mention the (often implicit) conditions of classical social contract theories—must itself be subject to moral and political argumentation, must itself be tested through a process in which genuine agreement is sought. In such testing, as I showed in chapter three, any proposed condition may be rejected on the grounds that it silences some point of view, renders invisible some aspect of experience, and so rules out possible moral or political positions prior to the very process that is supposed to establish acceptable principles.

Discourse theories, as I will refer to them here, attempt to avoid the problems of contractarian approaches by focusing on the process of argumentation, rather than positing a particular conception of the self—that is, a particular conception of rationality and motivation—that can be used to ground specific normative principles. Liberal interpretations of discourse focus on the discovery of shared principles, attempting to bracket the moral and evaluative differences among the participants in the discourse. Unfortunately, as I shall show in the next section of this chapter, this model of discourse constrains the considerations that participants can bring up, and thus may prestructure that process in ways that may be adverse to the needs and aspirations of certain groups. Once again, the liberal strategy fails to realize the promise of political community.

If we cannot hope to bridge the differences we face, can we perhaps transcend them? Rather than adopting a process through which differences are preserved by being subsumed under general principles all can accept, some argue that we should turn to what I earlier called "moral-transformative" theory. I will consider two versions of moral-transformative theory in this chapter. This first is Rousseau's, a model of moral transformation that imposes what I will call "social" constraints by specifying the kind of political and social context in which genuine agreement is possible. Although Rousseau's model cannot deal with the problem of moral pluralism, it is instructive in offering a particularly clear and accessible account of many features and problems shared by moral-transformative theory. The second version of moral-transformative theory I will examine is that of Seyla Benhabib, responding in part to inadequacies of both traditional contractarian theories and theories such as Rousseau's. Benhabib argues that we need to abandon the contractarian model and adopt instead the idea of a discourse in which people seek not merely to bracket, but also to overcome, their differences. Thus, such discourse must be as unconstrained as possible, keeping to a minimum the constraints that participants must observe. Unfortunately, as I will argue below, this approach will not work, for the very notion of "unconstrained discourse" is deeply problematic. The effort to make particular voices heard will necessarily silence, or at least burden, others.

Liberal Dialogue

Bruce Ackerman has offered such a persuasive interpretation of liberal dialogue that an examinination of its strengths and weaknesses reveals why this conception of discourse is ultimately inadequate. Ackerman begins with the assumption that moral pluralism—disagreement among people regarding the ends of life and principles of action they regard to be "true"—is the principal problem we face in creating a just political order. His starting point is a "simple model" of a society consisting of different groups of people "who have combined faith and reason in an effort to search out the moral truth," but where each group has come up with different answers. The problem then becomes: "How are the different groups to resolve their problem of mutual coexistence in a reasonable way?" (Ackerman 1989:9). Ackerman's answer is, in essence, that they must talk to one another—to engage in dialogue.

This requires, according to Ackerman, a conception of dialogue that enables "political participants to talk to one another in an appropriately neutral way" (23). Unfortunately, the history of efforts to develop such a conception is not encouraging, including Hobbes's effort to discover a sufficiently important common value under which to subsume other disagreements, Bentham's attempt to "translate" moral disagreements into the language of utility, and Rawls's effort to transcend moral disagreements in the "original position." The problem with all these approaches, according to Ackerman, is that they require participants in a dialogue to renounce or to misrepresent their core beliefs by constraining them to fit the preferred model of political or moral dialogue. What we need to do, according to him, is to develop a different strategy, one that does not offer a new framework to which all might converge, but that begins (and ends) with their existing beliefs. The point of this dialogue, Ackerman insists, is not to discover the truth, and so to break down the ideational barriers separating different groups from each other, but "to consider the way they might live together despite this ongoing disagreement" (10).

Ackerman's suggestion for such a strategy is what he calls "the path of conversational restraint": "We should simply say *nothing at all* about [any] disagreement ["about one or another dimension of the moral truth"] and put the moral ideals that divide us off the conversational agenda" (16). The intended outcome of such dialogues will be the discovery of moral beliefs shared by all parties to the conversation. According to Ackerman, only shared beliefs should be used "for the purposes of conflict resolution" (18). In this way, no one will be compelled to disavow important beliefs or values, and citizens will have "a way of reasonably responding to their continuing moral disagreement" (19).[1]

In many ways this idea of "conversational restraint" is attractive. That we should seek areas of agreement with others, and attempt to build on these areas rather than to impose our own views on others, is a moral idea at the heart of the "discourse" conception of moral and political legitimacy. Unfortunately, the strategy is fraught with difficulties. The most obvious, perhaps, is that the notion of "shared beliefs" is not altogether clear. Ackerman illustrates his argument by means of standard Venn diagrams, showing the shared beliefs as the intersection of two sets of beliefs, those of the two hypothetical groups who are parties to a dialogue. But this is not an appropriate model for beliefs, since their relationships are not extensional but intensional. Unlike, say, the intersection of the set of objects that are white and objects that are cats—viz., white cats—the "in-

---

[1] Conversational restraint applies only to "public" contexts. Ackerman insists that we do "not lose the chance to talk to one another about our deepest moral disagreements in countless other, more private, contexts" (18).

tersection" of two "sets" of beliefs may not unproblematically belong to each. Beliefs are not discrete objects like cats, but bear "internal" or conceptual relations to other beliefs. The meaning of a particular belief depends upon its place in a system of beliefs, and abstracting the belief from the system may distort its sense. This is particularly true in political and moral matters, where necessarily make use of "essentially contested concepts." The fact that two participants in a dialogue agree, for example, that "freedom" is an important value does not mean that they share a common belief.

This is not simply a quibble about the way in which Ackerman represents his argument, but it goes to the heart of the matter. For the key idea behind his strategy of "conversational restraint" is to avoid questions of "moral truth." But in the case of beliefs, it is not clear that we can even identify a particular belief without asking questions about its "truth," about its coherence, grounds, relationship to other beliefs, and so forth. Thus, to be barred from discussing the truth of contested beliefs may prevent us from discovering common ones. Indeed, one of the most important ways we actually discover beliefs we hold in common with others is by challenging beliefs that seem wrong, and coming to see the grounds on which they are held. In addition, it is at least possible that, in an unconstrained conversation, the area of agreement may come to be enlarged as we reassess our beliefs in light of the points raised by others.

Because we cannot separate the identification of a belief from the question of its truth, it is doubtful that "conversational restraint" can serve the purpose it is intended to serve, namely, to enable us to solve "our problems in coexistence in a way [that all participants] find reasonable" (10). Would participants in such a constrained dialogue find this limit on what they are allowed to say in defense of their views reasonable? What motive might someone have for adopting it? On the face of it, it appears to allow a veto to any group that, for whatever reason, objects to a given proposal. At the very least, would we not wish to require some test of sincerity before according such power over our common life? And do we not test sincerity by examining the grounds of beliefs, by testing them for consistency with other beliefs and behavior? By, in short, discourse aimed at discovering (something like) truth?

More seriously, we must ask whether this approach is apt to provide a sufficient area of agreement for coexistence on terms all regard as reasonable. What do we do when we face conflicts that we cannot resolve on the basis of shared principles? Under these circumstances the issue must be settled by imposition—by some kind of force. Given this alternative, isn't it more reasonable to abandon the strategy of "conversational restraint" and at least attempt to persuade others before we seek to coerce them (and be persuaded by them, before they may coerce us)? The strategy of conversational restraint seems capable only of discovering "preexisting" areas of agreement; the problem, however, may be to enlarge those areas if we seek to replace force and manipulation with relationships based on principles that all parties can freely accept.

Finally, Ackerman's model rests upon an unexamined distinction between "public" and "private," where the obligation of conversational restraint applies only to public, not private, dialogue. In our private lives we may offer the deepest grounds for our convictions and engage in discussion about whether these grounds are adequate. But in discussions of public policy these grounds are ruled out of court. But how are we to tell when we are in one realm, and when in the other? When is it appropriate to engage our fellow citizens in unrestrained dialogue, and when are we to censor ourselves? To one person, abortion is a private matter, but to another it may be a public one.

Ackerman's point is that authoritative decisions—those decisions ultimately sanctioned by the legitimate use of force—should only be based upon shared moral beliefs, not on positions that are rejected by some citizens. The result is that those spheres of life in which no moral position commands a consensus must be excluded from authoritative decision, being left to the "private" decisions of particular individuals. Thus, the problem of reasonable coexistence is supposedly solved so long as the state monopolizes the legitimate use of force and its power is employed only in support of consensually held principles.

But this is clearly inadequate as an examination of issues on which there is profound disagreement reveals. Take the abortion question, for example. The strategy of conversational restraint would have us resolve this issue by referring only to shared beliefs as decisional premises, such as the belief in a separation of church and state, and shared commitments to certain basic individual rights. And, to a large degree, the debate has been conducted in these terms—in terms of a shared public discourse of rights, including the right of a woman to control her own body, and the right of fetuses or unborn children to life. And in part because the debate has been framed in this way, it has in the main been decided in favor of the "pro-choice" position. Since the grounds for deciding that a fetus is a "person" are to a significant degree contested religious beliefs, they represent improper decisional premises for authoritative decision.

But this way of framing the debate, as Luker has shown so well, misrepresents issues. According to her analysis, what is at stake in this argument are two broadly opposed worldviews that involve fundamentally different conceptions of the ends of life. In her study of the women active in the "pro-life" movement, she found a widely shared set of beliefs about what constitutes proper and fulfilling roles for women and men, based upon the supposedly natural differences between the sexes. For these women, motherhood and nurturing were seen as essential and deeply valuable activities requiring full-time commitments and emotional qualities fundamentally different from those required by male activities. The ability to give life is what is distinctive to women, and it is in giving and sustaining life that women can find their full realization as persons. Legalized abortion, in their view, is one among a host of similar policies which undermines the possibilities of realizing these values. These policies include permitting teenagers access to contraception and abortion without parental consent, allowing sexual activity outside of marriage, and public support for those kinds of contraception and for small families which implicitly suggest that sexuality is desirable for nonprocreative purposes. In particular, Luker argues, they see abortion as

> intrinsically wrong because it takes a human life and what makes women special is their ability to nourish life. Second, it is wrong because *by giving women control over their fertility*, it breaks up an intricate set of social relationships between men and women that has traditionally surrounded (and in the ideal case protected) women and children. Third and finally, abortion is wrong because it fosters and supports a world view that deemphasizes (and therefore *downgrades*) the traditional roles of men and women. (Luker 1984:161–62)

Public policies regarding the family and divorce, contraception, and abortion have increasingly disrupted settled patterns of life, making it more and more difficult for women and men to pursue this vision of the proper ends of life.

The "pro-choice" position, according to Luker, is based upon a very different worldview, one in which reason and the human capacity to control and direct one's life hold a central place. In this view, men and women are seen as fundamentally equal. Both men and women must choose for themselves the ends they wish to pursue, including the balance they seek between such goods as family and career. For a woman to have the ability to choose in this way requires that she have control over her

79

own reproduction, including access to contraception and, when that fails, to abortion.

Given this diagnosis of the positions at stake in the argument over abortion, it is easy to see why those who support the "pro-life" position might find Ackerman's idea of conversational restraint problematic. To the extent that it prohibits them from articulating what is, in fact, the basis of their position, it structures the public debate in terms that are systematically stacked against them. In this case, either the supposedly shared language of rights and secularism is not actually shared, or the injunction against asserting disputed moral positions is a disguised form of imposition and not "an appropriately neutral device to enable political participants to talk to one another" (Ackerman 1989:12). Moreover, by illustrating the complex ways in which "public" policy bears upon "private" life, it suggests that the distinction between public and private discourse that Ackerman invokes is deeply problematic. If the participants in this debate are to be able to act on their values in their "private" lives, it is hard to see how they can refrain from voicing these values in public debate.

The Social Context of Discourse

The contractarian theories I examined in chapter two foundered on a problem as old as the social contract tradition in political theory, a tradition in which consent is taken to be the basis for political authority: the problem of determining exactly what constitutes agreement or consent.

Part of Rousseau's great originality is that he is the first to provide anything like an adequate account of the problem, one that he develops by extending the idea of the social contract. Thus, Rousseau imagines a "first convention" establishing society. But, unlike his predecessors, he attends to the way in which the formation of society transforms the issue of "consent" and its relationship to authority. Indeed, it affects the emergence and nature of morality itself. Rejecting Locke's idea that there is, by nature, a rational, moral law binding on all people, Rousseau recognizes that the deep problem we face in thinking about society in terms of the metaphor of the social contract is to understand how people could come to be bound by norms at all. If these norms are necessarily conventional, under what circumstances could people come to accept them? Or, in Rousseau's formulation of this question, the problem is to "find a form of association . . . [in] which each one, uniting with all, nevertheless obeys only himself and remains as free as before."[2]

Rousseau's answer is not without its obscurities, but its general form is reasonably clear: what we must do is to create a society whose laws are expressions of the "general will," and whose institutions are such that each citizen will come to identify with, and accept, the general will as an essential part (though not the whole) of his[3] own will. To the extent that this is achieved, then in conforming to the law one is acting in accordance with principles one has fully accepted, and so is free. This requires (among other things) that the citizens themselves make the laws through their own deliberations in the sovereign assembly, for it is only by actively participating in the creation of these rules that they will come to see them as expressions of their own will, and so find obedience to them to be compatible with their individual freedom. And because their relationships to their fellow citizens and to the society as a whole are regulated by principles that they fully accept, they are moral relationships.

But it is misleading to view the citizens of a polity based on the general will simply as "free," or, at least, "as free as they were before." For, as Rousseau argues, their "nature" is transformed by their coming to live in such an association, so that they come to have aspirations and needs that they did not have before: one ceases to be "a stupid, limited animal" and becomes "an intelligent being and a man." In particular, their idea of freedom alters: by coming to live with others under the general will, "man [becomes] truly master of himself." Prior to, or outside of, a society based on the general will, people mistakenly think freedom is doing what one wants, but that is to act under "the impulse of appetite," which Rousseau calls a form of "slavery" (SC 1.8.56). The sense in which we are free in political society—civil and moral freedom—is very different from what Rousseau calls "natural" freedom.

Rousseau's citizens, as authors of their own laws, give their continuing consent to the authority that binds them. But what of those who initially

---

[2] Rousseau (1978: book 1, chap. 6, p. 53). All subsequent references to the *Social Contract* (SC) in this chapter will be given by book, chapter, and page number in the Masters edition (thus, SC 1.6.53). Viroli (1988:23) has argued that Rousseau presupposes "an objective moral order and the existence of objective truth." My formulation, on the contrary, suggests that Rousseau rejects moral realism, but this difference is not really important. The crucial point is that even if there is an objective moral order, the construction of political society depends on human understandings or perceptions of that order, and so on agreement.

[3] I say "his" because Rousseau, notoriously, excluded women from citizenship.

form the social contract, those who (at least in our imagination) originally placed their persons and all their power "under the supreme direction of the general will"? Not having been transformed into "intelligent beings" who are "masters of themselves," how could they even understand what they were doing, let alone be said genuinely to consent to it?

On this matter Rousseau is disarmingly frank. It is, he insists, impossible "for an emerging people to appreciate . . . and follow the fundamental rules of statecraft, [because] the effect would have to become the cause; the social spirit, which should be the result of the institution, would have to preside over the founding of the institution itself; and men would have to be prior to the laws what they ought to become by means of the laws" (SC 2.7.69). Thus, the people could not themselves create the political institutions necessary for a society based on the general will. The design of these institutions must be the work of a "legislator" who deceives the people by making them believe that his proposals are the work of the gods, and so "persuading" them—without "convincing" them—to enact the foundational laws he proposes. The creation of moral relationships rests upon deception and, in a remarkable inversion of the Lockean account of consent, the original act of "consent" in creating the state can be seen to be deeply problematic, while the "consent" of future generations appears to be genuine.

But is it really genuine? If it results from a process of socialization which in turn rests upon the manipulation of the people by an elite, is it really different from the case of slaves who, coming to think of themselves as slaves as a result of being subjected to slavery, "consent" to the institution? Rousseau faults Aristotle for justifying slavery as "natural" on the grounds that he "mistook the effect for the cause," failing to see that "Slaves lose everything by their chains, even the desire to be rid of them" (SC 1.2.48). Can we not say the same thing about the "chains" of political authority, since even the general will society originates in deception? This sort of objection represents a general problem with the idea that legitimacy can be based upon consent, what we might call the problem of circularity. If our "consent" to a set of social conditions results from our having been socialized to those conditions, is that consent not spurious? In Rousseau's case, the crux of the problem has to do with how people come to develop an interest in, or to value, civil and moral freedom.

In a rich and suggestive discussion of Rousseau's account of autonomy and democracy, Joshua Cohen provides an answer to this question, but an answer that is not entirely satisfactory. He argues that "Rousseauian contractors" are not "rational, asocial, purely self-interested individuals," but are persons who have an interest in being autonomous. Because of this interest, he argues, there is an "anticipation of the general will—something universal—present within the contractual situation itself, and therefore a basis for that will in the nature of human beings" (Cohen 1986:284). In agreeing to establish a society "under the supreme direction of the general will," they advance their interest in rational freedom or autonomy. Because we wish to be free, we want to have a social order in which we can "affirm the framework of rules itself," and so we wish to "have a general will" (286).

Viewing moral freedom or autonomy as a "natural" end of persons enables us to escape the dilemma posed above, and in some ways it is reasonable to attribute at least a nascent interest in freedom to the contractors. After all, the social conditions in which the social contract is made are not those of the primitive state of nature in which humans are "stupid animals." When they have "reached the point where obstacles to their self-preservation in the state of nature prevail by their resistance over the forces each individual can use to maintain himself in that state" (SC 1.6.52), "much progress had to have been made, [and] industry and enlightenment acquired, transmitted, and increased from one age to the next."[4] In particular, "the first duties of civility" had come to be recognized, and with them the ideas of self-respect and mutual respect.

Nonetheless, there is a danger in taking freedom as a natural end. Like most appeals to nature, it runs the risk of begging the question. What appears to be most striking about Rousseau, at least compared to other contractarian thinkers, is his insistence upon the ways in which human motivations, needs, and capacities change with changing social circumstances, and the inadequacy of appeals to nature as a basis for explaining or prescribing forms of social and political order. While Rousseau attributes "free will" to human nature, it is only in (certain forms of) society that we come to value this freedom and to define ourselves in terms of it. Indeed, in the normal course of events—as depicted in the *Second Discourse*—such an interest will not (at least in general) develop, as people will increasingly define their interests in terms of reputation and social standing, and human relationships will increasingly be based upon force and domination. Under these circumstances, as Rousseau argues in the

---

[4] Rousseau (1986: part 2, para. 33, p. 184). All subsequent references to the *Second Discourse* (SD) will be given by section, paragraph number, and page number in the Gourevitch edition (thus, *SD* 2.33.184).

Second Discourse, the formation of the state can properly be described as the subjugation of "the whole of Mankind to labor, servitude and misery" in order to advance "the profit of a few ambitious men" (*SD* 2.33.184).

The difference between the state based on the general will and the state depicted in the *Second Discourse* is not in the quality of the consent to their original formation: both are based upon the deception of the people by the few. But in the former case, this deception is ultimately supposed to give way to knowledge; the citizens come to understand the basis of their institutions, develop an interest in civil and moral freedom, and make citizenship a core dimension of their identities. What is crucial is *not* that the contractors originally had an interest in moral freedom, but that they come to develop such an interest, and that the society provide scope for its realization.

Rousseau's argument, then, is not subject to the objection he makes to Aristotle's defense of slavery. If Rousseau is correct that the incapacity of slaves to direct and control their own lives is not "natural," but a result of their socialization as slaves, then an appeal to this incapacity cannot be used to justify the practice of slavery. But Rousseau's argument for the state based on the general will is not an argument from "nature." Once we recognize the social and historical character of our needs, capacities, and aspirations, we must realize that any norm or value we affirm will be in part the result of processes of socialization which we could not even in principle freely control or direct. What we can expect, however, is that we be free to investigate and to criticize these processes, and that we be willing to affirm or deny our moral and political beliefs even after we have understood how we came to acquire them. While we cannot fully avoid the circularity of consent in discourse-based theories, if these two conditions are met that circularity need not trouble us unduly.

Unfortunately, these conditions are not adequately met by Rousseau's theory. Rousseau focuses too narrowly on the impediments to agreement that are rooted in material inequality. As a result, he envisions a form of society in which the knowledge and understandings of the citizens are so constrained as to call into question the authenticity of their freedom. Rousseau's model, then, turns out to be a model of constrained discourse, one in which consensus on a general will is attained by constraints on the range of issues that are permitted to arise. These constraints call the genuineness of the consensus on the general will into question.

The key to Rousseau's argument is that citizens must come to have interests and aspirations that are broadly compatible in the sense that the realization of one person's interests will not seriously conflict with the realization of another's. "Why," asks Rousseau, "is the general will always right and why do all constantly want the happiness of each, if not because there is no one who does not apply this word *each* to himself, and does not think of himself as he votes for all?" (*SC* 2.4.62). If our interests were diametrically opposed, so that any principle that I could accept would prevent you from your satisfying your needs, then we could not agree on rules or principles to govern it. In that case, our relationship would necessarily be based on force and manipulation.

Because of scarcity, conflicts of interest will inevitably arise as people come into competition for a particular good. But if they share a framework of rules, they can appeal to those rules to settle their disputes. While the conflict over any particular object may involve a complete opposition of interests in that object, by appealing to shared principles and rules we transform the situation from one of pure conflict to one of (at least ideally) willing cooperation. If I can be satisfied that the appropriate rules have been observed (because, for example, I see them as just and because they are administered by a neutral party), I can accept the outcome, even when it goes against me.

A more fundamental problem for political order arises when we come to have needs or interests that are diametrically opposed not simply regarding particular objects, but as it were intrinsically. This occurs when we come to have needs based on "vanity" or "status," what Rousseau calls *amour-propre*. When people come to define themselves and, thus, their needs and interests in terms of their relative standing to others, such that each person sets "greater store by himself than by anyone else" (*SD*, note to 1.35.226), they will be unable to agree upon principles regulating their relationship because each desires only to be accorded superior status to others. At an extreme, when "blind ambition" and love of "domination" come to be the principal motives for action, "everything reverts to the sole Law of the stronger" (*SD* 2.56.197).

The source of vanity, in Rousseau's analysis, is inherent in social life—in our capacity to compare ourselves with others, and in the role of social comparison in the formation of self-consciousness and personal identity. But it is only with the development of personal dependence based upon material inequalities that needs based upon vanity come to play a major role in social life. People can enforce their demand for superior status only by controlling essential resources; by threatening to withhold these resources, they can force others to accord them the social recognition necessary to confirm their sense of themselves as superior to others. Without such confirmation, the view of oneself as superior will not become (an important) part of one's identity, and therefore needs based on vanity will remain (relatively) insignificant.[5]

Because mitigating material inequality is the key to limiting the negative effects of vanity, Rousseau insists upon material equality—"no citizen should be so opulent that he can buy another, and none so poor that he is constrained to sell himself" (SC 2.11.75). Although this formula is not very precise, the general line of argument is quite powerful: some measure of material equality is a necessary condition for the existence of a general will. But it is surely not sufficient, for needs and aspirations may be incompatible for reasons not (or, at least, not directly) connected with vanity, with the desire for domination or superiority. We live in a society characterized by moral pluralism, and so must contend not only with "class" divisions but also with disagreements rooted in differing conceptions of the aims and purposes of human life, and in different allegiances and attachments, differences that can lead to deep and enduring conflicts.

Rousseau offers us little in the way of understanding the sources of such differences, nor how they might be bridged. This is not surprising, for he did not believe that they would be significant in the kind of society he envisioned. He believed that material equality would be possible only in a relatively small and self-sufficient community, one without luxury, extensive commerce, and a flourishing artistic and scientific culture. In small, simple societies, the problem of moral pluralism would not present itself. Their size, the uniformity of social conditions, and the absence of a diversity of points of view and educational opportunities would mean that citizens would not be exposed to, nor be likely to develop, alternative possibilities, different ways of life, different aspirations. And to make sure of that, Rousseau advocates a number of practices—notably a civil religion and censorship—designed to prevent citizens from deviating from the mores and beliefs of the society.

The problem with this solution is that it works only by undermining the goal it tries to achieve. As Viroli points out, "In working to preserve a just social order and freedom of the individual, he proposes to use means which are in contradiction with the goals that he desires to attain"

---

[5] Viroli argues that the desire for prestige or eminence will be central to the society of the general will, but that in this society it will be tied to the practice of virtue, not wealth, and so will not have the deleterious consequences it has in civil society. While such motivations can be used to train young people to become virtuous, people who continue to have such motivations could hardly be regarded as genuinely virtuous. Many citizens in Rousseau's society would have to value virtue for its own sake, and not merely as a means to status.

(207). Thus, Rousseau's account violates the first condition necessary for a discourse-based theory of moral and political life, that citizens be free to criticize their arrangements and to explore alternatives.

Because citizens' social horizons are so deliberately limited by the structure of their society, their consensus does not satisfy the second condition I set out above—that participants affirm their moral beliefs even while realizing how they came to acquire them. Their consensus, while it may appear to them as reasonable and just, is rooted in constraints imposed upon them by the deliberate design of their institutions, constraints intended to prevent the emergence of issues and perspectives that could disrupt that consensus. Knowing that, it is difficult to see how *we* could agree to impose such constraints upon ourselves, for to do so would require us to engage in a kind of deliberate forgetting, to practice a kind of self-deception incompatible with the notion of free agreement.

The experience of the West over the past two hundred years does not bear out Rousseau's general social theory. As our societies have become wealthier, they have become more, not less, equal.[6] At the same time, moral pluralism has increased. Even if one believes that a moral community requires greater levels of equality than we have yet achieved, we must still face the problem of articulating rules or principles that can be accepted by people whose differences are based not on a need for domination, but in different views of the ends and purposes of life. For this we must go beyond the kind of argument Rousseau has to offer.

UNCONSTRAINED DISCOURSE

One obvious response to the inadequacies of constrained discourse is to turn to a model of unconstrained discourse oriented to the discovery of truth. Jürgen Habermas, Karl-Otto Apel, and others have articulated such a model in recent years, using it to develop what they call "communicative ethics." Seyla Benhabib has recently developed a valuable account of communicative ethics, drawing on their work. She argues that, at the most general level, communicative or discourse ethics "does not simulate a thought experiment for all beings capable of speech, and estab-

---

[6] This is obviously true considering social and political equality. The question of equality of wealth or income is more problematic, if only because of the difficulties of measurement and the need to fix a time frame (as inequality appears to increase with the onset of modern economic growth, but to fall thereafter). For a general discussion, see H. Phelps-Brown (1988).

lish what norms they ought to accept as binding. It requires that controversies over the validity of contested norms be settled through an argumentative process in which the *consensus of all concerned* decides upon the legitimacy of the controversial norm" (Benhabib 1986:315). For such a consensus to emerge, Benhabib argues, practical discourse would have to be viewed as a "moral-transformative process" (313). What is involved in moral-transformative discourse can best be seen by contrast with Rawls's account of justice as fairness, in which individuals agree on the choice of norms to govern the basic structure of their society under conditions that enable them to make choices in a suitably impartial manner. Benhabib characterizes this model as discourse oriented to a "generalized other" (in G. H. Mead's [1964] sense)—that is, discourse oriented to all other persons irrespective of their particular identities or relationships to the self. Such generalized discourse is intended to establish a "lowest common interest, while leaving the substantive conflict of interest untouched" (314). Generalized discourse does so because it adopts a particular strategy of argumentation, in which the participants abstract from their particular identities, seeking to find a set of values that they share with others at a fairly abstract level, one that transcends the particular issues that divide them. In Rawls's case, this is accomplished through the mechanism of the original position and the use of the "thin theory of the good." If successful, this model of discourse is supposed to lead to a consensus on the juridical framework within which conflicts arise.

Benhabib is critical of this model because it permits substantive conflicts to continue, leaving open the possibility that some people may find their needs and aspirations frustrated. The problem, in her analysis, is that needs and interests should not be taken as given but must be seen (at least in large part) as a result of the processes of socialization and the life experiences of individuals in particular social formations. "Generalized discourse," she argues, arbitrarily takes a particular and historically contingent configuration of interests as given, as beyond question and criticism. In particular, she endorses the argument of Habermas and others who hold that Rawls's approach "is biased toward the kind of needs fostered in a *specific* type of society, i.e., one characterized by social competitiveness and economic individualism," and so violates the discursive ideal in "that it declares once and for all that some potential voices (and the needs they express) will not be given an adequate hearing" (White 1988:72). Discourse should not be confined to finding rules that bridge the differences among given constellations of interests and identities, but should call into question the conflicting interests, needs, and aspirations that lead to conflict. She thus concludes that discourses should be "moral-transformative processes" through which "new needs and interests, such as can lead to a consensus among the participants, emerge" (Benhabib 1986:314).

The "moral-transformative" conception of discourse holds out the possibility that people can come to discover new needs and interests whose satisfaction for one person is compatible with (or even contributes to) their satisfaction for others. Such discourse would be oriented not to the "generalized other," but to the "concrete other"—to specific individuals with particular identities and aspirations with whom we would seek to establish a genuine community. By including the evaluation and criticism of needs—or, more precisely, "need interpretations"—in discourse, this model is intended to transform substantive conflicts of interest, rather than merely providing a juridical framework to adjudicate them.

Moral-transformative discourse, it would appear, must be based upon some account of human needs, for it will succeed only if "true" needs can be discovered and if, contrary to Hobbes, the needs of different persons turn out to be compatible. Benhabib (wisely) rejects both the "essentialist" understanding of human nature, according to which there is some determinate set of "true" needs that we can discover, and the view that our needs are impervious to discourse. Rather than attempting to develop criteria for "true" needs, Benhabib offers a more modest proposal, arguing that those needs "which do *not* permit linguistic articulation cannot be true." When we discover that we disagree with others about the norms that should govern our relationships, and enter into moral-transformative discourse with them to settle this disagreement, each will attempt to articulate the needs—the objectives, desires, projects, self-identity—that he or she holds, needs that lead one to advocate a particular norm or set of norms. Hopefully, we can come to discover, as a result of this effort, which of these needs are false by attending to "those silences, evasions, and displacements which point to the presence of an unmastered force in the life of an individual." By discovering that one's position is rooted in "the dark recesses of the psyche," one will be in a position to reevaluate one's claims as a result of this deeper self-understanding (338). Thus, moral-transformative discourse leads to a kind of self-transparency which can form the basis of a genuine community.

To achieve the goal of transparency, discourse must be unconstrained: all matters, including those stemming from "the dark recesses of the psyche," must be placed on the table, subject to public argumentation and analysis. Further, if discourses are to address such needs, they must be conducted by the actual parties to the relationships in question. There is no possibility here of representation, either in the sense of an "idealized discourse" along the lines of, say, Rawls's conception of the original position, or one involving representatives of different groups and interests. Representative or idealized discourses enable us to examine issues only from the standpoint of the "generalized other." They are necessarily based upon abstracting from the concrete particularity of individuals and their needs and can only establish an abstract equality and formal reciprocity which can at best provide a basis for a "community of rights and entitlements." But such a "community" gives expression only to a "lowest common interest," one that is compatible with substantive conflicts of interests and, therefore, with situations in which the needs of some groups and individuals are suppressed.

Thus, transformative discourses can be conducted only in the context of a participatory democracy in which we come to examine our relationships not only from the standpoint of the "generalized other" but also from the standpoint of the "concrete other," from a standpoint that "requires us to view each and every rational being as an individual with a concrete history, identity, and affective-emotional constitution" (341). Such discourses can establish a "community of needs and solidarity," a community in which we affirm not simply the abstract humanity of others but also their concrete individuality. "The moral categories that accompany such interactions are those of responsibility, bonding, and sharing. The corresponding moral feelings are those of love, care, sympathy, and solidarity" (341). In contrast to "late capitalist societies," in which "public life" is viewed only "from a legalistic-juridical perspective" (351), the ideal of moral-transformative discourse envisions a "politics of empowerment that extends both rights and entitlements while creating friendship and solidarity" (352).

This model of unconstrained discourse is obviously attractive. It speaks to the problems we encountered in examining Rousseau's and Ackerman's theories, and there is an intuitive plausibility to the idea that unconstrained discourse will enable all voices to be heard, voices that may have been silenced by the kinds of constraints we have examined above. But this appearance is deceptive; even if it is true that constrained discourse may be repressive in certain ways, it is false that unconstrained discourse is necessarily liberatory.

Benhabib's argument is open to a number of objections that have often been urged against theories resting on a distinction between true and false needs. Even the apparently modest claim—that needs we cannot articulate are necessarily false—is problematic. It is far from clear that only dark thoughts are to be found in the "dark recesses of the psyche" or that we should seek to overcome all "unmastered forces" in our lives. Sometimes we find ourselves driven in ways that frustrate our deepest commitments and projects by needs we do not understand, and in such cases the discovery and mastery of these needs will be liberating. But not all of our unarticulated needs are of this character. Some of those needs may be at the basis of our deepest commitments, our strongest bonds, and our capacity to love. Love, Wollheim has argued, "is a response . . . to a felt relation: intially to the relation of total dependence, and then to whatever relation we come to substitute for it" (1984:279). Rooted in our most basic and earliest experiences, the capacity for love and love itself is always in some ways opaque to us.

The kind of self-transparency that this model of discourse envisions is mistaken even as an ideal. Our capacity for self-transcendence, for distancing one's self from oneself and reflectively examining one's actions, motives, needs, and so forth, makes it possible for us to achieve some mastery over our own lives, some degree of freedom or self-determination. But this is necessarily limited, because no description of our needs and capacities, of our attachments and aspirations, could ever be complete, if only because the very process of apprehending them alters them, opening up new possibilities for insight and self-discovery. Our motivations and the meanings of what we say and do are not univocal, fixed things, but exist on a variety of levels, in complex relationships to various aspects of the self, and are fraught with ambiguity. In an important sense, then, we can never fully articulate our needs. Self-transparency therefore cannot be a condition of our needs being "true" or even "not false."

Supposing that these concerns could be answered, there is a much deeper objection to the idea of unconstrained discourse: it is at least potentially coercive, denying values or ideals that may be important to at least some participants in discourse. Viewed as a form of public discourse, unconstrained discourse rests upon the unacknowledged assumption that there is no limit to the claims others can make upon one to render one's needs transparent—not only to oneself but to them as well. Indeed, this assumption could be said to *constitute* moral-transformative discourse, distinguishing it from generalized discourses that are intended to establish common interests, and which therefore take individuals' need-interpretations as, to a large extent, given. In the context of a public discourse, when not only the "*goods* [we] desire" but the "*desires* themselves become legitimate topics of moral disputation" (Benhabib 1987:

93), discourse can itself become repressive by threatening important values. I will illustrate this by considering the values of privacy and personal integrity.

There are many reasons why people might wish to resist the demand that they render themselves transparent to others. Self-disclosure in a public setting subjects an individual to social pressures that can distort one's judgment and even one's feelings. Probing one's deepest desires and needs is difficult enough when there is a high level of mutual trust among the participants, such as between close friends or in psychotherapy; unless voluntarily entered into, such probing is virtually impossible. The implicit sanction of the disapproval of others, pressures to conform, and the fear of revealing one's weaknesses, or leaving oneself vulnerable in other ways, may make it necessary for individuals to withhold or even dissimulate their beliefs and feelings, and often can prevent them from recognizing their own needs. There is no question that critical reflection on one's desires and aspirations can be liberating and can enable people to overcome tension and conflicts with others. But public discourse is a setting in which one's normal psychological defenses and one's resistance to self-recognition are likely to be enhanced rather than diminished, setting back the goal of moral transformation.

A deeper reason for resisting self-disclosure in public discourse is that privacy is essential to autonomy and to a certain ideal of intimacy and friendship. As self-conscious beings, the meaning and significance of what we do and feel, and our ability to form a coherent identity, are deeply affected by the presence of others, as we come to observe ourselves through their eyes. In a complex society, we have to negotiate many different roles and social settings, responding to different roles and relating to different people in appropriate ways depending upon the context and the history one shares with them. To maintain a sense of self and a more or less coherent set of values and principles requires that we be able to control the ways in which we reveal ourselves to others. This is not a matter of manipulating others, or protecting ourselves against their power, although in a world in which many of the people with whom we must deal are strangers, we will often seek to avoid vulnerability by controlling self-disclosure. But even if we were mutually invulnerable, we would still reveal ourselves selectively. In part, that is because self-revelation is a gift of intimacy to another, a way of showing one's commitment to another person and of creating and sustaining a deep relationship with him or her. If one seeks to have this kind of intimacy in some relationships, certain forms of self-revelation will be inappropriate in others.

Further, we reveal ourselves selectively because doing so helps us to maintain control over our own identities. To an important extent, our identities are formed in interaction with others, as we observe ourselves through their eyes, thereby coming to see aspects of ourselves that might otherwise remain hidden. In responding to these experiences, we may recognize and acknowledge something about ourselves, as well as discover features that we might wish to change. In most relationships we respond to others only in terms of a limited part of ourselves, and so limit the extent to which our whole identity is implicated in any particular encounter. In that way we avoid the risk of being overwhelmed by the responses of others and preserve a "space" from which we can attempt to construct an identity that we can seek to express in different aspects of our lives.[7]

Personal autonomy and the cultivation of close, intimate relationships are not universal values, nor would I contend that they are "true" or demonstrable in some way, though they are widely held in societies in which moral pluralism has come to be a significant issue. What is problematic in unconstrained discourse is that it rests on assumptions that exclude or at least significantly disadvantage those for whom these are crucial values. If the problem with constrained models of discourse such as Ackerman's is that they implicitly and improperly deny certain needs or values, the same is true of unconstrained discourse. One way around this objection, then, would be to deny the validity of values such as privacy or the right to resist others' demands for self-disclosure. But Benhabib would not accept this solution, for she does not call for the abolition of any distinction between public and private, for the complete displacement of a community of rights and entitlement by a community of needs and solidarity. She acknowledges that "conceptions of the good life" may not be universalizable,[8] and so properly belong in the private sphere, since they cannot be settled by public debate. The dilemma is clear: we appear to require unconstrained discourse in order to settle what the boundaries of the private should be, but such discourse itself violates any such boundaries because it rests upon a demand for unlimited self-disclosure.

---

[7] In discussing the value of privacy I have drawn heavily upon the work of Benn (1988), chaps. 14–15.

[8] Benhabib 1987:94 (see also Benhabib 1989:148). Benhabib has argued (in a personal communication) that the interrogation of needs that occurs in public discourse should not be personal, but only involve a generalized discussion of needs. Thus, her conception of unconstrained discourse would not violate privacy.

If unconstrained discourse does not provide sufficient protection for the value of privacy, it must be emphasized that privacy is by no means an absolute value. While noncoercive discourse requires that we be permitted to resist the demand for self-disclosure, it does not license an absolute refusal to explore the reasons why someone may put forward a particular normative demand. Privacy can and has been used to justify forms of domination, or to prevent certain relationships from becoming the object of public concern. An obvious example is domestic violence, which has been implicitly condoned because of the importance of shielding family relationships from public view.

In addition to this bias against privacy, the model of unconstrained discourse implicitly structures the terms of moral and political argumentation against traditional or religious views of the world. As we have seen, moral-transformative discourse focuses on conflicts among the need-interpretations of the participants. But if we return for a moment to the discussion of abortion, we can see that, from the perspective of the pro-life position, this way of framing the argument is itself part of the problem. In their view, too much of our society's thinking on such matters is concerned with our "needs" to the exclusion of our "duties." Understanding this dispute in terms of conflicting interpretations of needs may well distort the self-interpretations of those holding the pro-life position, for whom the secular and anthropomorphic basis of discourse is itself problematic. When we take the position of the concrete other in this conflict, might we not find that it calls into question the very commitments that led us to moral-transformative discourse in the first place?

I suspect that Benhabib would answer this question in the negative. Communities based on the perspective of the concrete other, she assures us, "are not pre-given," but "are formed out of the action of the oppressed, the exploited, and the humiliated, and must be committed to universalist, egalitarian, and consensual ideals. Traditional ethnic, racial, and religious communities are neither necessarily nor primarily such communities of needs and solidarity" (1986:351). While this perspective "acknowledges the plurality of modes of being human, and differences among humans," it does not endorse "all these pluralities as morally and politically valid" (1987:81). Yet there is an obvious tension here, for the "standpoint of the concrete other" is also said to be "governed by the norms of *equity* and *complementary reciprocity*: each is entitled to expect and to assume from the other forms of behavior through which the other feels recognized and confirmed as a concrete, individual being with specific needs, talents and capacities" (1987:87). It appears, then, that the affirmation of the concrete other for which Benhabib calls is not a presupposition of discourse, but a result of discourse. In the present case, this transformation requires the abandonment of traditional and religiously based identities. But this appears to be inconsistent. Unless we posit either some form of essentialism or a very strong understanding of the possibilities of reason, we cannot expect rational argument alone to dislodge such traditional or religious identities. Translated into practice, then, the call for the "affirmation" of the concrete other is likely to lead either to an abandonment of the critical universalism that motivated the call in the first place or to a rejection of certain groups or positions as legitimate parties to the discourse.

The objections to moral-transformative discourse I have presented are largely conceptual, but we must also consider the contexts in which such moral-transformative discourses would take place. There is an obvious difference between intimate settings in which friends or lovers mutually explore their "affective-emotional constitution[s]," and reeducation camps or citizens' block committees. In Benhabib's model, moral-transformative discourse involves a commitment to forms of participatory democracy and a corresponding reduction in the use of representation. Even in democratic settings, however, there will be significant pressures on the individual. If the costs of nonparticipation are high, some may be forced to give political activity and self-disclosure a place in their lives that precludes self-realization for them, or at least frustrates their ability to satisfy their needs. If those sacrifices are too great, they would be forced to withdraw from politics and would instead suffer the tyranny of activists (see Elster 1986:122). Thus, moral-transformative discourse is at least potentially coercive, leading to institutional forms that involve domination or imposition. It is hard to see how any form of "discourse" could achieve a consensus that is genuinely free and uncoerced unless participants enjoy some rights of privacy and personal integrity, unless they can resist the demand for self-disclosure.

CONCLUSION

Rousseau, it might be argued, articulated one of the deepest problems with a discourse-based politics when he observed that, for such a politics to be possible, "men would have to be prior to laws what they ought to become by means of laws" (SC 2.7.69). For Rousseau, the circularity inherent in the idea of such a politics is sociological: to set up the institutions of a just political society, citizens must have developed traits of character and an understanding of themselves and the world that they could come to have only after such a society had been established. For the later thinkers examined in this chapter the circularity is conceptual: the conception of discourse they defend as adequate to the realization or discovery of consensual norms and values necessarily presupposes a particular set of norms or values, or at least delimits the range of positions which can be effectively articulated. Models of constrained discourse, by restricting the range of issues that are to be decided consensually through discussion, can effectively silence certain voices, or at least burden them by structuring a public language in which it is difficult to articulate their experiences and needs. On the other hand, models of unconstrained discourse rest upon a demand for self-disclosure which can threaten the privacy and personal integrity of participants in a way that can make discourse coercive.

I do not, however, wish to conclude that a discourse-based model of political and moral life is irredeemably flawed. My purpose in this chapter has been to uncover the limits of the discourse model, but I do not wish to argue that the existence of such limits vitiates it. No model of discourse can provide a procedure that can guarantee the truth or justice of the positions we take, and all forms of discourse are inherently limited because they are necessarily structured in certain ways.

Concretely, this means that any political arrangements may be experienced as unjust by some members of our society. There can be no "neutral" framework of the sort Ackerman seeks, a framework that can be used to resolve differences among people in a morally pluralist society. Nor can we hope to overcome these differences through the unconstrained, moral-transformative discourse Benhabib seeks. Both of these models involve their own silences and evasions, for both structure our collective decision-making in ways that, at the very least, may make it difficult for certain voices to be heard. Even if we (hopefully) suppose that there are enough commonalities to develop a basic framework of justice governing our interactions, there can be no guarantee that these commonalities will be more important to any particular group, on any given issue, than their differences. Thus, some may find the decision required by the framework on a specific issue to be oppressive. Because they may experience it as an imposition, in this respect they will find that their interactions with others do not realize the ideal of a moral relationship.

Since we must, in a sense, learn to live with the possibility of what we see as injustice, what model of discourse would serve us best in confronting our situation? We must, I think, reject the moral-transformative model of unconstrained discourse as a basis for our political lives in favor of a model that limits the public demand for self-disclosure and provides space for individual privacy. We should not have to defend or to justify every aspect of our existence, including our most intimate desires and beliefs, if it is going to be possible for us to participate freely in public discourse. Similarly, we must reject those models of constrained discourse, such as Rousseau's or Ackerman's, which seek to provide a final or a neutral framework for public life, since they can have the effect of permanently excluding certain voices and needs. What we require, I will argue in the next chapter, is a model of generalized discourse which protects the integrity of the participants in discourse, but which opens itself to criticism of its own presuppositions and assumptions, acknowledging the possibility of its own silences and evasions. Suitably formulated, political liberalism can answer this need.

Political Liberalism

TRADITIONAL LIBERALISM sought to provide a normative framework that would make political community possible in the face of moral pluralism. What is distinctive about political liberalism is, first, that it is not based on an "ontology" of human nature but is offered as a *strategy* to achieve political community. Second, it rejects the "prestructuring" of normative arguments characteristic of "contractarian" approaches, adopting instead a model of generalized discourse. Third, while rejecting the ideal of unconstrained discourse, it seeks to remain open to criticism of its fundamental presuppositions. It is open, but not unconstrained. In order to accommodate fundamental criticism, political liberalism must be "contextualized" to particular historical and institutional settings, within which the voices that have been excluded can be identified and, to the extent possible, provided a hearing. Finally, political liberalism explicitly recognizes the inherently tragic nature of political life: the fact that, in a morally pluralist world, there may be no framework of justice that all can accept to regulate their interactions. On some issues, we may face tragic conflicts, conflicts in which all parties justify their positions in terms of what they regard as fundamental moral considerations, which are opposed in ways that do not permit reconciliation. Under such circumstances, political community must give way to imposition: whatever decision is taken, some will experience the outcome as unjust but will be constrained to abide by its terms. Moreover, and more significantly, the institutions and practices that political liberalism supports or even requires may unfairly burden some citizens, leading them to experience those norms as impositions.

As a strategy to achieve political community in the face of moral pluralism, political liberalism, like other discourse-based theories, conceives of citizens as engaging in discussions with the aim of discovering norms they can accept. This conception of discourse is intended as a critical model for testing normative claims in a way that does not beg critical questions by prestructuring the "conversation" in such a way that only certain outcomes are possible. Political liberalism incorporates a model of generalized discourse, in which participants seek to abstract from their particular—and conflicting—identities and aspirations, in order to discover bases of agreement with others that "bracket" the particular issues that divide them. The process of bracketing or abstracting from particular identities protects individuals against demands for unreasonable self-disclosure, while at the same time discovering bases on which mutually acceptable norms of justice can be developed.

Political liberalism is also intended as a substantive political theory specifying (at least for an important range of cases) the kinds of practices and institutions necessary for political community. It is, obviously, not possible for a society to manage its affairs directly through purely discursive processes. Much of social life does not involve agreement in any specific sense. Rather individuals respond to the situations in which they find themselves, taking the behavior of others as parametric and creating social outcomes that no one intends. Even in cases where agreements are reached (consider, for example, the "agreement" of two individuals to become friends), they generally have little to do with the "philosophical conversations" envisioned by discourse theories.[1] Thus, we must go beyond the abstract notion of a generalized model of discourse to identify the practices and institutions that could be legitimated through discourse and that most closely approximate the ideal of discursive validation. Representative democracy and the recognition of a set of "agency rights" for each individual are two of the critical practices of political liberalism. Agency rights protect the integrity of each individual by providing space for individual privacy. Representative democracy secures all individuals formally equal voices in the shaping of their collective lives. More generally, political liberalism holds that democratic individuality is essential to create political community in the face of moral pluralism.

Much of the argument that I will offer in the rest of this book is intended to support that conclusion. In the remainder of this chapter, I will further develop the idea of political liberalism as a discourse-based theory, explaining how it is linked to the idea of agency rights, why it gives rise to the possibility of tragic conflict, and the sense in which its claims can be put forward as "true" or "rationally warranted." In the following chapters, I will examine some of the paradoxes and problems associated with the commitment to agency rights, in the economy and in the society and culture more generally. In these chapters I will be asking whether the framework I am proposing does not itself contain its own silences and evasions, suppressing certain voices and ruling out certain needs. In responding to these concerns, I will fill out the account of political liberalism sketched here.

[1] The phrase is Michael Walzer's (1989–90:182–96).

Discourse and Tragedy

Political liberalism attempts to escape the circularity of discourse models of political justification by initially adopting what amounts to a constrained model of discourse, but then it seeks to overcome these constraints by acknowledging their partial character and permitting them to be called into question. Conceiving of discourse as a two-stage process in this way means that "discourse" cannot function (as it does in most theories) as a purely methodological device for testing normative claims. Rather the discourse of political liberalism must be contextualized to particular historical settings, governed by a particular set of normative understandings, which can then be called into question. The transcendent aspirations of Rawls's original position or Habermas's ideal speech situation must be abandoned.

Given that our society is morally pluralistic, there can be no guarantee that any particular framework of justice, any particular model of generalized discourse can accommodate all of the voices that may seek to be heard, or which may over time come into existence. This means that we must be open to consider the values and aspirations, the needs and attachments, that any particular formulation of a framework of justice appears to suppress. There can be no universal or complete justification of any particular framework, because it is not possible for us to anticipate all the questions we will face, nor the ways in which people will come to define themselves and their attachments, and so come to discover norms, including norms that have long existed, that are unacceptable, and whose enforcement is experienced by them as a form of domination. Thus, our "generalized discourses" must be contextualized to specific social and historical settings in such a way as to allow the basic framework to be challenged. Each "we" must remain alive to the possibility that what "we" consider reasonable may be experienced by others as a form of imposition. But such possibilities can only be canvassed in a particular discursive context, framed by a specific structure of constraints, one in which dissenting voices will have to struggle to make themselves heard precisely because their demands will involve a violation of the established framework of rights and, in particular, the privacy that the model of generalized discourse is designed to secure.

This approach obviously disadvantages certain perspectives, but its aim is to secure a reasonable balance between the scope of discourse at any particular point in time and the need for openness. As I have argued above, in the absence of such a balance the resulting unconstrained discourse will be experienced as coercive to some participants. Unfortunately, we must also realize that there is a darker possibility that when the basic discourse on the framework of justice is reopened, we may discover that there is no possibility of genuine agreement, that "we" may have no choice but to impose our judgment on others, or experience their judgments as impositions on us. We may hope that such situations are rare, so those who experience them can nonetheless accept the system as a whole. Political liberalism is deeply committed to overcoming injustice and creating a political community whose norms are affirmed by all its members. But it has no formula to guarantee that result. We must live at least with the possibility of suffering injustice, or acting in ways that others experience as unjust.

These difficulties can be illustrated by returning to the issue of abortion. Assuming that our community of rights and duties includes the liberty of a woman to have an abortion, it may well be that many "pro-life" people find that the weight they attach to other aspects of their moral lives is greater than their commitment to the public framework of justice. Thus, they feel that this decision is not a reasonable one, but an imposition, and may even feel justified in resisting it. On the other hand, "pro-choice" supporters will certainly feel justified in their position, pointing to what they see as an important asymmetry between their situation and that of the "pro-life" group. While recognizing that public policies permitting women to assume a variety of roles may make it more difficult for groups that hold traditional values to flourish, pro-choice supporters will point out that they would be unable to achieve their ends at all if public policies are premised on some conception of women's "natural" roles as mothers and caretakers. Without the ability to control her reproductive activity, a woman cannot direct her life in accordance with her own choices among career, family, and other ends. Quite apart from the fact that this argument overstates the case—we are, after all, only talking about how the burden of risks is to be distributed among different groups, not absolute impossibilities—the real difficulty in this response is that it structures the question in a way that many pro-life supporters would find objectionable. By casting the issue as one of finding norms enabling people to realize their objectives, it defines the issue in the secular and anthropomorphic language that, for many pro-life people, is itself deeply problematic. It is by no means certain that such deep disagreements will necessarily arise but, should they do so, no model of discourse may be able to resolve them.[2]

[2] I do not mean to suggest that the issue of abortion is irresolvable; Ginsburg (1989) has

Not all conflict, nor even all moral conflict, is tragic. Many of our choices involve the sacrifice of one good in order to obtain another; we choose a particular career, thereby forgoing other possibilities; we choose to marry someone, sacrificing the freedom of an uncommitted life. But some (though not all) of the conflicts of political life can be genuinely tragic conflicts, at least from the perspective of political liberalism, given its aspiration to political community. In a political community, the norms under which we live and regulate our common affairs must be fully and freely accepted by all those who are subject to them. When we encounter a conflict between people whose moral commitments are so deeply opposed that they cannot find mutually acceptable rules to govern their relationships, when any rule will necessarily deny the ends sought by one of the groups, there is—at least in this area—no possibility of political community. Not only will one of the conflicting goods be denied, but we will also fail to achieve political community and our lives will be marked by the experience of injustice. For some participants, the conflict over abortion has this character, which we can witness in the mutual hostility and incomprehension of the opposed groups in front of abortion clinics. Less dramatic, but no less real, is the experience of Christian Science parents forced to provide medical treatment for their children, and so to violate their deeply held religious views.[3] Many of the issues explored in chapters five through Nine below involve a tragic, or potentially tragic, character.

POLITICAL THEORY WITHOUT FOUNDATIONS

Because political liberalism eschews the transcendent aspirations of traditional political theory, because it acknowledges the potentially tragic nature of political and moral conflict, and because it does not (as I shall argue below) entrench a particular set of institutional forms, there is a sense in which it can be said to be radically contingent. Because of its structure, political liberalism lacks secure foundations from which to defend its claims, for all its assumptions and principles are open to criticism and revision.

---

argued that the participants in this dispute share important values and beliefs, and cites the formation of a group to encourage dialogue among activists in the area she studied. Unfortunately, such efforts to encourage discourse have not yet been successful in resolving the issue in a way that is satisfactory to all parties.

[3] See Frohock (1992) for a sensitive exploration of these issues.

This acknowledgment of contingency raises the specter of relativism—a charge frequently directed at liberalism by its critics who often see its endorsement of pluralism as a self-refuting effort to defend the value of tolerance on the grounds that "all morality is merely subjective" (Sandel 1984:1). But this criticism is mistaken. Political liberalism does *not* hold that morality is subjective; instead, it insists that there are a plurality of moral and religious positions that are rationally defensible, that there is no "best" way to live that is rationally warranted. Far from denying the importance of rational assessment in moral and political matters, political liberalism insists on it, for political liberalism is rooted in the belief that it is through rational discourse that such questions must be settled. What it does deny is that such discourse is capable of producing uniquely correct answers to these questions. Political liberalism is committed to *pluralism*, not skepticism or relativism.

Given its acceptance of pluralism, how can it inspire conviction or recommend itself for adoption? Is it not just one of a plurality of political positions for which rational warrant can be given? What, if any, claim to uniqueness can it make for itself? In particular, how can it appeal to those who accept a foundationalist creed of any kind? Would they not find its acceptance of contingency to be antithetical to their deepest commitments? These questions have plagued political (and other varieties of) liberalism in the past; in one way, their import is to deny the inclusiveness that political liberalism claims, to deny that it embraces a wide range of moral positions, and to identify it with a narrow, modernist, and skeptical position, as partisan and one-sided as the political views it would displace. But these questions can be answered. Although political liberalism has a strong affinity to a modern, secular culture, it can be embraced on many grounds, including those who have deep and traditional religious beliefs.

It is easy to see how political liberalism is compatible with antirealist movements in philosophy and political theory, but it would be a mistake to see it as requiring or presupposing (or resting on!) such premises. Indeed, political liberalism is compatible with strong forms of moral realism that posit an objective order of moral facts to which our moral beliefs are supposed to correspond. Political liberalism insists upon fallibilism and pluralism, but neither of these positions is incompatible with realism. Indeed realism and fallibilism complement each other: the idea that our beliefs might be mistaken (and that we must therefore be open to further evidence and argument) lends itself to an obvious realist interpretation, for what is it for our beliefs to be mistaken but to fail to "correspond" to

103

the way things really are? Similarly, moral pluralism does not rule out moral realism. Even if we suppose that there is an independently existing realm of moral facts, it does not follow that all true moral values are compatible with each other, or that different values are commensurable and can be arranged in a correct hierarchy of value.

Nonetheless, while political liberalism is compatible with realism, it is perhaps best understood in terms of what Putnam calls "internal realism" or "pragmatic realism," which recognizes that objects don't exist independently of our conceptual scheme because "there are no standards for the use of even the logical notions apart from conceptual choices" (1987:35–36). In Putnam's view, no meaning can be given to talk of things in themselves, or to other familiar dualisms, such as the distinction between "truth" and "warranted assertibility" or between the properties of an object and those qualities (such as color) that are said to represent projections of the "mind" on the object. Nonetheless, once having adopted a conceptual scheme, what we can say depends not only on the scheme but on the world: "Our concepts may be culturally relative, but it does not follow that the truth or falsity of everything we say using those concepts is simply 'decided' by the culture" (20). Thus, internal realism incorporates "conceptual relativity," acknowledging that our explanations and descriptions are "relative" to particular conceptual schemes, and that our schemes "reflect our interests and choices." But it denies a more radical relativism that sees all judgments as conventional: "Our conceptual scheme restricts the 'space' of descriptions available to us; it does not predetermine the answers to our questions" (39). Because the questions we ask and the judgments we offer are necessarily framed within a particular conceptual scheme, the answers we offer, including the moral visions we hold, are subject to rational criticism. Such criticism cannot provide us with the "best" or uniquely correct version of all possible conceptual schemes, "but what we have are *better and worse* versions and that *is* objectivity" (77).

There is a strong affinity between political liberalism and internal realism. The possibility of rational criticism and the discovery of "better" versions—more adequate causal accounts of social processes, more adequate theories of justice, richer understandings of our psychological and emotional lives—makes rational discourse possible and gives it a point. At the same time, conceptual relativity provides an occasion for discourse because it recognizes the legitimacy of divergent views and judgments. Moreover, internal realism supports the strategy of generalized discourse, of bracketing disagreements and seeking common ground, because it offers no grounds for expecting that rational discourse will yield unitary answers to questions of political principle and practice. Internal realism is also compatible with the possibility of deep opposition and even mutual incomprehension—with the tragic possibilities of politics.

It is often argued that if we cannot guarantee the adequacy of what Rorty calls our "final vocabularies," then the process of rational justification would, at some point, have to run out, and at that point we could no longer rely on reason. Instead, our commitments would be based on only our own acts of will, the choice of one of Weber's warring gods. Thus, Putnam speaks of reaching a point where "I have to say with Wittgenstein: 'This is where my spade is turned. This is what I do, this is what I say' " (85). Rorty makes a similar point, though in more sociologically realistic terms, counseling us to abandon the false quest for "objectivity" and to make solidarity "our *only* comfort" (1985:14). We must, he insists, embrace ethnocentrism, "we must in practice privilege our own group." But whether justification ends with an act of individual self-assertion or an affirmation of a collectivity and its claims, the upshot is the same: a retreat to commitment.

There is, however, a certain exaggeration in this picture. It has to do both with the idea of a "final vocabulary" and the idea of merely willful choice. In the formalized languages of logic or some branches of philosophy and science, the notion of a final vocabulary (or conceptual scheme, research program, and so forth) is reasonably well defined. Putnam, for example, offers the example of a "Carnap world" in which there are three individuals, and contrasts it with the "same" world, which he identifies with "some Polish logicians," in which both the original individuals and sets composed of groupings of those individuals are considered objects. In Carnap's language, the world contains just three objects, whereas in language of the Polish logician, the world contains seven objects.[4] In a case such as this, the boundaries of the languages are clearly marked, and there are more or less definitive rules specifying the uses and operation of various terms, including logical primitives. Here, the notion of a "final vocabulary" is reasonably well defined.

But when we are dealing with natural languages, whose terms are notoriously "open-textured," the idea of a "final vocabulary" is deeply problematic. There are, obviously, paradigmatic uses of terms in any lan-

---

[4] In the world of the Polish logician there are three sets each containing one of Carnap's individuals, plus three sets of two of the original individuals, plus one set of all three individuals, where each set counts as one "object," making a total of seven objects (Putnam 1987:18).

guage, uses that make it possible for us to learn a language and to use it to communicate. But even these uses can always be subverted. In the face of novelty, we have to extend and so alter those terms in unpredictable ways; and speakers can always use inherited terms creatively, drawing on analogies, inventing metaphors, coining new words, importing terms from other languages, speaking playfully. Similarly, even highly artificial final vocabularies are never without bridges to other vocabularies. Formalized languages are always defined in terms of, and tacitly presuppose, a natural language, and it is in terms of the natural language that we can see the ways in which the formalizations are opposed (as in Putnam's example above). And the vocabularies of different cultures must be translatable from one to the other, if they are to be recognizable as vocabularies at all.

Even when the contrasted vocabularies involve intellectual constructions, scientific paradigms or research programs, and philosophical systems, the notion of a "final vocabulary" is questionable. Rorty mentions the contrast between Aristotelian and Galilean mechanics, Romantic poetry, and socialist politics (1989:6). But in all these cases, the identification of the meaning and use of these vocabularies is an interpretative (and contested) activity, even among their users, let alone among historians and critics.

Moreover, even if we suppose that the idea of a "final vocabulary" made sense in this context, the idea of willfully choosing one does not. Take the case of Aristotelian physics, for instance. Its proponents did not and could not *choose* it. In the first place, this system is *our* historical reconstruction, created for our purposes and revised as our purposes and understandings change. In the second place, this vocabulary was the medium through which its proponents made choices, not an object of choice itself. Nor can we choose Aristotelian physics over, say, Newtonian or Einsteinian physics. There is no possibility of adopting so-called final vocabularies from the distant past. When we look at such systems we have what Williams calls a "notional confrontation." Aristotelian physics is not a real option for us: we could not adopt it in our "actual historical circumstances and retain [our] hold on reality" without engaging in "extensive self-deception" (1985:160–61).

In the second class of cases Rorty mentions, "Romantic poetry," there is no need or occasion for "choosing" between the supposedly final vocabularies. I can adopt the idiom of Romantic poetry without abandoning other genres; their coexistence enriches my life, and to choose among them would be to impoverish myself. It may, of course, be true that one cannot create works in certain idioms today, if only because today one would be deliberately adopting a particular idiom when earlier artists or poets were forging it. They were creating rules and conventions, rather than following them. But this merely confirms the point that there are few, if any, occasions for the choice of final vocabularies, at least in the aesthetic and expressive areas of our lives.

Rorty's third example, socialist politics, brings us closer to the concerns of this book, and it strikingly illustrates what is problematic both with the idea of a "final vocabulary" and with the idea of merely willful choice. In one sense, everyone must speak the idiom of socialist politics, insofar as it has become part of the language of modern political life throughout the world, but it is far from clear that it is a distinct "final vocabulary." Not only are there vast differences between, say, Stalin and Michael Harrington, but the socialist idioms at best comprise only some of the "words in which we tell, sometimes prospectively and sometimes retrospectively, the story of our lives" (Rorty 1989:73). The other, nonsocialist words we speak provide criteria that we can use to evaluate and criticize the idiom of socialist politics. The choice of this idiom is not, then, a criterion-less choice.

We do not have to accept philosophical foundationalism to find Rorty's devaluation of "notions of truth, rationality, and moral obligation" in favor of "metaphor and self-creation" (44) to be problematic. Metaphor and self-creation are not opposed to truth, rationality, and moral obligation, and they are to be found as much within as between so-called final vocabularies. Our disputes are rarely, if ever, conducted at the level of "final vocabularies," and so we rarely if ever reach a point where justification by reason "runs out." On the other hand, even among people who share a "final vocabulary," there are any number of occasions in which disputes cannot be resolved—at least not within the practical constraints of available time and energy to deal with the issue. And this is true of particular issues of "fact" as well as broader explanatory claims or normative disagreements.[5] There are, then, points at which we may have nothing more to say, places where we invoke our commitments or solidarity over reason and objectivity. But that is not because reason runs out, but because time, energy, patience, or goodwill are exhausted.

This is true even in those rare and localized areas of knowledge where we have a deductively integrated structure of reasons, dangling from a set

---

[5] Consider, for example, the difficulty of resolving legal disputes, including particular factual claims, among lawyers who have undergone extensive training to equip them with a shared vocabulary.

of highest-order premises or "skyhooks." Once we reach the skyhook, there will be nothing more to say in the same mode, but that does not mean that reason has run out. As Mill argues in his famous defense of utilitarianism, the fact that "ultimate ends are not amenable to direct proof" does not mean that their acceptance or rejection "must depend on blind impulse, or arbitrary choice" (Mill 1951:5). Rather, as Mill writes, "Considerations may be presented capable of determining the intellect either to give or withhold its assent to the doctrine; and this is equivalent of proof" (6).

The range of considerations "capable of determining the intellect" is extremely broad, at least in moral and political discourse. It includes the use of metaphors and imaginative portrayals intended to induce appropriate feelings or emotional responses in our audience. It includes drawing on analogies and precedents, and showing how the issue in question coheres with other judgments and beliefs. None of these appeals will be definitive, none unanswerable. Because the world does not split "itself up, on its own initiative, into sentence-shaped chunks called 'facts' " (Rorty 1989:5), there is no guarantee of agreement, even ultimate agreement. But neither do we reach "bedrock," a point from which there is nothing more to be said, a point where reason literally runs out. Political liberalism accommodates contingency without abandoning the commitment to rationality, a commitment expressed in its model of discourse, which accepts certain constraints but also which, acknowledging the ways in which these constraints may silence certain voices, holds open the possibility of their being challenged and revised.

AGENCY RIGHTS

Political liberalism is based on a strategy of generalized discourse, but one that seeks to remain open to criticisms of its own presuppositions. But it also involves—like all political theories—certain substantive commitments. Foremost among these is a commitment to the notion of agency, which is implicit in the idea of discourse itself. It is hard for us, raised in contemporary democratic societies, not to think of ourselves as agents, as beings who are at least sometimes "doers," who control and direct some of our actions according to our purposes and beliefs. Indeed, that we think of ourselves as agents is central to our identities. We claim credit for what we do well and, less happily, sometimes accept responsibility for what we do badly. We offer excuses for misdeeds that separate them from our will—I did not know, my hand slipped, I was stopped: the passive voice attests to the moral role of agency in such assessments. We resent being treated like "children," in ways that deny our ability to direct and control our lives. We make plans and promises, we punish and reward, we blame and praise. We structure many of our institutions in ways designed to make officeholders explain themselves. We elect officials and try to hold them accountable. We sue when others damage us, holding them liable for what they do and for negligence in failing to attend to matters under their control. Some have even argued that our understanding of nature and causality is also rooted in our experience of ourselves as agents.[6] The list could go on and on, so pervasive is agency to our ways of life.

The liberal strategy begins with the assumption that the sense of oneself as an agent is widely shared in our society, and that it is significant to (virtually) everyone. There is, of course, nothing natural or necessary in people understanding themselves in these terms. We can, with some stretch of the imagination, and drawing on other but equally central aspects of ourselves that appear to us as "given," form some sense of what a world would be like in which agency was not an important part of the practices and self-understandings of society. We can study anthropological accounts of other societies or read literature in which fate plays a central role, or we can take seriously the deterministic assumptions of certain forms of social science to gain a sense of a life "beyond freedom and dignity."[7] Our seeing ourselves as agents is contingent, a result of our particular history, our society's having been shaped by specific economic and political factors. But though it is contingent, it is nevertheless fundamental to our thoughts and practices.

One source of the centrality of the concept of agency is the role of discourse in our lives. The idea of agency appears to be presupposed by the very idea of discourse itself. We could hardly engage in discourse with the purpose of determining the mutual acceptability of the rules govern-

---

[6] See, e.g., von Wright (1971:65–66), and Habermas's notion of natural scientific knowledge as answering to the human interest "in technical control over objectified processes" (1971:309).

[7] See Gaus (1990:383f.) for a fascinating use of Geertz's work on Bali to explain the concept and significance of "self-directed" agency. For a particularly insightful and illuminating exploration of issues of fate and their relationship to agency in ethics, see Williams (1981) and Nussbaum (1986). The reference to social science, of course, is to Skinner (1953; 1971). In raising these possibilities, I do not wish to argue that there are societies in which people do not experience themselves as agents in any way (or in terms that we would regard as those of agency).

ing our common affairs unless we saw ourselves as capable of forming judgments on the basis of reasons. Nor would this activity have any point unless we were, and understood ourselves to be, capable of controlling our conduct on the basis of our judgments. Anthropologists may describe societies where people do not view themselves in this way, and the literary imaginations may conjure yet other worlds, but in none of these worlds can the idea of testing normative claims through discourse have a place.

Agency not only is part of our self-descriptions, but it also carries normative weight. Participants in a discourse must value their capacities for agency, as any decision or agreement must respect the agency of the participants. As O'Neill has argued, if people with different moral visions are "to share principles, action on the principles must leave the agency of each member of the plurality intact" (1988:718); for no

> plurality can choose to live by principles that aim to destroy, undercut or erode the agency (of whatever determinate shape) of some of its members. Those who become victims of action on such principles not merely *do not* act on their oppressor's principles; they *cannot* do so. Victims cannot share the principles on which others destroy or limit their very capacities to act on principles. (1989:213)

This is not to say that the capacity to make choices and to act on principles will not sometimes be experienced as a burden, nor that some people might on occasion welcome the removal of this burden. The desire to "escape from freedom" is one of the best-known explanations for the rise of fascism, though the massive level of coercion employed in that process suggests that the desire was far from universal. That explanation has more plausibility on the smaller scale of a Jonestown or other more or less self-contained groups united by unquestioning adherence to the ideas and commands of a leader. But where people abandon (or have failed to form) a conception of themselves as agents, they will also reject the idea that the principles of their social order should reflect the free agreement of those who are subject to them.

If the outcomes of discourse must respect the agency of the participants, then each member of society must possess those rights necessary to the exercise of the capacities for agency. We have already reviewed several theories that ground rights in the concept of agency. Although political liberalism rejects the essentialist claims of these theories, it can appropriate much of their analysis of the connection between agency and rights. Respecting persons' capacity for agency requires, in the most general terms, responding to them in terms of their abilities of rational self-direction, by giving them reasons for acting and not attempting to control their behavior through force and manipulation.[8] Specifying this general formula more concretely can only be done in specific contexts, considering the various ways in which one's agency might be undermined; this in turn depends on what O'Neill calls its "determinate shape"—the specific identities and self-representations through which capacities for self-direction are understood and even constituted. At a minimum, however, it would have to include rights to bodily integrity, or freedom from physical coercion and the right to control the use and powers of one's body; rights necessary to participate in discourse, including communication and self-expression; rights of privacy, including the right to resist self-disclosure; and rights to certain resources or goods without which one could not exercise the powers of agency.[9]

Obviously, these formulae are imprecise, at best pointing or even gesturing in a certain direction. But at this juncture I am not interested in specifying them further, but in explicating and defending a rights-based approach in general. It is important to note, however, that the list above includes both what Martin Golding has called "option rights" and "welfare rights."[10] In Golding's account, option rights "correspond to spheres of individual sovereignty, as it were, in which the individual is morally free to act on the basis of his own choices." Such rights are limited, but within these limits they imply "some kind of rightful control over the actions of others." Option rights, then, are conceived in terms of a "capacity or power," as having an "active character," and so they can be ascribed only to beings who possess capacities for self-direction. Welfare rights, by contrast, "are entitlements to goods," and can be ascribed to any entities that can be said to have interests, including animals. Many specific rights, such as the right to property, are a compound of both option and welfare rights—an entitlement to a particular good, and the liberty to make certain uses of it.

Both option and welfare rights lend themselves to what Feinberg has called "the characteristic use" of rights, which "is to be claimed, demanded, affirmed, insisted upon." In Feinberg's account, it is this dimension of healthy self-assertion or self-respect which having rights makes possible. Because I have a right, I can insist that others show due regard

---

[8] See chapter three above for a discussion of efforts to derive rights from the concept of agency.

[9] Other rights, such as liberty and property, grounded on agency will be discussed briefly in chapter six.

[10] See Golding (1984:122–24). This terminology is developed in Golding (1986:521–49).

to me, and can "feel in some fundamental way the equal of anyone" (Feinberg 1970:252). The assertion of both welfare and option rights can thus contribute to a person's sense of worth or self-respect, and why the denial of rights accorded to others is experienced as a loss of dignity. That is one of the reasons why so much of contemporary political conflict—particularly the demands of newly emergent groups such as workers, women, and racial minorities—is conducted in the language of rights. Because rights are attached to agency, and because the experience of oneself as an agent is (virtually) universal, any breach of equality in the extension of rights is experienced as an injury.

OBLIGATION AND IDEALIZATION

I have been arguing that agency rights are deeply entrenched in the self-understandings of our society and that they are necessary to the idea of discourse, but they are equally crucial to accommodating moral pluralism because they provide "space" within which individuals and groups can pursue their different ends and commitments. The importance of the connection between agency rights and moral pluralism can be seen by considering an alternative position, one that begins with a commitment to respecting the agency of others, but that rejects the limited primacy political liberalism would give to rights. O'Neill argues that we should take "obligations," not rights, to be primary in our moral and political lives. Of course, since rights are correlative with obligations, she allows that, once having identified basic obligations, we "may also identify the entitlements that are the reciprocals of these obligations" (1989:215). But since there are important obligations that are not correlative with rights—such as the obligation of charity or the duty to cultivate certain virtues—she contends that an approach that privileges rights will fail to provide space for them.

O'Neill's criticisms are persuasive only against approaches in which rights are taken to be the exclusive occupants of moral and political space. This is not the case for the theory I am proposing, which views basic agency rights as only one element of the moral landscape. The limited primacy of agency rights I have defended does not necessarily exclude obligations of charity or virtue from our public lives.

Nonetheless, political liberalism insists upon the relative primacy of agency rights, as opposed to the imperfect obligations of charity and virtue, in political life. Duties of charity and virtue depend on determinate conceptions of the ends of life and ideals of excellence that are often deeply contested, while such rights as bodily integrity, freedom of thought and communication, and privacy protect values that are widely held and are (in some form) implicit in any concept of human agency. O'Neill is correct to point out that liberalism has over time come to place increasing emphasis on rights (and their corresponding obligations) over imperfect obligations and the cultivation of virtue, but this reflects the possibilities of reasoned, noncoerced agreement in a morally pluralist world. That is why the political status of imperfect obligations is much more problematic than the obligations associated with agency rights.[11] Needless to say, in our personal lives the place of virtue and imperfect obligations should loom far larger. A moral life consisting only in the assertion of one's own rights and the observance of the rights of others would not only be puerile, it would lack a sense of direction and appropriate connectedness to others.

A more serious objection to rights-based theories holds that they too incorporate a particular, and contested, view of the ends of life. As O'Neill puts it, they rest upon an "idealization" of human capacities and relationships. Rather than beginning with a minimal concept of agency, they implicitly privilege an "ideal of citizenship" that "prizes the mutual independence of citizens," an ideal in which "*Moralität*" is "not merely the only shared culture but ultimately the only public culture" (1988:713). The problem is not that these theories are abstract, but that they are idealizations that go beyond simplification to incorporate "predicates that are not even approximately true of the agents to whom the model is supposed to apply" (1989:210), as when they assume that human rationality can be modeled by "rational economic man" or an "ideal moral spectator." Such idealization, "masquerading as abstraction[,] produces theories that may appear to apply widely, but in fact covertly exclude from their scope those who do not match a certain ideal. They privilege certain sorts of human agent and life by presenting their specific characteristics as universal ideals" (1989:210). Although ostensibly designed to cope with the problem of moral diversity, such idealizing theories subvert that purpose by excluding a whole range of moral views not only from an account of

[11] See "The Great Maxims of Justice and Charity" in O'Neill (1989), chap. 12. To some degree, O'Neill's critique of modern liberalism for neglecting imperfect obligations and virtues is based upon a selective reading of liberal theories. Rawls, for example, has argued that certain "political virtues" are properly promoted in a liberal polity (see, e.g., Rawls 1988). More important, however, like many critics she neglects the limited scope of liberal theorizing, criticizing it for its inadequacies as a complete ethical system, when the entire point of the theory is to provide only a partial ethical system—one confined to the political sphere—in order to accommodate moral disagreement among comprehensive ethical systems.

justice but from human life—and do so without engaging in any real argument or analysis of the merits of this exclusion (1988:713).

O'Neill is deeply critical of the notion of "consent," arguing that the fact that people consent to an arrangement—even in the absence of coercion or deception—does not necessarily indicate that the arrangement is consistent with their exercise of agency. Normal humans, as opposed to the idealized selves inhabiting the state of nature or the original position, are vulnerable in various ways, and so are subject to various forms of manipulation. She even goes so far as to argue that "genuine" consent is "undermined by the very institutions that most readily secure an appearance of consent" (1989:217), such as intimate sexual relationships, employment relationships, and "market economies and democratic politics" generally (1986:148).[12] The mere fact of consent, then, is not sufficient to ensure that institutions and practices realize the ideal of a moral community.

These arguments raise fatal objections to some classical contractarian views that purport to set out necessary and sufficient conditions for a just political order. Taking an idealized model of agency as the basis for political order may cause us to overlook important ways in which nonideal persons are vulnerable, and so lead us to endorse institutions (such as unregulated market societies with a "minimal" state) that often function in such a way as to undercut the capacity for agency. We must be sensitive to the ways in which the appearance of consent may disguise its absence. But not all versions of contractarianism rest on such an improper use of idealizations. When Rawls, for example, utilizes an idealized conception of agency to determine what "ideally" rational and knowledgeable persons would accept or agree to in framing the rules of social cooperation, he does not assume that he is framing principles *for* ideally rational individuals. On the contrary, he recognizes a variety of human vulnerabilities, and the rules are framed accordingly. For example, he rules out certain norms partly on the grounds that they would involve severe "strains of commitment." Actual individuals, he argues, would not have the will or moral fortitude to live up to their demands, and so ideally rational individuals, recognizing such weaknesses, would not accept them (1971: 176–78). In general, the point of such idealizations in the construction of a social theory is to identify and reject those rules or social practices that would be accepted only because those subject to them were mistaken or irrational. The purpose of the idealization is precisely to protect us against common vulnerabilities.

O'Neill would like to avoid relying upon idealizations of the person,

---

[12] Actually, she does not specify what institutions she has in mind; the first examples are taken from O'Neill 1985 (reprinted in O'Neill 1989).

whose hypothetical consent in the "original position" or a "presocial" contractual stage defines legitimate social arrangements. At the same time, she is sensitive to the danger that the actual "consent" of people in particular settings may reflect various forms of oppression. Thus, she would have us appeal "to the *possible consent of actual agents*" (1989: 217, emphasis in original). The criterion we should use is "that any arrangements or offers could have been refused or renegotiated," for "Only action and policies that guarantee the refusability by actual agents of institutions, offers and involvements that others propose can ensure consent that is not merely nominal but legitimating" (217). But how are we to know when someone has a "guarantee" that he or she can refuse proposed institutions, offers, or involvements? O'Neill does not pose this question, but how else could we answer it but to say that refusal is possible only when one has an "acceptable" alternative and is in a position to realize it? But what constitutes an acceptable alternative? Gandhi notoriously said that European Jews should not have used violence to resist the Nazis since, if all else failed, they "should have offered themselves to the butcher's knife. They should have thrown themselves into the sea from cliffs" (quoted in Ashe 1968:341). Given the ideals he accepted, this was apparently an acceptable alternative under the circumstances. We cannot even begin to identify acceptable alternatives, and the capacities and resources an agent would have to have in order to know what the alternatives were, without using a particular conception of the person—and the ideals associated with it.

The problem of defining acceptable alternatives is much more difficult when we turn from individual interactions to consider the design of institutions, in which numerous individuals with different capacities and vulnerabilities will participate. When should those of us who accept a particular institution feel it necessary to respect another's objections to it and agree to reform or disband it? And what, in the face of this conflict, should we put in its place? Perhaps someone's refusal is purely self-interested, reflecting a grab for power and control over others? Perhaps it stems from irrational desires, or mere willfulness? While O'Neill is correct to stress that any idealization carries with it the possibility of unreasonable and unjust exclusions, we cannot simply dispense with idealizations altogether. The "possible consent of actual agents," like any counterfactual claim, can only be judged through the use of theoretical constructions utilizing a particular view of human capacities and ends. This carries the risk of excluding those whose aspirations and needs cannot be expressed in those terms, but it is a necessary risk anyone interested in consent as the basis of political life must take.

Agency Rights and Institutions

Agency rights protect the conditions for discourse, and they are essential to the creation of political community under conditions of moral pluralism. Agency rights—particularly in the form of option rights—create what could be called "free social space," activities that are not subject to authoritative direction or control. In a pluralist world, free social space allows people to express their different identities and to pursue their various ends. But the decision to organize a society in which there is an extensive area of free social space has important consequences for the kinds of institutions that can be created and for the ends that the society can hope to realize.

Perhaps the most obvious consequence is that significant areas of social life will necessarily exhibit an unplanned, unintended character. Because individuals are permitted to act on their own judgments in these areas, their actions will be coordinated (to the extent that they are coordinated at all) only in a piecemeal and unplanned manner. Sometimes the overall pattern of activity that emerges will be reasonably stable and contribute to the reproduction of familiar social forms: for example, there is no central arrangement of marriages in any society, but the number that occur in any given year can be predicted with considerable accuracy based on variables such as the number of people in certain age cohorts and the general level of economic well-being at the time. But in other cases, particularly where agency rights are extensive and include important economic and cultural activities, social outcomes will be unpredictable, leading to significant social changes that may profoundly affect the lives of everyone.[13]

In free social space people will generally have to take the behavior of others as "given" in making their own choices. Since I will be able to influence the actions of only a few individuals, I will generally have to make the best guess I can as to what most people will do, and act accordingly. In choosing to study engineering, for example, I will have to predict

[13] Of course, unplanned and uncontrolled social change occurs in the absence of a system of agency rights as well. Moreover, even in societies in which agency rights are insignificant, there will always be a certain area of "free social space." To the extent that a system of social rules is closed by the principle that actions that are not forbidden are permitted, even quite elaborate systems that regulate vast areas of life will leave many unregulated actions (though they may be so narrowly constrained that they do not disturb the stable reproduction of the social order). Systems based on an extensive system of agency rights are distinctive in the degree to which they are open to uncontrolled processes of internally generated change.

as best I can how many others will be making the same choices and what opportunities will be available once I have completed my training. If my guesses are wrong, I may find that the competition is too stiff for the few jobs that exist (or, more happily, that firms are falling all over themselves making me offers). Not only will there always be considerable uncertainty attaching to important choices, but different people will, for purely arbitrary reasons, find themselves in quite different positions in terms of their ability to realize their goals. On a hot day in the summer, lots of people will swelter in their cars as they sit in traffic jams leading to the beaches. But some, whose tastes run against the grain, will breeze along as they head for town. On the other hand, people with minority tastes may sometimes find it difficult to satisfy their interests; consider the lover of classical music who only has an AM radio in a typical American city. In the presence of free social space, outcomes for society and for its individual members will be contingent; sometimes we—collectively or individually—will welcome the result, sometimes lament it. And because of that contingency, the result will often have little to do with the character or virtue of those who experience it.[14]

The contingency associated with a system of agency rights can be troubling. While it is possible to take collective action to address the unintended effects of individual (and corporate) actions, there are severe limits to the effectiveness of such efforts. In the first place, collective action in a system in which there is significant free social space often has unintended consequences, as people respond to the new situation created by government policy. Measures to reduce poverty, for example, by raising the minimum wage, may cause increased unemployment, possibly exacerbating the original problem. Similarly, highway construction may aggravate, rather than reduce, congestion because it encourages people to move further out and drive longer distances. Second, collective action tends to be reactive. Rather than shaping our world through our collective choices, in much of our political activity we simply adapt to it. Consider, for example, conservatives who have (reluctantly) come to support policies such as providing birth control information and devices in schools, having resigned themselves to the impossibility of altering teenagers' sexual behav-

---

[14] Cohen (1989) advocates a form of utilitarianism that would redress all disadvantages resulting from luck (and so cancel all the advantages), including even those "disadvantages" due to the fact that one has come to have "expensive tastes," and so finds it difficult to achieve the same level of well-being as others. It is difficult even to conceive of such a monumental task, and even harder to see how realizing it could be consistent with institutions that provide scope for the exercise of agency rights.

ior, and who wish to avoid some of the worst consequences of it. Third, collective action often has only a meliorative character, addressing problems only after they have developed. Unemployment compensation may ease the strains caused by the business cycle, but it never restores the losses, either economic or psychic, that the unemployed suffer. Finally, political activity itself is a further source of contingency in social life. Political outcomes depend in part on choices that various actors make, taking the behavior of others as given, and miscalculations in this area can be as costly as in any other sphere of social life. Moreover, in many cases, individuals utilize the free social space created by a system of political rights to advance their own ideals or interests, and winning or losing in politics, as in other areas, often has more to do with chance than with desert.

These contingencies, inherent in a system in which agency rights play a central role, pose serious challenges to political liberalism. They raise the possibility that the institutions of a liberal society—such as the market or the practices of representative government—will function in such a way that some people will find their wants frustrated and their aspirations blocked. Some may find themselves unable to pursue satisfying lives because, for example, they are unable to acquire the necessary resources, or because the opportunities for political participation are too limited. To the extent that these blockages are systematic in nature, political liberalism may be convicted of injustice in its own terms. Thus, a defense of political liberalism requires an examination of its characteristic institutions, and the pattern of exclusion they appear to involve. Conducting such an examination is by no means a straightforward task, as it is difficult to separate the framework of agency rights from the specific institutional and historical context in which it is employed.

Much of contemporary political theory is informed by what might be called an "instrumentalist" account of political and social institutions. In this account, institutions are viewed as structures that a society might create in order to achieve the various goals it has set for itself. Lindblom, in a well-known discussion, argues that there are certain "elemental mechanisms for social control that all politico-economic systems employ," which can be combined in various ways to produce different institutional structures or regimes with different characteristics (1977:11). Depending upon our aims—how much we value efficiency, say, as compared to popular control of elites—we would opt for one system over another. Of course, there are constraints on the building of regimes; for example, certain structures of authority may require technologies of communication that may not be available, or the scale of economic organization which is required for efficiency may preclude certain form of citizen participation in governance. An understanding of these constraints, of the actual as opposed to imagined possibilities, could significantly affect our aims, as we come to recognize that certain objectives are incompatible and thus to accept the need to establish priorities among them.[15]

For many purposes, this is a useful, even indispensable way of thinking about political issues. It permits a certain freedom for normative analysis by temporarily enabling us to set aside some difficult questions, allowing us to focus more clearly on what we mean by, and what we value in, equality or freedom or justice. But, as many critics have argued, the instrumental view of social institutions is deeply flawed. The sharp separation of "values" or "ends" and "institutional means" on which it rests is largely untenable, since the theory that specifies the range of possible institutions that could exist under given circumstances will also sharply delimit the range of "values" or "ends" that could be rationally adopted. That is why we seldom find people disagreeing about "normative" questions who do not disagree at least as profoundly about "empirical" issues as well.[16]

But there is an even deeper problem with the instrumentalist view of institutions: it neglects the fact that the norms defining an institution are often of intrinsic, and not simply instrumental, value to their participants. In important ways we come to define ourselves through the roles we play in different practices, and the expectations—particularly the rights and duties—that constitute these roles often become part of our identities. In some cases the values we hold from an "external" perspective may be reinforced by those that are "internal" to the institution. For instance, the experience of ourselves as equal citizens may lend added weight to the value of equality which we might hold on other grounds. In other cases, however, they may be in some tension with each other. Hayek, for exam-

---

[15] This is why Rawls would endow those in the "original position" with the best available social science knowledge, so that they could choose principles of justice that would incorporate the necessary priorities and "trade-offs."

[16] For one (of many) accounts of the connections between the "empirical" and the "normative" aspects of social theories, see Moon (1977). This should not be taken to support skepticism about our values or our knowledge; research and rational discourse may enable us to overcome such disagreements. But given the complexity of the issues involved, there is no reason to think that such resolution could occur within the constraints of time that we face in political life. That, of course, is one more reason recommending the liberal strategy, since it is intended to minimize the extent of agreement required for a just political order to exist.

ple, argues that a "market society" (or capitalism) is justified in part for the essentially instrumental reason that it provides everyone "the best chance of achieving their different and largely unknown particular ends." Unfortunately, in his view, it often leads people to construe the payments they receive for their services as "rewards" that they "deserve," which in turn leads them to demand public policies that undercut the market order itself (Hayek 1976:114, 93–96).

The possible conflict between the "external" purposes that justify an institution and its "internal" values and expectations may pose significant difficulties for liberal theories of politics. Seeking to accommodate a wide variety of moral positions within a political community, liberals are attracted to institutional structures that incorporate agency rights and so provide scope for people to pursue their different purposes and ideals. Organizing social activities through voluntary associations and markets, for example, is generally seen as preferable to compulsory, collectivist forms of activity. But structures that may be justified because they serve agency rights will seldom if ever only serve agency rights. They will also have a complex set of internal norms and standards which will inevitably come to have moral significance for the members of the society. Even when the need to conform to these norms, or to live up to these standards, does not undercut the justifying purpose of the institution, it may involve a host of commitments that go well beyond the commitment to the relatively minimal shared set of norms and values that liberals seek.

As I will show in the next chapter, these complications are especially evident in the economy, where the commitment to agency rights lends support to institutions such as markets and private property for structuring economic activity. Although these institutions provide scope for the exercise of agency rights, they cause a level of inequality and insecurity that tends to undermine the value of agency itself. But, as I shall show in chapters seven and eight, the issues raised by the commitment to agency rights involve more general concerns as well, affecting all aspects of society and culture. Having, as it were, presented deep objections to the strategy of accommodating pluralism through creating free social space, in chapter nine I will consider an alternative strategy, one that places its faith in an ideal of "democracy as collective freedom." Although this is an ideal that is, in many ways, appealing to political liberals, I will show that it is deeply flawed, and that we must therefore live with the antinomies of political liberalism.

Rights, Private Property, and Welfare

POLITICAL LIBERALISM takes agency as its provisional starting point, and asks what exclusions may lurk there, and how it must be amended to include all voices in the discourse necessary to constituting a political community. This self-critical process does not proceed in a vacuum: we do not seek a standpoint that is universally inclusive, but to address the particular objections and frustrations that arise in specific institutional contexts. Because liberalism has emerged in "market" societies, one of the most vexing questions has to do with property rights. In particular, doesn't a society constructed on the basis of agency rights alone exclude all but the well-endowed from full citizenship? Those without significant property are exposed to contingencies that can in effect force them to serve the interests and purposes of others, and leave them in desperate straits when the wealthy and powerful no longer need whatever services they can offer. Why, then, should they be willing to accept a public order constituted only on this basis?

This objection obviously assumes that agency rights include a right to property and do not support a right to welfare—an assumption that has been vigorously defended by important schools of liberal thought. In this chapter I will show that this assumption is wrong. While some system of property rights, particularly property in one's own person, one's body, energy, and abilities, may be essential, agency does not establish the sweeping rights of appropriation that have often been claimed for it. Moreover, and more significantly, at least in a society organized in part through a system of property rights and markets, the commitment to agency requires a set of welfare rights, rights to those opportunities and goods that are necessary to full membership in a society. Political liberalism requires that the state be a welfare state. I will take up these issues in the next three sections of this chapter, in which I will argue that political liberalism is compatible with the extensive use of markets only if it is combined with a more or less extensive system of welfare provision.

Suppose I can establish these claims. Do I thereby exonerate the liberal strategy of this charge of exclusion? Not entirely, for there may be real limits to the ability of the welfare state to guarantee the rights necessary for the exercise of agency. The very formulation of the issue in these terms

121

appears to carry with it a set of exclusions, not only of possible ways of life and the goods they embody but possibly also of persons—if not necessarily for their whole lives, then at least for significant periods—who seek only to enjoy the opportunities available to others. But, as I shall argue, there may be no way of assuring their inclusion without sacrificing other important ends and principles. It may not be possible, even in principle, to realize fully the ideal of a moral community. I will take up the limits of welfare rights in the last section of this chapter.

Agency Rights and the System of Natural Liberty

The idea that agency rights include a right to private appropriation and use, not only of one's own body and its powers but also of the resources available in the world, has often been taken as the hallmark and even the origin of liberal theory. Although I think this account wrong, it is easy to see its appeal. If we accept individual freedom as one of our basic premises, we must recognize the claim of each person to control his or her activities and the exercise of his or her capacities. From this perspective, it is at least a prima facie violation of a person's integrity to use his or her body or to control his or her actions without the person's consent. There may, of course, be circumstances in which this can be done—conscription for national defense in a just war, perhaps. But such occasions would have to be limited, or the value of individual liberty would be vitiated. This means that individuals must have at least a presumptive transactive freedom, the right to enter into agreements with each other regarding the control and direction of their activities and the right to refuse to do so if that is their wish. Following an argument by Gerald Cohen (1986a; 1986b), we can also see that this freedom is empty unless it is accompanied with at least the possibility of some kind of right in external objects as well, for virtually no human activity, let alone activity involving more than one person, can take place without objects and a space within which it can occur. If the individuals involved could not establish legitimate control over the required objects and an appropriate space, then they could hardly exercise their freedom to direct their own activities.

This sketch of an argument obviously does not establish the need even for a minimal set of property rights; to justify a system of property rights would require a demonstration that the powers of agency could only be exercised adequately in a social order embodying those rights. But it does suggest why there is an affinity between the commitment to agency and to a minimal set of property rights, including the right to control one's own body and powers, the right to transact with others regarding the use of one's powers, and a system of rights in external objects, including land, that provides scope for personal activity. These rights secure some of the crucial conditions for exercising the powers of agency. But it must be emphasized that this set of rights is minimal. It does not necessarily require the rights associated with full ownership (which include use, alienability, and bequest), nor does it prohibit extensive forms of taxation and regulation of transactions. Many in the "classical contractarian" tradition have held that a much stronger set of property rights can be defended through appeals to human agency and allied notions. Although I have already shown the inadequacies of the classical contractarian form of argument, it is worth looking more closely at some of their derivations of what we might call "strong" property rights to see what light they shed on the role that the conception of agency plays in the strategy of political liberalism.

One of the most powerful arguments has been offered by Gauthier, who views property rights as among the rights that must be imputed to individuals in order to define an "initial bargaining position," that is, the context within which individuals come to agree upon the norms that govern their interactions and constrain the pursuit of their interests. His specific argument takes the form of an appeal to a "state of nature" in which there are no property rights, but all resources are "common" in the sense that they are unowned and available to all for use. Under these conditions, Gauthier argues, an exclusive right of appropriation could be established. For someone to take something and claim it as private property would not harm others since "Exclusive rights of possession may afford benefits to all, because they give individuals the security needed for it to be profitable to themselves to use the resources available to human beings in more efficient and productive ways" (1986:216). On the other hand, denying this right of exclusive appropriation, by either seizing what another has taken for one's own use or by seizing it and causing it to revert to common use, would be harmful, since the person who had invested his or her energy and time into the object in question would lose the investment. Thus, because appropriation is not harmful to others, and because seizing what someone had appropriated would be harmful, Gauthier concludes that property can be created in the state of nature.

This justification for strong property in the state of nature rests on its superiority to the only alternative Gauthier considers, common use. These may be the only alternatives in the "state of nature," but in society various forms of centrally planned and cooperative management of resources could be established. To justify a right of exclusive appropriation in society, as opposed merely to a hypothetical state of nature, Gauthier must show that his rational contractors would choose a system of private property over the other alternatives. If some alternative system were superior to private property, then rational contractors would certainly adopt it. To be superior, according to Gauthier, a system would have to pass two tests: first, everyone would have to be better off than in a state of nature with private property; second, the division of this "co-operative surplus" should impartially relate "each person's contribution to co-operation to the benefit he derives from it" (1986:156). Since the gains from social cooperation are so large, it is hard to imagine the first condition not being satisfied—even the now discredited central planning systems of the USSR and Eastern Europe surely pass that test!

If the state of nature was an actual historical period, a system of cooperative management of resources might not pass the second test, since a cooperative system might not preserve the disproportionate gains of the wealthy at the time society is formed. The rich might not be willing to abandon their specific holdings at the time the social contract is signed, because their share of the "cooperative surplus" would not be proportional to the wealth they contribute to the stock of socially managed resources. But the state of nature is not an historical stage of social evolution, but a hypothetical construct used to assess social arrangements. In a purely hypothetical state of nature, no one has specific holdings, and so no one could claim that the division of the social surplus fails to reflect his or her initial contributions. Indeed, the highly inegalitarian distribution of income resulting from a system of private appropriation would argue against adopting a system of private property.

Gauthier's defense of strong property rights, then, depends upon an equivocation in his argument. When the "initial bargaining position" is taken to refer to an actually existing state of nature, it can be stretched to support a strong right to exclusive possession. But when it is used only as a hypothetical construct to test existing practices, it does not uniquely support such rights.

The failure of Gauthier's attempt suggests the advisability of a more direct approach, one that derives strong property rights directly from the concept of agency and agency rights. This is the route that Lomansky takes. He begins with what he calls the "fundamental moral imperative of a well-ordered society," which he formulates as, "Each person is to have an equal right to the most extensive basic liberty compatible with a similar liberty for others" (1987:102). This right is based upon the notion that people are "project pursuers," and so require freedom and "a regime of rights that responds to the incommensurability of personal value by maintenance of an order that is neutral among persons" (121) in order to realize their essential ends.

Because we could hardly pursue any projects without being able to control and use objects in the world, some form of private appropriation may be, as I suggested above, a necessary correlate of the commitment to agency. But this consideration does not uniquely support a system of strong property rights. Indeed, it could be used to support an egalitarian distribution of property or an extensive set of welfare rights, in which people were entitled to those things necessary to the realization of the basic ends they have set for themselves. But that, in Lomansky's view, would be wrong, since it would impose upon "the collectivity a duty to bring about the attainment by each project pursuer of [the] material requisites for successful project pursuit" (122). As members of the collectivity, each of us would have to support other people's projects even when one is "indifferent or antipathetic" to them (123). This would violate neutrality by requiring "that others undertake the service of [a particular individual's] ends" (122). Only a system of private appropriation, in which individuals are responsible for themselves, is genuinely neutral or impartial among persons. Unlike collective arrangements, a strong property system does not require the collectivity to embrace anyone's projects.

The difficulty with this argument is the move from "providing others with resources" to "supporting their projects." When I refrain from interfering with your liberty, I contribute to your ability to pursue your own projects, but I do not thereby approve of what you do. But neither do I approve of your activities when I give you the means to pursue them. In neither case am I personally committed to, nor does my action constitute endorsement of, your ends. As long as the collectivity, in providing resources to its members, only seeks to enable them to pursue projects of their own choice, it is hard to see how its actions violate neutrality, any more than it violates neutrality when it protects its members against interference from others. Indeed, protection against interference is itself a form of the provision of resources.[1]

The law, Lomansky argues, "must not be designed so as to favor the ability of one group of individuals over the ability of another" (124). A

---

[1] I should point out that Lomansky does not reject the use of taxation to provide aid, but he sharply limits the scope of welfare rights to "cases of extreme exigency" (128).

system of private appropriation obviously advantages certain groups over others—those whose parents are wealthy, those who have talents or skills in great demand, those who do not suffer from natural or socially imposed disabilities. Unless we can adduce additional considerations, it is hard to see why neutrality would not be served better through egalitarian distributions rather than a system of private appropriation.[2] There may be other reasons for a system of private property, including private property in the means of production, but it is hard to see how the mere concept of agency establishes strong property as a basic right in the way intended by Gauthier and Lomansky.

AGENCY RIGHTS AND MARKETS

At the beginning of this chapter I suggested that certain kinds of property rights, including rights in one's own body and its powers, as well as a limited form of property in external things, could be supported by an appeal to the concept of agency. But I have argued that attempts to go beyond this, to "strong property," are unsuccessful, at least insofar as they rest on considerations of rational agency alone. If capitalism, or a "system of natural liberty," is to be justified, other grounds must be found besides those offered by the concept of agency. Nonetheless, the limited property rights supported by the concept of agency are compatible with an economy organized to a significant degree through markets, in which the norms governing property are defined to make market transactions possible. This is not, once again, to say that agency rights *require* a market society; to argue that would require a systematic examination of

---

[2] Lomansky offers another argument for property rights that, like Gauthier's, appears to depend upon the assumption that the state of nature was an historical stage. He writes that "persons *come to* [emphasis added] civil society with things that are theirs. A socially defined system of property rights must be responsive to what persons have." Although he is using "theirs" and "have" merely in the sense of something like physical possession, this argument is patently false when applied to external goods. No one "comes to" civil society, for we all start *in* civil society. Whatever we "have" has been determined to a significant degree by the preexisting rules of civil society. It is obviously circular to use the results of the existence of these rules to validate them. But how, Lomansky asks, can collectivities acquire the right to determine who should get what? If individuals cannot appropriate things as property, how can collectivities do so? The answer, as Rousseau pointed out long ago, is that they cannot: "But as the force of the City is incomparably greater than that of a private individual, public possession is by that very fact stronger and more irrevocable, without being more legitimate, at least as far as foreigners are concerned" (1978:56).

alternative institutional structures, demonstrating that all other arrangements were incompatible with the exercise of the powers of agency. For now, I would like to sketch a provisional case for markets, and then consider the objection that market society excludes all but the well-endowed from full citizenship.

The most obvious area in which markets might be justified is, somewhat paradoxically, labor. I say "paradoxically" because there has always been considerable resistance to the commodification of labor. Polanyi called it (along with land and money) a "fictitious" commodity (1957:75–6), and Marx's vitriolic views on the subject are well known. Moreover, labor is not and cannot be completely commodified because it is inseparable from the person who performs it; thus, its sale and purchase are always hedged in by significant restrictions. Nonetheless, it is hard to see how we could avoid creating a labor market in a large-scale society so long as people are free to withhold their labor, so long as we cannot use their powers or their bodies without their consent. This is particularly true in a system characterized by an advanced division of labor, in which individuals are free to prepare themselves for, and to enter, different lines of work. When people are free to withhold their services, they will work only if they are persuaded to do so. In many cases, of course, socially necessary tasks will be performed by people who accept personal responsibility for doing them; domestic production and volunteer work are vitally important and absorb considerable amounts of time and energy. But short of a stunning change in motivations and behavior there will remain a vast array of tasks which people will perform only if they are induced to do so, and the obvious inducement is to pay them.

These considerations rule out the kind of utopian (or dystopian) vision of a Bellamy (1982), who would organize economic production along military lines, simply assigning people to various jobs in accordance with the organization's needs. They also support, though not as strongly, the right of people to produce goods and services independently, or in cooperatives or small firms. Even a centrally planned economy in which all production is controlled by state agencies could provide a sort of labor market, in which different agencies compete to attract workers, and workers are legally free to enter different lines of work or to acquire the training to do so. But such a system would provide work only in hierarchically organized, usually bureaucratized, structures, thereby denying people the choice of other settings in which the experience and social relations available in work would be different, such as self-employment

127

or cooperative work in small groups. There may be reasons for restricting choices in this way, but it constitutes an infringement of liberty and rules out certain kinds of ends, or ways of life that are important for many people, and so considerations of agency speak against doing so, even if not conclusively. If these options are to be available, people must have the right to have or to acquire property not only in their own bodies and powers but also to a limited extent in the means of production.

In addition to the rights to control one's own activities and to acquire the tools and materials needed for self-employment, cooperative, or small-scale production, the exercise of agency requires that one be permitted to acquire the things that are necessary to the various projects or purposes we might adopt.[3] Obviously, not everything necessary to one's projects must be individually possessed; I can pursue my interest in art by visiting museums, and the collective experience of attending a concert or play may be an essential part of the value it has for me. Nonetheless, for a great many purposes, individual control over objects and space will be necessary. I could hardly paint without possessing a canvas, nor put on a play without access to a theater. Moreover, if one is to be able to realize projects that are distinctive to oneself, one must have the possibility of acquiring different types of objects (and different types of objects at different times, as one's projects change). Otherwise, the exercise of capacities for self-direction will be nugatory, as only minor variations in activities and lifestyles will be possible, and control over what is produced can be used to suppress particular ways of life—as state socialist regimes once tried to suppress religious practices by prohibiting the production of required texts and objects.

A system in which markets play a central role in organizing production *can* meet these requirements.[4] This does not mean that capitalism is justified, as various forms of decentralized or market socialism would also be acceptable.[5] But whatever the particular set of property rules, a market system incorporates the liberty to engage in different forms of productive

[3] I avoid using the terms "production" and "consumption" here, since as normally employed they presuppose a particular institutional context, and so would beg the very question at issue here. For example, an activity such as domestic gardening is normally classed as a consumption, or leisure-time activity, since it is unpaid work, but it might instead be thought of as a form of production.

[4] To ensure that a market system satisfies these requirements we would have to make certain additional assumptions about the degree of competitiveness, appropriate state policies enforcing contracts and regulations controlling externalities and providing public goods, etc. But these issues are not critical given the level of generality of the argument here.

[5] See, for example, Miller (1990) and Nove (1983).

activity and to withdraw one's services when one finds the terms and conditions of work to be unacceptable, and it orients production to consumer demand. Moreover, market exchange institutionalizes a form of reciprocity; neither party to an exchange has authority over the other, but each must orient his or her behavior to the needs and interests of the other in order to induce the other's cooperation. Unlike hierarchical systems in which most production is organized through "command," reasonably competitive markets tend to realize the value of mutuality, since exchanges will occur only when both parties benefit.[6]

This sketch of a justification of markets is no doubt familiar—as familiar as the objections to markets with which this chapter began. These objections include the charge that markets generate inequality, in which some inevitably come to have great wealth while others, with little to offer in exchange, find it difficult or impossible to meet their basic needs. Reduced to desperation, they may be forced to accept degrading or hazardous terms and conditions of work, or be compelled to accept a kind of dependency that makes a mockery of the idea of agency. In dire cases, they may suffer not only an undeserved exile from society but physical pain and even death. If the market is an institutional form through which agency can be realized, it may also deny agency.

This is a serious moral contradiction, which advocates of the "minimal state" have consistently been unwilling to face. Its solution requires that we extend the set of rights that the commitment to agency requires, to include "positive" or "welfare rights." I take up this extension in the next section.

Welfare Rights

The standard argument for welfare rights begins with the observation that, without access to certain basic resources, it is impossible to exercise the powers of agency. Thus, the protection of a person's capacities for agency requires that these resources be provided to individuals as a matter of right. Although this argument has considerable force, it is inadequate because it abstracts from the institutional context in which the issue of welfare rights arises. Obviously, various kinds of physical deprivation, illness, lack of education, and insecurity constitute threats to agency,

---

[6] Strictly speaking, voluntary exchange will occur only when each party believes that it will benefit, compared to available alternatives. Of course, they may be mistaken, and the alternatives may be quite bleak.

threats that welfare rights are designed to alleviate. But the institutional context in which these threats arise is crucial, since it will affect both the character of the threat and its relationship to other values. In a market society, these threats often take the form of unemployment, as a result of disability, old age, or a lack of demand. But that does not mean that we can simply provide income or services to those in need without undermining their status and self-respect, given the institutions of a market society. What is demeaning about receiving welfare in a market society is in part the invidious distinction that it makes between those who receive it and those who do not. Even if one has a right to receive a benefit, if the need to exercise that right is a sign of failure, it will be stigmatizing to do so.

This is not to say that any particular person who receives benefits will necessarily experience a loss of self-esteem. "Self-esteem" is a very broad concept; as used by social psychologists, it refers to the "generally favorable or unfavorable, positive or negative, pro or con feeling toward [oneself] as a whole" (Rosenberg 1979:21). In this "global" sense, there are many bases on which a person may come to consider oneself "a person of worth" (54), including the favorable appraisals received from family and friends, comparisons made with others, and attainments in valued activities. Since we have at least some freedom in selecting those against whom we might compare ourselves, and in selecting those activities we deem important, it is possible for particular individuals to have high self-esteem, even if most people in the society hold them in little regard. In an extreme case, for example, delinquents or criminals may take pride in qualities and skills that others condemn.

This very general sense of self-esteem is important and has considerable relevance to an evaluation of the justice or desirability of a social and political order. But just because it is so general, and can be affected in particular cases by so many idiosyncratic factors, it is necessary to focus on more specific concepts. Although the notion of self-respect is often used synonymously with self-esteem, I will use it in a narrower sense to refer to one's belief that one lives up to certain standards that define what it is to be a person of worth, a person entitled to respect. For most people, self-respect is a crucial component of the more global feelings of self-esteem, but it expresses a more narrowly moral judgment of the self.

In using the concept of self-respect in this way, I am following Walzer, who argues that self-respect is dependent upon one's measuring up to a standard (1983:274). It is a concept that is essentially tied to notions of worth and honor: to have self-respect is to have "proper regard for the dignity of one's person or position," where dignity is "the quality of being worthy or honorable."[7] Because self-respect requires that one hold and live up to standards, it is expressed in the language of duties and ideals of excellence, rather than in the language of rights. Thus, self-respect is an achievement, earned by living in a way that is worthy or honorable, not a good that one can have simply by virtue of being a person. As something to be achieved, self-respect cannot be guaranteed: it is always possible for a person to fail to measure up, and so to lose his or her self-respect.

Like global self-esteem, the standards that a particular individual uses in assessing his or her moral worth are variable. But in any society, there will be standards that are at least implicit, if not explicit, in its practices and institutions, that define the kinds of character, actions, and attainments that are worthy or honorable, and that specify the groups of individuals who are subject to these standards. These standards are often part of the expectations of certain important social roles such as "mother" or "friend"; in other cases they include general expectations applying to nearly everyone, quite apart from their particular roles.

For most people, living up to these standards is essential to their coming to have a sense of self-respect. Although there are some escape hatches, few will succeed in finding identities that will avoid incorporating many of these expectations into their own sense of what they must be. But even if that were possible, it would not be relevant to an account of how a society could be a moral or political community. If the practices of a society are to be acceptable to its members, and if most people find their identities at least in part in these practices, then it must be possible for them to maintain their self-respect in terms of the standards implicit in these practices. Unless they can do so, it is hard to see what could motivate them to accept the society's norms as valid or legitimate.

There are, it goes without saying, a great many standards or norms to which we must measure up if we are to achieve self-respect. Among these standards in our society is "self-sufficiency," which requires that able-bodied individuals provide for their own needs and those of their families.[8] That we have this expectation is a legacy of our past, and not by any means a necessary feature of social organization as such. It is deeply affected by other institutions of our society, in particular, the family (and

---

[7] Quoted phrases are from the Oxford English Dictionary.

[8] To specify this standard precisely would require some elaboration. The expectation of self-support has traditionally differed for men and women, and there is considerable ambivalence about its relationship to inherited wealth. It does not require that one's livelihood derive solely from one's own efforts, but wealth that is "self-made" commands much greater prestige than wealth that is inherited.

associated gender roles) and the centrality of markets in economic life. It both expresses and reflects social understandings of work, vocation, and other values. And the meaning of this standard changes with the changing context of practices and concepts in which it is embedded.

Self-sufficiency or independence is best seen not as a value in its own right, but as grounded in our understanding of ourselves as morally equal, autonomous agents, whose relationships are governed (in part) by a norm of reciprocity. This self-understanding is central to the justification of markets; not only do markets provide scope for autonomy in the choice of work and forms of consumption, but the principle of exchange embodies the ideal of reciprocity. On the other hand, dependence in the context of civil society violates the ideal of reciprocity. Even when it does not involve a relationship of moral inequality, premised on the subordination of one person to another, the dependent person receives something without offering anything in return. As Hegel put it, for people to receive their subsistence from the state "directly, not by means of their work, . . . would violate the principle of civil society and the feeling of individual independence and self-respect in its individual members" (1952:150). That is why the need to exercise one's right to welfare can be, in our society, a sign of failure. While it is certainly true that the way in which welfare is administered may exacerbate the stigma associated with receiving it, as long as people are expected to support themselves the fundamental cause of that stigma will remain.

Many of the discussions of self-respect in contemporary political and moral theory neglect the fact that self-respect is something that must be achieved, and at least implicitly see it only as a matter of status and individual rights. For example, Sachs (1981) lists a number of ways in which one's self-respect might be threatened—by having one's wishes arbitrarily disregarded, by having one's rights flouted, and by being used or degraded (348). All of these are, of course, threats to a person's self-respect, but what is striking about this list is that they all involve situations in which the person is passive, is acted upon, rather than active. But one does not really lose self-respect simply by having one's rights or dignity violated, but in failing to respond appropriately to such violations. It is not the improper treatment, but one's own acquiescence in it that constitutes a loss of *self*-respect. A person who has self-respect will demand to be treated with respect: to that extent, self-respect does involve questions of rights and status. But even here self-respect must be earned by asserting one's rights, by refusing to allow others to disregard, to use, or to degrade oneself.

In his penetrating discussion of the concept of self-respect, Walzer points out that, in our society today, to treat someone with respect is to treat them as an equal. The "democratic revolution" has created a single set of norms, where "the experience [of self-respect] is connected now to a sense of one's ability to shape and control the work (and the life) one shares with others." In a democracy, "there is one norm of proper regard for the entire population of citizens" (1983:277). Today, self-respect is a complex function of membership in a democratic society "and depends upon equal respect among the members" (278).

It is important, however, not to misunderstand the role of equal respect and equal rights. If equal rights and equal respect are now necessary conditions of self-respect, they are not sufficient. Self-respect is not a matter of occupying a status or having certain rights. Rather it requires that one perform certain duties or, better, live up to some ideal. One cannot achieve self-respect simply by having one's rightful claims recognized— claims for equal respect, for a share in directing the lives we share with them, or for certain goods. Indeed, the opposite may be more nearly true: that a condition of asserting one's rights depends upon one's having self-respect, that is to say, feeling oneself to be worthy of exercising these rights. And that depends upon one's being able to live up to certain standards. To have self-respect we must be accorded the rights of citizens; to gain self-respect requires that we perform the duties of citizens.

This poses a serious dilemma for a theory of welfare rights in a market society. For if the society is partially based on the norm that people should be self-supporting, then how can the state provide them with the means of subsistence without violating their self-respect? Walzer describes the welfare state as an effort "to guarantee effective membership" in society, thus helping to make self-respect possible. But if self-respect requires that one satisfy one's own needs (and the needs of one's family), then how can the state meet these needs in a way that won't be degrading to the people whom it benefits? What is crucial is not only that certain welfare rights be guaranteed but also that they be institutionalized in appropriate ways, so that their implementation is consistent with the self-respect of recipients. In modern liberal societies, this is done—imperfectly—in three principal ways: macroeconomic management to achieve "full" employment; the universal provision of services; and social insurance.

To the extent that economic management is successful, most people will usually be able to provide for their basic needs by themselves. But even if we could guarantee full employment all the time, there would still be a set of important needs that would not be met. Quite apart from cyclical changes in employment and economic activity, in a dynamic economy jobs will continually disappear. Even if new ones are promptly created, the period of transition will involve hardships for workers and their families. Moreover, many will suffer from illness and disabilities that impair their capacity for work, and everyone faces retirement and old age. In addition to these widely shared contingencies, there are also certain needs that must be satisfied for anyone to be able to participate in the life of the community. The most obvious, perhaps, is education. Although education is, from a narrowly economistic viewpoint, a form of capital investment whose returns accrue mainly to the person involved, it is so essential to citizenship that it is never entirely left to be provided by the market.

In responding to these contingencies and needs, the welfare state employs the principles of universal provision and social insurance. In some areas—education is the obvious example—public provision of a (nearly) universally consumed service enables everyone to receive the service without stigma. Consuming a universally provided service, like enjoying a universally accorded right, does not, of course, enable a person to achieve self-respect, since these activities do not involve a performance or achievement. At the same time, when a need can be met through some form of universal provision, such programs will not threaten the individual's self-respect.

In other areas, where it is necessary to respond to differential needs, the use of the principle of social insurance enables people to receive differential benefits without violating the idea of reciprocity which is fundamental to our sense of ourselves as moral equals. Two obvious examples are social security and unemployment compensation. Both of these systems are set up as insurance schemes, so that those who collect benefits under them see themselves as (and, to a large extent, are in fact) receiving something to which they have a right just because they have contributed their fair share to providing the benefit in question. Of course, an active commitment to economic management is intended to reduce the extent to which many services will be necessary at all.

The use of these principles in providing public services may be older than the welfare state itself. What is distinctive about the welfare state is the generalization of services provided on these principles to cover most aspects of life. This generalization is essential if citizens are to protect themselves against the contingencies of illness, disability, old age, unemployment, and so forth—and to protect themselves in a way that enables them to maintain their membership and dignity in society.

Economic management, the universal provision of services, and social insurance have enabled us to make considerable progress in overcoming the moral breach in civil society to which markets inevitably give rise. However, there is a very real limit to how effective this strategy for securing welfare rights can be. The continued existence of poverty raises the obvious question of whether the welfare state can, even in principle, realize its own ideals. This is not to suggest that we can not do more than we do, especially in the United States, where the level of provision is far below what justice requires. Nor is it to suggest that the welfare state is illegitimate, that it should be abandoned and replaced by something better. Rather these limits point to the limitations of political liberalism itself, to the tragic dimension of political life.

The Limits of Welfare Rights

The key to the success of the welfare state is its ability to maintain full employment for those who are capable of working. As many commentators have pointed out, those who are able to secure full-time, year-round work are almost certainly able to avoid poverty, and most are able to secure a decent standard of living (see, for example, Mead 1992: chap. 3). For those who cannot escape poverty in spite of their work effort, liberal justice requires that their incomes be supplemented.[9] Others who are too young, too old, or disabled can be provided for through categorical programs that are not stigmatizing because the beneficiaries are not expected to provide for themselves. Those who are capable of work, but who are unemployed, constitute the most difficult problem for the liberal welfare state. Unfortunately, the commitment to full employment, symbolized in the United States by the 1946 Full Employment Act, has been eroded by a growing skepticism that government policy can achieve it without creating serious threats (particularly inflation) to long-term growth and stabil-

---

[9] They must be supplemented in a way that is consistent with self-respect, of course. There are a variety of policies which could accomplish that objective, utilizing the income tax system. Ellwood (1988) describes a number of policies for "making work pay"; these policies also address the problem of single-parent families, who require support from the absent parent, including a child-support assurance scheme. Measures such as these are essential to guarantee the provision of welfare rights in a nonstigmatizing manner.

135

ity. Our inability to maintain full employment would not be so serious if it meant only that the length of time between jobs was somewhat greater than it otherwise would be. But in times of high unemployment, those workers whose skills and personal characteristics make them less desirable to employers may be unable to find work for very long periods of time. Thus they often become discouraged and drop out of the workforce. The efforts to address this problem with training and work experience programs have not, to say the least, met with uniform success. While there is scope in this area for further social experimentation, it is certainly possible that the practical obstacles in the way of full employment through the normal labor market are insurmountable. This is the crux of the moral problem with which the welfare state grapples, for people who have been unemployed for a considerable period of time or who have dropped out of the workforce entirely suffer a kind of moral exile from society. Unable to meet their basic needs either through their own earnings or through programs of social insurance or universal provision, they are branded as human failures. They are forced to rely on social assistance, "welfare" in the narrow sense of the word, which would be socially stigmatizing even if it provided a reasonable level of benefits.

To deal with these problems, many have proposed an alternative approach, one that would establish a right to work and make the government the employer of last resort. People seeking work who could not find a job in the regular labor market could, in this vision, be given employment by the state. David Ellwood has argued that such a program should replace all long-term social assistance in our country (1988:238), and Lester Thurow has proposed using a guaranteed jobs program to achieve other goals as well, such as narrowing the wage gap between men and women and between high- and low-wage workers (1981:203–207). Unfortunately, there are serious obstacles in the way of any program designed to secure a right to work or to realize the social rights of citizenship through employment. Providing a guaranteed job to anyone who wants one means, in effect, that people cannot be fired from these jobs. If a job is guaranteed, someone who is fired would have the right to be automatically rehired. Unless these jobs were to involve significantly lower levels of pay and/or social prestige, they would be more desirable than comparable jobs in the normal labor market because they would involve lower levels of work discipline, because employees would not be subject to dismissal for poor performance. If these jobs came with equal pay and benefits, workers would have an incentive to leave regular jobs and enter the job program, defeating the purpose of the program as an adjunct to the market economy.[10] Thus, it is hard to see how we can have a system of guaranteed jobs without having a systematic difference in pay and in status between these and regular jobs, which would at least partially defeat the point of the program—to enable people to meet their needs without stigmatization. Moreover, if an employment program were to replace long-term welfare support, it would incorporate a coercive element, as people would in effect be forced to accept the jobs to which they were assigned in order to meet their essential needs. Thus, providing jobs in this way may come only at serious (though not necessarily prohibitive) cost to other values, particularly the self-respect of those who have no alternative but to take them.[11]

These difficulties can be illustrated by considering the experience of countries that have vigorously followed a program of employment creation and job training. Perhaps more than any other country, Sweden has attempted to combine the provision of social welfare with employment, thereby minimizing the extent to which social assistance must be used to meet basic needs. It has, accordingly, developed "active labor market policies" designed to provide work for all who need it, and it has provided generous unemployment compensation for those without work. The program of unemployment compensation, however, does not simply function as a guarantee of welfare rights but also as a mechanism of social control and discipline. Under the Swedish program, benefits are denied to those who refuse to accept work or a place in a training program, or if they leave their jobs for reasons deemed unacceptable.

In a study of how the system enforces these rules, Anna Christensen found "a structure in which the helping and supporting function [of the welfare state] is intrinsically associated with the controlling and repressive functions" (1980:174). Authorities have significant discretion over clients, in many cases without any clear statutory authority. For example, people have been denied benefits for refusing to participate in "general working-life-oriented courses," even though there is "no clear evidence"

---

[10] Consider, in this context, the experience of state socialist countries, where there were no jobs outside of the guaranteed jobs program, and where work discipline and productivity were very low. Significantly, when reforms were adopted (such as allowing private agricultural plots or cooperatives) that made regular jobs available, these jobs commanded significantly higher remuneration and required significantly greater productivity and work discipline.

[11] For a discussion of the difficulties of a guaranteed jobs program, see Elster (1988).

137

that such courses have any real impact on employability (173). Those who undertake educational programs judged not to lead to employment can also be refused benefits. In one particularly egregious case, a

> girl without hips and legs, without thumbs and many other thalidomide handicaps, managed despite the terrible difficulties facing her to complete a course of study at the People's High School and to train in a pottery workshop. The authorities reproached her for not taking a more directly vocational course like other young people of her age, and for spending her time instead on "leisure-time" activities. They withdrew her sickness benefit, her sole means of support. (Christiansen 1984:29)

People who refuse, on grounds of health or safety, to take a position, must obtain a medical certificate, which may only be granted on the basis of some "deficiency in [the] individual"; one cannot object, for example, to the general structure of the job itself. A very high premium has been placed on ensuring the geographical and occupational mobility of workers. There is "no legal protection" for such interests as staying in one's "customary occupation" or "in getting a job corresponding to [one's] vocational training/education" (1980:163). Nor are human relationships beyond the immediate nuclear family protected, as "Swedish labour market policy, as revealed in actual administration during the sixties, had its brutal side. Families were split up or were torn away from their social environments and planked down in residential districts in another part of the country. The older generation was left alone in sparsely populated areas of northern Sweden to manage as best it could" (164). Even the need to care for children can be compromised, as "All forms of child care must be accepted, even forms which in other contexts are not considered to fulfil the societal norms" (166).

These mechanisms of social control may themselves be experienced as demeaning, as individuals are required to conform much of their lives to the requirements of a wage-labor system. But at least the system has assigned people to productive jobs. Increasingly, however, a significant part of the population is required to take positions in training programs or in relief work. Christensen argues that "Wage labor as *sysselsattning* (the Swedish term has exactly the meaning of 'keeping people occupied')" is fundamentally "humiliating" (1984:25). "In the language of everyday life it is only unruly children, fidgety old people and perhaps apathetic teenagers who have to be kept occupied by others. Today the whole population has to be kept occupied" (27). Although in many ways Sweden's welfare and employment programs have been enormously successful in overcoming poverty and sustaining a sense of social solidarity, this success has not been without its costs, involving the imposition of disciplinary controls designed to structure much of social life around the paradigm of wage labor.[12] Swedish welfare programs have been able to hold the loyalty of Swedish society, but it is not difficult to see why other societies, particularly larger and more diverse countries, have been reluctant to adopt it.

The principal alternative to tying the provision of welfare rights to employment is to provide support to people directly, as a right of citizenship, quite apart from their role as workers. Unfortunately, programs based on universal provision and social insurance are incapable of meeting the needs of all citizens. Social insurance is limited to particular contingencies, such as unemployment and old age, and presupposes that recipients have been able to make contributions to the scheme in order to earn benefits. Thus, there will always be significant gaps in social insurance programs, as people find themselves in need but not qualified for the program's benefits. Universal programs can meet some of these needs, but in most cases are inadequate. Such programs are usually designed to satisfy a particular need, such as education, health care, or the cost of raising children. For these reasons, all welfare states rely upon selective programs in which eligibility is determined by means-testing, rather than the principles of universality and social insurance, to provide a floor under incomes. But because these programs violate the norm of reciprocity, accepting support under them can be stigmatizing. This has led to what has been called a "two-tier" welfare system, in which some people are served through socially validated programs such as social security and tax-supported private provision, while other people are subjected to stigmatized, means-tested programs.

It has been argued that such a two-tier system is an inevitable result of taking individual rights as our point of departure. By tying welfare provision to individual rights, and defining these rights and associated responsibilities in individual terms, this system classifies people on the basis of their success in the market, and rewards some while stigmatizing others. If the only people who had to resort to the residual, means-tested pro-

[12] I should note that the expectation of self-sufficiency does not require the universalization of the paradigm of wage labor. Self-employment and work in cooperative organizations are obvious alternatives. Perhaps more significant, the high degree of social organization—and state direction—that is necessary to the Swedish model tends to drive out voluntary and nonprofit but private organizations as well. For a critical discussion of the relationship between employment and self-respect presented here, see Arneson (1990).

grams were those who had failed, for reasons that were entirely their own responsibility, to meet the expectations of self-support and reciprocity, the system would not be unjust in its treatment of citizens, at least in terms of its own norms. But these norms are themselves objectionable, since they necessarily give rise to a group of people who are the objects of contempt, whose self-respect is undermined, and whose links with others and whose membership in society is thereby strained or even severed.

This objection to the way in which the welfare state has been structured can be sharpened by considering an alternative program which, according to studies by William Simon, had been presented by "social workers during and after the New Deal" (1985:1). According to Simon, "social work jurisprudence" rejected what he calls "classical legalism," which is based on the value of "individual independence" understood as autarchy or self-sufficiency. In this view, threats to independence are to be contained by "absolute or categorical" rights "designed to create zones of nonaccountability" prescribing "certain and unbreachable boundaries of autonomy" which were to be enforced regardless of consequences to others (10). Classical legalism was also based on a theory of just distribution, in which property can rightfully be held only when it results from individual effort and voluntary exchange. The specific legal rules of society, in this view, are supposed to realize these ends (10). By contrast, social work jurisprudence took "interdependence" to be fundamental to the human condition and saw autonomy and individuality as a social product. Rather than seeing rights as absolute and categorical, they understood rights to be conditional and dialectical. The recognition of a particular claim as a legal right, then, should result from a political process through which competing concerns are compromised, rather than being conceived of as following from some abstract or general characterization of human capacities or ends, such as autonomy or independence (15).

From these premises, the social work doctrine concluded that "Need was not only a legitimate principle of distribution, but also a more fundamental one than the classical principles of effort and exchange, since some minimal level of material welfare was a prerequisite to the kind of autonomy presupposed by classical principles" (Simon 1986:1437). By basing entitlements on need rather than social insurance contributions, we would achieve a much greater degree of equalization than is possible in the present system, since transfers would be closely targeted to the worst-off. And because most people would receive help in this way, receipt of need-based assistance would not be stigmatizing; we would no longer have a two-track system in which the poor would be isolated.

There can be no question that the redistributive potential of welfare systems based on contributory principles, or which provide benefits universally, is quite limited compared to those in which benefits are targeted on the basis of need, when need is defined in terms of income.[13] Nor is there any reason in principle why the liberal strategy as I have defined it could not yield a needs-oriented welfare system. The essential rights that the discourse model rests upon do not include the strong property and contract rights central to private law jurisprudence or libertarian versions of liberalism. Redistribution based on need, so long as it did not violate the weak property rights described above, is certainly something that people could decide through democratic processes. Indeed, the American welfare state is characterized by an unusually high degree of categorical assistance. Relatively generous assistance is provided to the blind, the disabled, and the aged in the form of income support based on need, and in the form of special programs to meet particular expenses. As Simon himself argues, "The most dependent beneficiaries have generally been treated best, in terms of both generosity of benefits and manner of administration" (1986:1508). Contrary to the view that the American system is premised upon the value of independence, he acknowledges that "*unambiguous dependence* is not regarded as degrading or contemptible per se" (1509; emphasis in original).

The problem arises with the extension of support to "able-bodied, working-age adults" (1509), and the reason for that is that extending support to the able-bodied violates the expectation of *reciprocity* in relationships among equals. Children, the elderly, and the disabled are believed to be incapable of providing services in exchange for what they receive, and so they are not expected to do so. But when the able-bodied receive support without providing anything in turn, they are seen as free riders, exploiting the other members of society.

It is a caricature of most (though not all) libertarian views, let alone other liberal positions, to see independence in the sense of autarchy or self-sufficiency as a fundamental or intrinsic value. Virtually all libertar-

---

[13] At least in theory. The experience of social democratic countries suggests that means-testing for income-support programs will be politically supported, and will not lead to the isolation of beneficiaries, only where social insurance and universal programs are extensive, where nearly everyone is a beneficiary, and where these programs generate a significant degree of redistribution. See the comparison Esping-Andersen (1990) presents of different welfare state regimes, and Olsson's observation that Sweden's "solidaristic" welfare system has survived the crisis of the post-1973 period, while New Zealand's more egalitarian and redistributive model was radically undermined in the same period (1990:33–34).

ian theorists recognize that, for most of us, in realizing our basic projects we will be deeply dependent on others, and will enter into relationships and commitments that will significantly restrict what we are free to do.[14] Their much-celebrated arguments for property, contracts, and markets would make no sense if autarchy were a conceivable goal, for these are all forms through which dependence on others is created. For libertarians and classical liberals, the evil is not dependence but coercion. They insist that we be free to determine our projects and commitments, rather than having them imposed on us. If we are to be free in this way, then we need a certain degree of independence from others, but independence is necessary only because of the commitments to freedom and to reciprocity in relationships among moral equals.[15]

The liberal commitment to reciprocity allows significant scope for need-based entitlements, which is a possible method to provide the conditions necessary to exercise the powers of agency. So long as one is unable to meet these conditions oneself, due to factors beyond one's control such as disability or age, the liberal strategy requires that they be met, and no stigma should be attached to receiving such assistance. This applies not merely to satisfying basic needs; other important goods can be distributed on the basis of need without stigmatizing recipients. A program is stigmatizing only when it in some way singles out its recipients as having failed to meet some duty or expectation, for it is the failure to meet expectations that constitutes the reproach or disgrace that stigmatization involves. Many targeted programs do not raise issues of stigma at all. To take an obvious example, need-based scholarships for university students are not demeaning, for there is no expectation that students (or their families) should be able to provide higher education for themselves, and the value

[14] An obvious exception is Ayn Rand, who has advocated a kind of self-sufficiency extending even to the level of personal identity and emotions. See, for example, Rand (1964) and (1968).

[15] There are, in many liberal cultures, other reasons for valuing independence in the sense employed here, notably the so-called "work ethic," the widespread view that work is a principal vehicle for self-realization and identity. Where systematic work in a vocation is widely held as an ideal of excellence in a society, those who do not work will not only be seen as violating the expectation of reciprocity but will also be held in contempt as lacking in virtue. Such contempt will be directed not only toward the "undeserving poor" but also toward wealthy rentiers. It should be noted that "work" need not be in the form of paid employment; voluntary social service and certain forms of domestic work are also acceptable. Much of the opposition to welfare provision in America stems from attitudes toward work as central to human excellence and/or flourishing, attitudes that do not derive from liberal values.

attached to "equality of opportunity" specifically licenses support for educational programs of all sorts.

Reciprocity is also consistent with significant redistribution. Simon argues that the redistributive aspects of contributory programs are in tension with the logic of liberal rights, but if we think of the key idea as reciprocity, then we can see that there are numerous grounds for setting aside the results of market exchange. The justification of the market is that it permits both a significant degree of freedom to use one's assets—property, energy, talents, skills—as one wishes, and to acquire things that enable one to realize the way of life one values (within the scope permitted by one's assets), and it instantiates reciprocity. However, the market does this imperfectly, providing all kinds of opportunities for enrichment that are not only undeserved but involve the exploitation of weak bargaining positions of others. What is crucial is not that each person be guaranteed whatever he or she can acquire, but that there be some reciprocity between persons, a reasonable balance of the distribution of burdens and benefits in their relationships. That ideal will often require regulations of market activity and redistribution of income from market exchanges.

If reciprocity rather than independence is the critical value in this context, then a system of welfare provision that looks only at needs will encounter the same problems of undermining self-respect that were discussed above. Contrary to Simon's argument, the issue is not what proportion of the society receives benefits under a program, but whether the receipt of benefits is compatible with the norms defining the major institutions and practices of the society. Shifting to a purely needs-based system would require a significant redefinition of the understanding of reciprocity and the displacement of market processes in important areas of economic activity. So long as these changes were made in ways that respected basic agency rights, they would be consistent with the liberal strategy. Unfortunately, it may not be possible to effect such changes because of the limits on the possible institutional forms through which they could be realized. The alternative is a more centralized system relying on planning to coordinate economic activities, but the record of such systems is hardly encouraging, to say the least. The various and in many ways attractive schemes of market socialism that have been proposed in recent years would not solve the problems outlined above, since they arise only when people cannot meet their needs through market exchange.

The introduction of a needs-based system, and the conception of "interdependence" with which it has been associated, can all too easily threaten basic agency rights. In his discussion of social work jurisprudence, Simon acknowledges the importance of such rights, which he calls interests "in individual nonaccountability or immunity that might limit the kind of inquiry and dialogue implicit in the dialectical notion of right" (1985:15). If we allow that rights are conditional, not absolute, and arise through collective or political processes of discussion and choice, these processes must already incorporate certain basic rights if the resulting decisions are to reflect the noncoerced choices of the participants. Simon suggests that these rights might best be dealt with "under the rubric of privacy" (15), and insists that social work jurisprudence "did not embrace paternalism," as social workers were supposed to "honor" the choices of clients (19). But there is a deep tension between the view that "the autonomy of the claimant [for welfare] is a goal . . . of the system," and that the social worker should therefore "assist the client toward a more reflective and articulate understanding of her interests through a vaguely psychotherapeutic discourse" (15, 17). Simon correctly notes that those seeking welfare are often subject to pressures that impair their capacities in important ways, but these very infirmities, not to mention the radical difference in power between the client and the social worker, make this "discourse" at least potentially coercive. Rights, in Simon's view, do "not constitute a fortress for the individual against the state, but rather an encounter between the individual and the state in which the identity of each [is] partly up for grabs" (17). In a dialogue between clients and providers, one suspects that their identities will never be *equally* "up for grabs."[16]

The provision of welfare rights based on a conception of agency does create a pattern of exclusions, in which some people are, at least at certain points in their lives, treated in ways that undermine their membership in the political community. But this does not constitute a reason for rejecting this approach unless we can find a superior alternative. And, at least in the United States, far more could—and should—be done to realize welfare rights without stigmatization by expanding universal programs and social insurance, by providing expanded training and employment programs, and by policies designed to provide adequate child support and to supplement the earnings of low-paid workers. Switching to a needs-based system of provision would fail to integrate the able-bodied long-term unemployed into the community, and by weakening the place of rights in the system it would create new opportunities for coercive interventions and exclusions.

[16] For a critical account of the tutelary and disciplinary impact of the social work model of welfare, see Polsky (1991).

144

Conclusion

Political liberalism requires a set of agency rights, including both welfare rights and option rights. Without such rights, effective participation in discourse would be impossible, and the ideal of political community could not be realized. But the characteristic institutions through which these rights are established—notably, markets—carry with them their own exclusions, as some will find themselves unable to meet their needs due to the normal operation of these institutions. Moreover, market society is premised upon certain norms, perhaps the most important being reciprocity, which create serious barriers to the direct realization of welfare rights, as policies to provide needed income and services may undermine the self-respect of their intended beneficiaries. Other policies, such as guaranteed jobs programs, also involve significant costs, such as disciplinary controls or the necessity to take jobs that involve significantly less pay and status than comparable work available to others. A welfare state is necessary, but it will inevitably fall short of its promise. To the extent that the suffering it produces (or fails to ameliorate) is widely distributed in the society, these limits may not weigh heavily upon us. But to the extent that some bear a disproportionate share of these burdens, the ideal of political community will have been compromised. In this area, political liberalism must acknowledge its own limitations.

Citizenship and Gender

THE SUSPICION THAT exclusions lurk in the liberal strategy has always focused on liberalism's support of property and markets, but the issues raised in that context can and have been extended to the commitment to agency rights in general. In recent years some of the deepest and most perplexing objections to the liberal strategy concern gender. There is a certain irony here, since feminists, like the advocates of other oppressed and disadvantaged groups, have often invoked the language of rights. Indeed, the first major theoretical statements of a feminist position were articulated within a liberal framework by Mary Wollstonecraft, Harriet Taylor, and John Stuart Mill. But many contemporary feminists deny that the liberal commitment to universal rights and citizenship is adequate to overcome the forms of oppression from which women have historically suffered. Some argue that the very distinction between "public" and "private" that is central to liberal theory—and to any theory in which individual rights are a fundamental constituent—works to perpetuate male domination. Far from ending the oppression of women, these critics contend that the complete realization of liberal principles would intensify it.

CITIZENSHIP: REPUBLICAN AND LIBERAL CONCEPTIONS

The idea of citizenship is not a liberal invention but has its home in the civic republican or civic humanist traditions of modern political thought. At the risk of caricature, the republican conception of citizenship, ultimately deriving from Aristotle, conceives of the citizen as someone who has both the capacity and the responsibility to contribute to the common good of the commonwealth or city. This common good is conceived largely in terms of the realization of the human good, or the good of man, to use the traditional and revealing phrase. The political association, as the most inclusive association, is aimed at the highest good, the good for man, and so it has the task of directing and allocating various partial or lesser goods.

The capacity to contribute to the common good involves three qualities, stressed in varying degrees by various republican thinkers: (1) *inde-*

pendence, in the sense that the citizen, not being dependent upon others for his livelihood, can give his own judgment as to the direction of public affairs; because of his independence, he will not be controlled by others in exercising the office of citizenship; (2) *capacity for deliberation*, in the sense that the citizen, understood to have the requisite level of rationality and knowledge, is able to provide useful counsel, to understand the laws, and conform to them; and (3) *capacity to bear arms*, in the sense that the citizen is able to contribute to the defense of the commonwealth from its enemies. Each of these capacities, understood to be necessary to the demanding role of citizenship, tends to be exclusionary, both in terms of class and gender.

In contrast to republican ideals, the logic of discourse-based legitimation is inclusionary. We can see this strain toward universality in the contradictions Rousseau is driven to in reconciling his deeply republican understanding of political life and his notion of the general will, which (as I suggested in chapter four) is at least implicitly a discourse-based conception of legitimacy. Rousseau insists that the laws must be expressions of the general will—they must be the result of deliberations in which everyone has an equal voice, and they must be equally binding on all. But he also recognizes that his notion of citizenship is very demanding: "The better constituted the state, the more public affairs dominate private ones in the minds of the citizens" (1978:102). But if that is the case, who is to do the necessary work of social reproduction, of providing for the material needs of the society? In Rousseau's example of the ideal form of political life, Sparta, the answer was slaves (and women). In Rousseau's words, "What! Freedom can only be maintained with the support of servitude? Perhaps. The two extremes meet. . . . There are some unfortunate situations when one cannot preserve one's freedom except at the expense of others, and when the citizen can only be perfectly free if the slave is completely enslaved" (1978:103). Rousseau, of course, does not endorse slavery, but he does—notoriously—insist upon the exclusion of women.

Only universal citizenship can be consistently sustained in a discourse-based view of legitimation. In Rousseau's language, any exclusion from the assembly means that its actions cannot be expressions of the general will and are therefore not binding on those who are excluded. And, as I argued in chapter five, universal citizenship requires respect for "agency rights," even if they may be contested through discourse itself. Thus all who are capable of intentional or responsible action are, in principle, participants in discourse, which can be expected to yield only those norms or principles that accord equal treatment and respect to each party. The only legitimate basis for exclusion is someone's incapacity for

147

responsible action—that is, immaturity, and more or less severe mental incompetence or mental illness.

The universalization of the status of citizenship leads to what we might call a "thinning" or shrinkage of its moral and political significance. When citizenship is a demanding role, requiring difficult performances and the cultivation of a range of virtues, there will be many who are incapable of meetings its expectations. As citizenship becomes more universal and the bases for exclusion are narrowed, its exercise becomes less strenuous and its activities occupy a smaller place in most people's lives.[1] This poses a dilemma for those who are critical of politics in contemporary liberal societies, and who yearn for a more participatory form of democracy where citizen involvement would be a major activity for most people. Such critics are attracted to the republican ideal of citizenship, but are unable to countenance the exclusions that appear to come with it. Thus, Hannah Pitkin laments the fact that "From the political ideals of ancient Athens to their recent revival by Hannah Arendt, republican activism seems to be linked to 'manly' heroism and military glory, and to disdain for the household, the private, the personal, and sensual" (1984:5).

The story of the extension—and the thinning—of citizenship has been told many times. One of the most compelling accounts is by T. H. Marshall (1977), who traces the emergence of universal citizenship by observing three successive phases, the first involving the general extension of civil rights, the second the universalization of the suffrage, and the third the growth of the welfare state and the creation of what he calls the "social rights of citizenship."[2] His picture of citizenship today presents a clear contrast to the republican ideal. Far from requiring a life of strenuous involvement, open only to a qualified few, citizenship is now a matter of universal right, including the right to have one's basic needs met by the commonwealth, and any duties of citizenship are scarcely noted. It is a far

[1] Political activities may be very important to many people and, as the growth of modern nationalism suggests, political identities can be of enormous significance. But just because citizenship is a role that virtually all are able and expected to play, meeting its demands could hardly occupy much time and energy for the average person.

[2] Like so much of social science, Marshall's account is blind to issues of gender, as he depicts these phases as an historical succession, the completion or virtual completion of one laying the basis for the realization of the next. His stages describe the gradual extension of the rights associated with citizenship for men, but they ignore the experience of women (and, I might add, other nonclass-based exclusions), who often were able to claim various welfare rights (e.g., widow's pensions) before they were entitled to political or even full civil rights.

cry from Machiavelli's image of civic brothers, marching off to battle against the forces of the Pope, men who loved their native city more than they cared about the salvation of their souls.

If citizenship in liberal theory (and, increasingly, practice) is no longer a demanding role, explicitly requiring qualities that exclude much of the population, might it nonetheless be true that it is still not genuinely universal, that its formal universality surreptitiously excludes many people, particularly women? Just because liberal citizenship is based on a narrow conception of the person, does it perhaps exclude a vital range of moral experiences that are particularly associated with women? And does this mean that full participation in public life is not, in reality, open to women in liberal societies?

FALSE UNIVERSALITY: PUBLIC AND PRIVATE

The charge of false universality is often made against classical social contract theories, and rightly so, I might add. Historically, social contract thinkers excluded women from the social contract, so that the resulting understanding of the polity was one that confirms or licenses male domination. Hobbes, with his usual boldness and directness, explained why men have dominion over their children, in spite of the fact that "there is not always [much] difference of strength or prudence between the man and the woman." The reason is that "for the most part Commonwealths have been erected by the Fathers, not by the Mothers of families" (1909:103).

But the critical question is not whether certain contractarian theories exclude women, but whether the very metaphor of the social contract and, more generally, the liberal project itself, necessarily does so. According to some critics, the process of abstracting from differences among participants in discourse in order to discover commonalities leads to a set of principles which privilege men at the expense of women. As these critics correctly point out, the liberal version of discourse-based legitimation leads to a division of social life between two spheres—the public, which is governed by universal norms founded on common or shared ends, and the private, which is the sphere of particularity and difference, where agents pursue their own particular ends. They go on to argue that the distinction between public and private must be understood as a separation between the political sphere and the sphere of the household, in which women are tacitly confined. These two spheres are grounded in opposing principles of association. In political life, citizens relate to each other as free individuals; the household, on the other hand, is governed by the principle of natural subordination, in which women are dominated by men. For example, as Pateman (1983:284) points out, Locke argues that rulership in the family "naturally falls to the Man's share, as the abler and the stronger" (Locke 1970:339). Although the liberal project began as an attack upon patriarchy, it was, in Pateman's interpretation, only an attack upon the political power of fathers. The new social contract, with its separation of the public and private, rests upon a prior "sexual contract" in which, as Pateman puts it, male sex-right is secured. The social contract, then, constitutes a "civil fraternity" of male citizens that not only upholds "civil laws that secure their freedom" but also realizes their "common interest *as men* in . . . ensuring that the law of male sex-right remains operative" (1988:102–103). This "original political right," which is obscured by the story of the social contract and the supposed distinction between patriarchal and political power that it introduces, "is a man's right to have sexual access to a woman's body" (95).

Because the liberal project issues in a "separation of family and politics or private and public" (Pateman 1988:21), a separation that obscures the political character of male domination in both the public and the private realms, Pateman argues that the separation of public and private itself must be rejected. Joining many feminist critics, she insists that "the personal is the political." Emancipation requires the transcendence of the liberal dichotomy of public and private. Freedom cannot be achieved by the progressive extension of the formal rights of citizenship to women, because such an extension would not transform the context of male domination in which these rights are set, and so they would remain merely formal. Liberal universality is therefore false universality. The continued existence of forms of male domination in the so-called private sphere—of domestic violence, marital and other forms of rape, pornography, prostitution, and, most recently, surrogate motherhood—bear grim testimony to its falsity.

It is easy to see the force of this line of criticism when applied to the civic republican tradition I briefly outlined above (and many who develop these arguments recognize that it is republicanism that is their main target, though they tend to draw rather sweeping conclusions from their limited analyses; see, for example, Young 1987). But as a criticism of the liberal project, the argument fails because it conflates the republican conception of the distinction between public and private with the liberal conception. For republicans, following the lead of classical thinkers, the distinction between public and private is a distinction between the type of rule that is required in each sphere, between rule over equals and rule over inferiors. In this conception, the individual is understood as, in a certain sense, an "accident" of social institutions. The individual is subsumed on the one hand by the family, which as an entity holds property and has its own gods, religious rituals, slaves, and retainers. On the other hand, the individual is also subsumed in the polity. The distinction between private and public is a distinction between the household and the political association. It is a distinction of institutional context and of the forms of rule appropriate within each sphere.

The liberal conception of public/private, by contrast, is—as we might expect—individualist: it is the distinction between those activities that are properly subject to authoritative direction and control (i.e., rulership) and those not so subject. It is a distinction between areas where rulership is legitimate and where it is not. Locke offered an explicit statement of the distinction between public and private in his *Letter Concerning Toleration*, though remarkably enough it is never cited in these discussions. What Locke said was,

> The commonwealth seems to me to be . . . constituted only for the procuring, preserving, and advancing civil interests. . . . Civil interests I call life, liberty, health, and indolency of body; and the possession of outward things such as money, lands, houses, furniture, and the like. . . . [T]he whole jurisdiction of the magistrate reaches only to these civil concernments; and . . . all civil power, right and dominion is bounded and confined to the only care of promoting these things; and . . . it neither can nor ought in any manner . . . be extended to the salvation of souls. (1955:17)

Thus, many activities and concerns that fall within the household—for example, the treatment of various family members (not to mention furniture)—are, in the liberal conception, properly part of the public sphere, while various activities that were once public—notably, religious worship and festivals—are, in the liberal conception, private. The liberal distinction between public and private does not depend on whether an activity is conducted in the presence of unrelated "others," but on the whether it is the kind of activity that the civil authority may regulate.

To understand Locke, and the liberal argument generally, we must make a distinction between the public and private spheres, on the one

151

hand, and political and nonpolitical forms of power on the other. The former, as we have seen, has to do with the types of activities which may properly be subject to authoritative control as against those which the government may not regulate. The latter distinction has to do with the kinds of powers that may be exercised by one person over another. For Locke, and for liberals generally, political power is the "Right of making Laws with Penalties of Death, and consequently all less Penalties" (1970: 286), while nonpolitical forms of power, such as paternal or parental power, do not include such sanctions. To the extent that a nonpolitical exercise of power impinges on someone's civil interests, on one's life, liberty, health, indolency of body, or possessions, it falls within the public sphere, within the jurisdiction of the magistrate. As such, it may be regulated by civil laws, which must secure everyone their rights. In particular, the powers of parents and of the father and husband in the household fall within the public sphere, and so ought to be regulated by the political authority, as Locke clearly recognized (1970:339–40).

The liberal distinction of public and private is not, as Pateman and others suggest, a distinction between family and politics. Inasmuch as human rights can be violated in the personal sphere, the liberal agrees that the personal is the political. Liberalism requires that the civil authority step in to prevent domestic violence, marital rape, and child abuse: privacy does not protect activities that violate the rights of others, no matter where they are conducted. Although liberals have not always been consistent in these matters, the liberal strategy itself is not exclusive in the way these critics suggest.

In some ways it is unfortunate that this distinction has come to be marked by the terms "public" and "private," because it is almost inevitable that they will cause confusion. In many of its uses, "public" refers to activities or objects that are observable or accessible to people generally, while "private" refers to things that are secluded from others. But when used to mark the liberal distinction, these connotations may almost be reversed. Making religion private—that is, not subject to political jurisdiction or control—enables people to practice their religion publicly or openly. Similarly, making sexual preference private in this sense would enable (or, at least, goes some way to enable) people to "come out of the closet," as they would no longer be forced to keep their sexual orientation secret. It is often the case that an important reason for making something "private" in this sense is so that it can become "public" in the ordinary, nonpolitical sense of the term, as Locke understood well.

FALSE UNIVERSALITY: JUSTICE VS. CARE

Even if the liberal distinction of public and private does not necessarily exclude women from public life, some critics have held that liberal theory is not genuinely inclusive because it fails to incorporate the moral experiences and orientations that are characteristically associated with women. One prominent line of criticism holds that the liberal strategy is one-sided, incorporating only what the critics call the "justice perspective" and excluding the "perspective of care." Because it is one-sided in this way, political liberalism effectively excludes or marginalizes women's experience, thereby denying women a voice in the public sphere and reproducing the sexist divisions associated with classical and republican theories.

Much of this discussion in recent years has been inspired by Gilligan's study, *In a Different Voice*, where the opposition of "justice" and "care" as two basic and (at least in our society) gendered moral orientations was first articulated. These orientations are said to correspond to two different ways of understanding moral problems and relationships. From the justice perspective, "the organizing dimension of relationship" is "inequality/equality," leading relationships to be seen in terms of "hierarchy or balance." In this view, "the self as moral agent" is in the foreground, "judging the conflicting claims of self and others against a standard of equality and equal respect." By contrast, from the care perspective relationships are understood in terms of "attachment/detachment" and are seen in terms of a "network or web." Relationships are placed in the foreground, and "the self as moral agent perceives and responds to the perception of need." From a justice perspective we ask "What is just?" while from a care perspective we ask "How to respond?" (Gilligan 1987:22–23).

Gilligan's studies were originally intended as a contribution to developmental psychology; her principal interest was to identify the stages through which individuals develop the moral, cognitive, and emotional capacities of adulthood, and to assess the psychological factors associated with different processes of maturation. However, many social theorists and philosophers have argued that her work points to inadequacies in traditional moral theory, "especially liberal-democratic theory" (Baier 1987:45). Baier, for example, contends that a "model of a decent community different from the liberal one is involved in the version of moral

153

maturity that Gilligan voices." Specifically, it constitutes a "challenge to the individualism of the Western tradition, to the fairly entrenched belief in the possibility and desirability of each person pursuing his own good in his own way, constrained only by a minimal formal common good, namely a working legal apparatus that enforces contracts and protects individuals from undue interference by others" (48). A care perspective reminds us, Baier argues, that society cannot function unless at least some people are connected with others in a deeper and more powerful way, and respond to them by meeting their needs and sustaining the texture of their interconnected lives. This is particularly true for young children, the elderly, and others who are weak and dependent, whose very survival depends upon such relationships with others. From this perspective the liberal tradition never really projected a society of free contractors, for "the liberal morality for right-holders was surreptitiously supplemented by a different set of demands made on domestic workers," a largely female "moral proletariat" whose nurturance and caretaking made the official morality of liberalism possible (50). These defects of liberalism cannot be cured by according equal "rights" to women, for if this were genuinely to occur, it would merely expose the fact that liberal "rules do little to protect the young or the dying or the starving or any of the relatively powerless against neglect" (53).

Liberal morality is not an adequate minimal morality because it does not demand enough of us, and it does not do so in part because it is based upon a misleading conceptualization of the nature of morality and society. In particular, the liberal strategy conceives of moral relationships as those between equals, and so has little to say regarding those whose natural vulnerabilities are so great that they cannot effectively speak for themselves. Moreover, it is based on a voluntarist conception of society, which exaggerates "the scope of choice" and fails to attend to "unchosen relations" (54). Finally, it is too rationalistic, failing to attend to the ways in which our feelings and emotional ties must be positively expressed if we are to meet our responsibilities and maintain our connections with others. It is not enough, for example, to respond to children with self-control, but we must also cultivate "desirable forms of emotion" in our dealings with them (55).

A similar set of arguments has been advanced by other social theorists. Virginia Held, for example, has attacked the "contractual view of human relationships," insisting that we would do better to take the relationship between a "mothering person and child" as the "primary social relation" and as our model for society. Citing Gilman's *Herland*, Held invokes the vision of a society in which people care for one another, seeking to advance the other's good and valuing the "shared joy," "mutual affection," and "bonds of trust and hope" that such relationships provide. Central to this vision is "the morality of being responsive to the needs of actual, particular others in relations with us," as opposed to "the morality of following abstract, universal rules" (1987:133).

Perhaps the most radical statement of this general position is Sara Ruddick's *Maternal Thinking*, in which she argues that the experience and practice of "mothering" gives rise to a particular mode of reasoning, to "specific metaphysical attitudes, cognitive capacities, and conceptions of virtue" (1989:61). "Maternal thinking," according to Ruddick, does not involve the same drive to abstraction, transcendence, and the denial of the body which characterizes traditional, masculine thinking, including political and moral theorizing. Rather, it is associated with a "morality of love," with a "mode of reasoning [that] is contextual and narrative," whose aim is "to respond to peoples' real needs" and manifests itself in the virtue of caring (1987:240). Both maternal thinking and the morality of love are largely invisible because they have been excluded by "the prevailing ideals of transcendent reason." "Although meant to include any 'rational' person," the dominant understandings of "reason" in our society actually "serve as instruments of exclusion" (244). One result of this exclusion is the failure to employ the resources of maternal thinking in the service of peace. For there is a deep connection between "maternal practices" and the "ideals of nonviolence" (1989:161). Implicit in these practices is "a conception of conflict and its resolution that can serve as an alternative to a conception that dominates public negotiation." In this dominant conception, relatively equal parties are conceived of as making minimal concessions to each other with the objective of becoming "free from fear of the other and [living] alone, independently, in 'peace' " (178). Maternal nonviolence, by contrast, rests on the ideal of creating and sustaining connections among parties whose powers are not equal, in the face of changing circumstances and needs. Rather than seeking independence and resisting exchange, maternal nonviolence is founded on "giving and receiving while remaining in connection" (181). For that reason, it promises a more genuine and stable peace. The dominant mode of reasoning gives rise to what Ruddick calls "the strategy of mutual concession." But this strategy is "both exploitative and inherently unstable" (178). It is exploitative because it does not admit those who are power-

155

less. It is unstable because the power positions of the conflicting groups are constantly changing in ways that give rise to new conflicts and the need for new bargains if violence is to be avoided.

These are powerful critiques. With their suggestion that the generalizing strategy of discourse excludes certain voices and moral visions, and their claim that it is inefficacious in achieving moral community, they challenge the central claims of political liberalism. They are certainly effective against some versions of traditional moral theory, particularly in their insistence that justice is not enough and in their critique of deracinated understandings of human nature and character. To the extent that philosophers have tended to define the moral life entirely in terms of general rules and duties owed to others, or rights that one can demand of others, these critiques are telling. But political liberalism is much less ambitious than these traditional theories. It does not seek to offer a complete or comprehensive morality, nor a system of values applying to all aspects of one's life and society. Rather its objective is to provide a set of principles that can regulate interactions among people whose moral beliefs and values conflict in significant ways. There will, therefore, be vast areas of life about which it is necessarily and properly silent. Nor, as I have argued above, does it rest on an "ontology" or theory of human nature of the sort that has often been employed to ground traditional moral theories. While the liberal strategy presupposes some very general conception of the person—particularly the idea of agency—it does not embody a particular conception of the person. That the resulting set of principles is incomplete, and the conception of the person on which it rests completely inadequate, are limitations necessary if political liberalism is to be successful in achieving its aim of providing a basis on which people with importantly different values can live together in a just society.

The metaphor of discourse and agreement, critical to the discourse-based model of liberalism that I propose, is designed to test the acceptability of the institutions and practices of a society by determining whether they could win the free, uncoerced agreement of those subject to them. Thus, it does not project a model of society as a union of instrumentally rational egoists, as Held fears, nor does it suppose that the only basis on which agreement could be achieved is self-interest, narrowly understood. It makes no pretence of offering a model of human nature or revealing the 'essence' of human rationality, emotions, or motivation. It is, instead, a strategy employed to produce a workable and worthy arrangement whereby people of different values and ways of life can live together.

156

But is not the generalizing strategy, as I have described it, subject to the objection that it excludes certain voices, particularly the morality of love? And can an integrated, coherent society exist if that is not part of its public morality? Given the description of the liberal strategy as resting on a "generalized model of discourse," I have to agree that it stands in a certain tension with the "ethic of care," given the particularism of the latter. To the extent that "maternal knowledge tends to be expressed in stories whose maxims make sense of individual and community life, but are not universal laws" (Ruddick 1987:245), there may be features of this style of reasoning which cannot fully be accommodated in generalized discourses. Since the point of such discourse is to bracket areas of disagreement in search of commonalities, much of the particular affections, histories, and ideals that give meaning to these narratives will be lost. This point, however, should not be exaggerated, since the differences between "universal" and "particular" is a matter of degree and varies with context. Without being embedded in a number of narratives, without its connection to a range of particular judgments and practices, a "universal" statement or principle will not even be intelligible.

There is, then, a certain priority to the general that is inherent in the liberal strategy; moral visions in which particularistic attachments are central are deliberately excluded, along with the incompatible ideals and ends held by members of a society. But far from silencing these voices, this strategy provides them a place where they can be heard. For it is hard to see how they can become part of a shared public life under the circumstances of moral pluralism. While Ruddick is undoubtedly correct to see a deep connection between nonviolence and maternal thinking,[3] her argument that this mode of thought promises a more effective way of dealing with conflict is, even in its own terms, problematic. The promise of maternal thinking is that it is based on sustaining connections among people of unequal power; it is this that in large part gives rise to maternal nonviolence. But such connections are precisely what may be and often are lacking, particularly in the context of international relations that Ruddick discusses. In those settings, even the liberal strategy of creating a moral or political community may be impossible, as the parties may not even accord mutual respect to those with whom they are in conflict. Similarly, Held's image of a "noncontractual society," however attractive in many respects, begs the question at issue, as it presupposes the mutuality

[3] Significantly, Gandhi also saw such a connection and sought to enhance the "feminine" aspects of his own personality in order to become a better *satyagrahi*. Unlike Ruddick, Gandhi appeared to understand gender differences in essentialist terms.

and connectedness whose absence is the occasion for liberal theorizing in the first place. There may be situations in which the morality of love could constitute the public morality of a society, and in such a society there might be no point of talking about the "liberal strategy."[4] Nonetheless, it is significant that the generalized model of discourse I have advocated would yield a morality of love as the public morality of society since the background of relationships and responsibility for others would be shared, and so appear "general" to its members.[5]

No doubt it is true that basing the public morality of a society largely on "justice" to the (relative) exclusion of "care," of particularistic attachments and relationships, will affect the way in which "love" is understood in that society. In liberal societies, the demands of justice tend increasingly to take priority over the ethic of care; the moral value of sustaining relationships, for example, will be assessed by reference to the quality of those relationships, particularly whether they are based upon mutual respect and a just sharing of its burdens and responsibilities. Love is compatible with domination and exploitation; it can be used to legitimize, even make obligatory, paternalistic interference with a person's choices; and it can give rise to and express dependence and infantile needs. Certainly the justice perspective cannot be exclusive; it does not exhaust our moral lives. The priority of justice in public life, however, does not preclude the ethic of care, but it does help to block the use of "love" to legitimize domination.

Arguments such as these have been advanced at least since Mill's essay *On the Subjection of Women*. They have gradually been insinuated into social and legal practices, as domestic violence, marital rape, child abuse, reform of divorce and family law, and other related issues have come to be addressed. Behavior that had previously been more or less accepted within certain relationships has come to be condemned, and there has been pressure to change some institutional structures, particularly mar-

---

[4] There is an obvious attraction in the idea that love and care could be the basis for social relationships, and this ideal has figured in any number of religious visions and utopian tracts. But actual human communities based on ties of love are often oppressive, and there is no reason why justice and mutual respect cannot provide the soil in which deep and abiding love can grow.

[5] The morality of love discussed here should be distinguished from other ways in which people have argued that love should enter into the public morality of a society. The Christian concept of *agape*, for example, is an impersonal, nonparticularistic form of love, distinct both from liberal respect for persons and the ethic of care advocated by some feminist critics of liberalism. Perhaps even further removed from the ideals of these authors are various kinds of love of nation, clan, or race that continue to inspire powerful political movements.

riage and family, to accord better with a public morality informed largely by liberal conceptions of justice.[6] The priority of justice has also affected the "conventions and standards" that govern our emotional lives. One of the most striking areas in which this has occurred is in the expression of anger. In early eighteenth-century America, in both work and family settings, "there were no explicit reproving standards" on the expression of anger "save when its expression contravened hierarchy," leading to a situation in which the "public expression of the emotion was relatively common" (Stearns and Stearns 1986:27). By the late eighteenth century, however, new standards requiring restraint on the expression of anger developed. Stearns and Stearns argue that these changes in social norms "led people to change their emotional perceptions of their own emotions," so that the very character and meaning of anger has changed over time (15–16).[7] Far from reflecting an erosion of the ethic of love, these changes were accompanied by "new ideals of romantic love in courtship and loving attachment between parents and children" (28) and a changing "imagery of key family members." Thus, "babies began to evolve from greedy beasts into cuddly creatures against whom anger could not be legitimately directed; emphasis on the cantankerousness and avarice of the elderly began to yield to the rosy-cheeked warmth of the stereotypical modern grandparent" (29). The concern with greater affection within the family developed at the same time as the commitment to greater equality in familial relationships developed.

Baier is certainly correct to insist on the need for more than justice, on the moral importance of connections among people transcending the requirements of a public morality of justice. But this does not mean that an ethic of care must be made part of the public morality of society. Within a framework of justice, the work of love and the sustaining of particular attachments can be enhanced and therefore flourish.

There is, moreover, an important sense in which the ethic of care does enter into the formulation of principles of justice, a sense brought out in Okin's critical examination of Rawls's theory of justice. While acknowledging that Rawls has failed to address issues of gender in his work, Okin argues that implicit in his theory of justice is a powerful critique of the "gender system," "the deeply entrenched social institutionalization of sex

---

[6] See Friedman (1987) for a perceptive discussion of these issues.

[7] Stearns and Stearns distinguish between the emotional experience of anger and the conventions and standards through which anger is evaluated. Though their work concentrates on the identification of changing norms relating to anger, it strongly suggests that the emotion of anger itself is not a fixed entity that exists unchanged throughout history, but one that evolves over time.

159

difference" (Okin 1987:43). Not only do Rawlsian principles rule out the "ascriptive designation of positions and expectations of behavior in accordance with the inborn characteristic of sex" (Okin 1989a:103), but she suggests that the Rawlsian construction of justice could only yield "a fully human theory of justice" in a world in which "the social factors influencing the differences presently found between the sexes" were "replaced by genderless institutions and customs" (107). That is because Rawls's construction requires that we be able to place ourselves in the situation of others, viewing the world from their perspective, which may be difficult or even impossible in a gendered society, where men and women differ "in their basic psychologies, conceptions of the self in relation to others, and experiences of moral development" (106). Rather than rejecting this approach, Okin would have feminists exploit the "feminist *potential* of Rawls's method" (108).

In Okin's analysis, the basic error in the feminist critiques of ideals of justice is that they rest on a false dichotomy between care and justice. According to Okin, this dichotomy is suggested by the way in which Rawls sometimes describes his theory, particularly by his (early) formulations of the "original position" in which participants were supposed to be instrumentally rational beings seeking to advance their individual (or familial) interests in "primary goods," but were assumed to be ignorant of their particular ends and capacities, social positions, and identities. This view of the person as radically separated from others gave rise to the criticism that this method of thinking neglected vital aspects of our moral lives, and led to the affirmation of "care" or "difference" as an opposed moral position. The problem, however, is in the way in which the "original position" was described, and not in the ideal of impartiality or universality. Indeed, as Okin correctly argues, "for real people, who of course *know* who they are, to think *as if* in the original position requires that they have well-developed capacities for empathy, care, and concern for others—certainly not self-interest and instrumental rationality" (1989b: 248). The justice perspective, in Okin's view, necessarily incorporates the concern with care and with otherness, with relationships and connectedness between people, for it is only among people who have such concerns and are able to act on them that genuinely universal norms could emerge in a situation in which people were free to debate and decide upon the principles governing their common affairs.

This line of argument is right in insisting that what the liberal strategy requires of us is *not* the capacity "to be a disembodied nobody," but the ability "to think from the point of view of everybody, of every 'concrete other' " (Okin 1989b:248). In actual dialogues leading to genuine agreement, the participants would have to have the capacity for empathy, to be cognizant of the different experiences and needs of others, and to treat others' concerns as equally important as their own. Without these capacities, it is difficult to imagine that people with different and in some ways opposed ends could engage in the imaginative and creative work required to find norms that they could all accept, and to develop the mutual trust required on those (surely frequent) occasions where accepting a norm or proposal meant that one would sacrifice some of one's interests. Thus, when we turn our attention to the *process* through which we can reach agreement, and the motivations and capacities required by that process, we can see that "justice perspective" incorporates some of the concerns of those who stress the importance of care and relating to others. The *desire* to find such principles and the *will* to live in accordance with them are expressions of a kind of care and relatedness to others that political liberalism both requires and fosters.

Nonetheless, there are important distinctions here that Okin's account tends improperly to collapse. While she is correct to argue that the dichotomy between justice and care is overdrawn, there is a significant difference between an ethical orientation that seeks to accommodate differences among individuals from one that seeks to sustain patterns of attachment with, and concern for, others. To treat someone justly is not the same thing as to care for someone, and in a morally pluralist society there will be many people to whom we owe the duties of justice, but for whom we will lack more than a minimal sense of attachment. In part, this will be due to the sheer scale on which such societies are organized, requiring us to interact with strangers. But in part it is due to the fact of moral pluralism itself, for those whose commitments are very different from our own will always be strangers to us. The reach of justice will necessarily be greater than that of care.

Okin is critical of Rawls's formulation of the idea of a free, uncoerced agreement. Rawls conceives of such an agreement in terms of the "original position," in which agents are pictured as mutually disinterested in the sense that they have no interest in advancing the other's good or end and are ignorant of their own particular ends, capacities, and identities. Under these circumstances they seek arrangements that will give them as large as possible a share of the "primary goods" they require to realize whatever ends they happen to have.

Okin argues that this conception is inconsistent with the empathy and mutuality that is required for concrete persons actually to reach agreement. But the point of Rawls's construction is not to describe the psychological traits people must have if they are to reach agreement, but to de-

161

pict the criteria of a fair or just agreement. This formulation of the original position represents the kinds of factors that should not influence decisions, and specifies the bases on which decisions should be made. By ruling out knowledge of our ends and capacities, Rawls intends to ensure that the resulting agreement does not reflect any partiality, does not benefit some at the expense of others. By insisting upon disinterestedness, he rules out both envy, my wish that you should be worse off even if it does not make me better off, as well as exploitative relationships, in which I am able to exploit your affection or concern for me to induce you to sacrifice your other ends and purposes in order to advance mine. Obviously, we can never be ignorant in the ways this model requires, and (most of us) have ties of affection and identity that make us liable to exploitation and moral weaknesses that can give rise to envy. Rawls's conditions are clearly counterfactual, intended to represent the idea of a fair agreement by setting out the grounds on which such an agreement could properly be made. They are not meant as descriptions of the psychological states of those who enter into such an agreement.

There are, as I argued above, a number of serious objections to Rawls's model, but underlying it and the liberal strategy as I have presented it here is the idea that, at least in pluralist societies, there are deep differences among people, differences that can and do lead to conflicts. These differences do not in any way preclude our having a developed sense of justice, and the capacities of empathy and respect for others, which can enable us to understand our differences and to seek (and often find) fair and reasonable ways of living and interacting with each other. Because these differences cannot be overcome, fair principles of social cooperation are necessary, and these principles will be rooted in a commitment to do justice to others, rather than in a sense of mutual identification and concern. It is a mistake to suppose that justice is radically opposed to care, but these terms do express an important difference of moral orientation, even if they both must find a place in a full human life.[8]

---

[8] These considerations also lead me to be skeptical of Okin's claim that agreement on principles of justice is possible only among "persons whose psychological and moral development is in all essentials identical" (1989a:107). The wager on which the liberal strategy is based is that people can reach agreements even if they do not do so for the same reason. We often succeed in coordinating our behavior around common practices and expectations, even though their meanings are quite different for the different parties. If Okin were right, the liberal strategy would be doomed.

Are Rights Exclusive?

THE LAST TWO CHAPTERS have reviewed charges that political liberalism, because of the primacy it accords agency rights, silences the voices of women and of those without property or valued skills. For some critics, these exclusions are only two examples of many, for they see agency itself as a form of exclusion. In this view, a social order based on agency does not provide individuals with the social space within which they can pursue their different ideals and ends, nor does the commitment to equality of agency rights and equal treatment secure the moral equality of persons. On the contrary, they contend that a system of rights intended to foster and protect agency cannot accommodate "difference" and that it functions in such a way as to create systematic patterns of social inequality and domination. These arguments, then, generalize the claims examined in the last two chapters; not only does a commitment to agency and agency rights harbor exclusions based on class and gender but, according to these critics, it burdens people whose ethnic or cultural identities are different from the "norm," as well as those who are "different" because of age, physical or mental disability, or other personal characteristics. In this chapter I will examine these arguments. In many cases I will show that they rest on an inadequate reading of the case for agency rights, and in other cases I will argue that traditional concepts of rights can be extended to accommodate the objections that have been raised. In some cases, however, these arguments point out important limits to the liberal strategy, limits that can pose the possibility of tragic conflict and unjust imposition.

RIGHTS AND DIFFERENCE

The demand for equal rights has been central to modern emancipatory movements including those against slavery, racism, and religious persecution, as well as struggles to restrict the power of the state and to institute democracy. But equal rights seem irrelevant to the needs of those members of the moral-political community who are unable even in principle to speak for themselves. These include young children, people who are mentally ill or retarded, and people who are suffering from various neurological disorders such as Alzheimer's, or who are comatose, and so forth. None of these individuals can, even in principle, participate in the discursive structure for testing moral relationships. If we are to bring them within the rubric of political liberalism (or any discourse-based theory), we would have to think of them as "virtual participants" in discourse, imputing a set of interests to them and assessing the legitimacy of our treatment of them in terms of these interests. Any such imputation, of course, would have to rest upon some conception or "idealization" of the person.

In some ways, having to make such imputations can be viewed as an example of the problem of circularity and the counterfactual nature of agreement or consent discussed in chapter four. Because it is always possible that any actual agreement might reflect a false consensus, because many people do not have the verbal skills and self-confidence to engage in such discourse, and because very few people ever actually take part in critical discourses testing the rules under which they live, we are always in the position of having to judge whether a particular set of rules could survive discursive testing. But we are not without resources to tackle this problem even in the case of those with diminished capacities, for these conditions affect all of us. We were all once children, and disease, disability, and mental illness are hazards we all face; mental retardation is a matter of degree and varies with the type of activity in question. Children grow up to be adults and can demand an accounting for the ways in which they were treated; often people who are ill recover and find their voices. None of these conditions is unalterably "other," alien forms to which "we" cannot relate—which is not to say that it does not require considerable effort, imagination, and empathy to do so.

These connections and continuities, and the shared risks that we all face of being disabled in these ways (or having someone we love or identify with being so affected), make it possible for us to understand and sometimes to speak for others. I know that I could suffer from Alzheimer's, or that a child of mine could be retarded. In extreme cases, there can be no direct reciprocity between those who suffer these disabilities and others, but the connections and shared risks make them part of our moral community, in the sense that it is still meaningful to demand that the only rules to which they should be subjected are those to which they could, in some extended sense, be said to accept.

But even if these individuals are part of our moral community, even if we have a basis for imaginative identification with them, can we use the modified liberal strategy to determine the principles that should govern our relationships with them? In particular, what is the relevance of the idea of agency to people whose capacities for agency are severely undeveloped or damaged? This has always been a difficult issue for theorists who begin with some notion of agency as the basis for moral norms.[1] One response is to see agency as the "normal" condition, and claim that children and the mentally ill have a right to those resources and forms of treatment that would enable them to act as agents when and if they can. Morris, for example, asserts that "When an individual is ill he is entitled to that assistance which will make it possible for him to resume his functioning as a person" (1976:57). But this response is altogether too facile, if only because we often do not know how to provide such assistance, and in many cases there is no hope of recovery. Too often ineffective, uncaring, and even brutal treatment is rationalized on the grounds that it is intended to help recovery.

Even when we know how to help, the goal of enabling someone to realize the capacities of agency is too "thin" to govern our behavior. Like it or not, we cannot merely aim at assisting someone to "resume his functioning as a person" without "assisting" him or her to function as a particular kind of person. This is most obvious in the case of children, where even the limited purposes of public life require a fuller account of human functioning than the bare conception of agency provides. In designing educational or health programs, for example, we seek to ensure that children will develop not only minimal capacities for choice and deliberative, self-controlled behavior; they should also be full citizens, capable of concerted action with others in the public realm. They should be able to function effectively in the economy, earning an income and managing a household. The same considerations apply to the mentally ill. One requires a great deal more than the mere capacity for agency to live in our— or any—society, and some account must be given of the further choices we must make in responding to children and others whose capacity for agency is undeveloped or damaged. In framing policies in these areas, we obviously cannot be limited to a normative framework of agency and agency rights. Indeed it has often been argued that this framework is irrelevant, that children and the mentally or psychologically incompetent cannot and should not be accorded agency rights at all.

[1] Criticizing moral theories that take agency in general, and particularly the capacity for rationality or "the faculty of discourse," as the basis for moral inclusion, Bentham insists that "the question is not, Can they *reason*? nor, Can they *talk*? but, Can they *suffer*?" (1948:412n; emphasis in original).

165

"Natural" differences have often been used to deny agency rights to those thought incapable of exercising such rights; in many cases, these judgments have reflected socially constituted hierarchies and patterns of stigmatization, and the denial of agency rights has simply legitimized such patterns of domination. The liberal strategy is premised upon the widest possible extension of agency rights, and thus upon minimizing the differences in capacities among different persons. So long as a person is capable of the minimal conditions of agency, including the ability to observe the duties of self-restraint that are entailed by agency rights, he or she must be accorded the same rights as others. The logic of this position leads to a progressive extension of rights throughout the community, as barriers based on religion, race, class, age, and sex are dismantled, at least in law. Even in the case of mental illness or retardation, this strategy has borne fruit, as a changing understanding of the conditions of agency and the abilities of the mentally ill and retarded have undercut justifications for earlier exclusions. By stressing the ways in which a retarded person can be self-sufficient and function effectively in various settings, the justifications for involuntary confinement to institutions that offered little by way of treatment or opportunities for growth have been discredited. By recognizing that the juvenile justice system frequently fails to provide either justice or appropriate treatment, the justifications for denying basic rights of due process to juveniles have been undercut.

There is, however, an internal limit to this strategy. Focusing on the ways in which previously excluded groups are similar to other citizens provides the basis for extending basic rights to them. But when the groups in question suffer important disabilities, this strategy can make a mockery of their common humanity. We have, for example, emptied the psychiatric hospitals, on the grounds that the involuntary confinement of people who are not a threat to themselves or others violates their rights. But one consequence is that many (though by no means all) of these people have simply been abandoned; they suffer from homelessness and victimization by others and lack the means to anything like a decent life. Responding to this situation, we point to the ways in which the mentally ill are "different," and claim on their behalf special rights—rights to halfway houses and community mental health facilities, to social services and medical care. But this very effort to base special rights on the grounds of "difference" calls into question the extension of agency rights on the grounds of similarity. It seems as if we are trying to have it both ways (see, for example, Minow 1990:108, 139, 144).

Martha Minow calls this problem the "dilemma of difference." It is posed by the question, "When does treating people differently emphasize their differences and stigmatize or hinder them on that basis? and when does treating people the same become insensitive to their difference and likely to stigmatize or hinder them on *that* basis?" (20; emphasis in original). Such dilemmas often result from unstated background assumptions, in which the situation and experiences of one group are tacitly taken as the standard to which others are expected to conform. Although "equal treatment" meets the formal criteria of equality, because of the way in which certain groups or perspectives are privileged, it can deny the substance of equality and be "deeply exclusionary" (152).

An example of a formally equal, but substantively unequal, rule is a court decision upholding the legitimacy of employers' denying health benefits for pregnancy, claiming that, "since women could be both pregnant and nonpregnant, these were not instances of sex discrimination" (57). While it may be true that this ruling does not burden all women, since at any point in time some women are not (and some may never become) pregnant, it is "only from a vantage point that regards men as the norm [that] the exclusion of pregnancy from health insurance coverage [would] seem unproblematic and free of gender discrimination" (57). Even when rulings do not go against women—when, for example, they are guaranteed leaves for pregnancy—the judicial and political treatment of these issues presupposes "a work world that treats as the model worker the traditional male employee who has a full-time wife and mother to care for his home and children. The very phrase 'special treatment,' when used to describe pregnancy or maternity leave, posits men as the norm and women as different or deviant from the norm. The problem was not women, or pregnancy, but the effort to fit women's experience and needs into categories forged with men in mind" (58).[2]

Basing political order at least in part on agency does raise important issues of exclusion since it takes the capacities of "normal" adults as the norm and not everyone can perform in those ways. Those who are too young or too ill or who suffer from severe mental deficiencies pose a gen-

---

[2] It would be easy to argue that these examples do not really involve any dilemmas of difference. In the case of insurance benefits for pregnancy, the Court's interpretation is obviously strained, and one could well conclude that it fails the test of formal equality. Similarly, defining the norms governing the workplace in order to enable *women* to meet their family responsibilities violates formal equality by assigning roles to women on ascriptive grounds.

uine "dilemma of difference," for their incapacities prevent their enjoying the full complement of agency rights, and their distinctive needs require that they be accorded special rights. The denial of full agency rights should not be thought of as a harm, since—by hypothesis—they are incapable of managing the attendant responsibilities. Not only would they fail to meet their duties toward others, but their inability to direct their own lives means that the freedom full agency rights provide would be a travesty, detracting from their ability to live lives of dignity and well-being.[3] Thus, it is not a criticism of this approach that it sets up a "two-track" system, where the "second track" is "for those who do not fit, those defined in opposition to competent and self-defining individuals" (260). To assign full agency rights, and to deny special rights, to the very young and the incompetent is not to respect them but to mock them.

It cannot be emphasized enough that determining what bundle of special and agency rights they should be accorded is very difficult, and potentially contentious, involving both disputed judgments about what kinds of lives are worthy of being led, and about the costs of provision. Because the mentally ill and the retarded have often inspired fear and hostility, these issues must be approached with special care and concern. But these are by no means insuperable difficulties for political liberalism. What we seek in a political theory is not an algorithm for generating "correct" answers to the problems of political life, a set of techniques that will forever free us from the need to think and make judgments. It is easy enough to say that in these "marginal" cases the liberal strategy becomes strained precisely because such people bear both similarities and differences to the "standard" cases for which the strategy is designed. But sometimes looking at something from the margins can lead us to see problems that are less obvious, though no less important, at the center. Although it is easier to begin with the assumption of a capacity for agency for most adults, the presence of "others" reminds us that this capacity is by no means our only trait, nor even perhaps our most central or crucial trait, around which we might organize our moral and political lives.

Take, for example, the case of children, who lack the capacities of agency but who gradually acquire them as they grow up. In our society,

---

[3] Some have denied that there are any people who fall into this category, contending that our concepts of mental illness or retardation are arbitrary, designating people whose lives do not accord with the dominant values of the society, rather than people who "naturally" or genuinely lack certain capacities. In the happy event that this were true, the dilemma of difference would not arise.

very young children are accorded no option rights, but are placed entirely in the hands of their parents.[4] As they mature, they acquire other rights, including option rights, and come to be subject to various duties and responsibilities. Because children differ from adults in being "incapable of exercising choice for personal ends and of protecting personal freedom from the pressure and power of others" (Minow 1990:299–300), their legal and moral status must, in the conventional picture, differ from that of adults. Minow, however, rejects this approach completely, insisting that inquiry into the ways that children differ from adults "wrongly suggests that such differences are real and discoverable, rather than contingent upon social interpretations and choices" (303).

Her response, however, is problematic in positing an opposition between differences being "real" and being subject to "social interpretation." Obviously, what will count as a difference will depend on social choices and interpretations—on the kinds of categories we use, and on the purposes for which we introduce these distinctions. But they are *also* discovered. Once we have certain categories, we discover whether two objects, individuated in terms of these categories, differ in certain respects.[5] There is nothing in the nature of things that makes it necessary for us to organize our social life in terms of a concept of agency, but once having done so, the differences between children and adults will be real. And if (or to the extent that) they are not, then differences in the ways we treat them will be unjustified (at least so far as those differences rest on appeals to agency). It is precisely the fact that alleged differences are often imaginary that explains the revolutionary power of theories of rights based on agency. In this way, justifications for the exclusion of nonpropertied men, of women, and of ethnic and religious minorities have over and over again been shown to rest on false claims about their capacities.

Minow and others have exploited the difficulties surrounding the "dilemma of difference" to produce a more generalized case against liberalism. Minow criticizes what she calls the "rights approach," arguing

---

[4] Children have welfare rights. Parents, for example, do not simply have duties to provide for their children's well-being, but children have rights against their parents for such provision. In failing to meet these duties, the parent not only does a wrong, but wrongs the child by depriving him or her of things to which the child is entitled. At least part of the basis of the parent's having this duty is the child's right, a right rooted in part in the child's own well-being. (There may be other grounds for parental obligation; failure to provide for one's children might be thought of as a form of cruelty, causing unnecessary suffering, for example.)

[5] See the discussion of "internal realism" in chapter five, above.

169

that it rests on an "unstated norm, based on one group of people" (108), thereby "debasing those defined as different" (111).[6] According to her, the rights approach defines people as "rational, autonomous individual[s]" who are separated from others, and whose social relationships result from their free and unencumbered choices (150). Those who do not meet these criteria are effectively excluded from the design of a society based on these assumptions.

To some degree, these criticisms reflect the same errors that we found in Sandel's critique of Rawls—confusing an analytic construct designed to solve a specific, limited problem with a general philosophical anthropology. For example, Minow criticizes Rawls as excluding those who "identify themselves as members of groups first, rather than as autonomous individuals," since "Affiliation and identification with others, based on traits not shared by all persons, is precisely what Rawls would have participants leave behind in the process of imagining the social contract" (151). There is nothing in Rawls or in the liberal strategy of generalized discourse that precludes identities based on particularistic attachments. Take, for example, the situation in Northern Ireland, where particularistic attachments create a setting in which even the semblance of order can be maintained only through violence and imposition. If that outcome is to be avoided, the parties must find enough commonalities to erect an agreed framework of norms and principles to govern their common affairs, and to do so they must be able to bracket those issues that divide them. Political liberalism does not rest on the patently absurd belief that individuals "have wants, desires, and needs independent of social context, relationships with others, or historical setting," or that the individual "is distinguishable from his or her situation and social, political, and religious identities" (150–51). Rather it insists that in the absence of a significant "overlapping" of these identities, political community of any kind will be impossible, and that the recognition of what we share, based

---

[6] In taking her argument to be a general critique of social theory which privileges agency rights, I may be misrepresenting Minow's position, since her concern in this book is with the use of the judiciary as an agent of social change, and her critique of the "rights approach" rests to an important extent on her judgment that it limits the kinds of social problems the judiciary can recognize, and the remedies it can impose. In her analysis, judges are precluded from questioning the background institutions and practices within which cases arise, and from ordering major rearrangements of basic institutional structures of our society. (She does, however, offer at least the outlines of a more general critique: see 148–56.) I would argue that, if a theory of rights imposes such limits on the judiciary, that might well be taken to be one of its virtues, since a democratically elected legislature is the appropriate institution to deal with these larger issues.

in part on a common understanding of ourselves as agents, can provide such an overlap, at least under favorable circumstances. Far from excluding those who show "any sign of difference, any shred of situated perspective," political liberalism seeks to embrace as much difference as possible by creating a political community that allows social space within which groups and individuals can express and cultivate their differences. But it is only possible to do this if the public sphere is *not* constituted on the basis of particularistic attachments and identities, nor on disputed conceptions of the good.

An even more central criticism of the rights approach charges that the conception of the individual as an agent, and the idea of agency rights as securing the capacities of agency, fails to acknowledge that these capacities are inherently social. Not only are they formed and exercised in society, but they only exist in and through social relationships. If we are to talk of rights, Minow argues, we should only talk of "rights in relationship." Similarly, Nedelsky insists that the "characteristic problem of autonomy in the modern state is not . . . to shield individuals from the collective, to set up legal barriers around the individual which the state cannot cross, but to ensure the autonomy of individuals when they are *within* the legitimate sphere of collective power" (1989:13; emphasis in original). The image of rights as limits, as "a wall . . . between the individual and those around him" reflects the perverse ideal that the "most perfectly autonomous man is . . . the most perfectly isolated" (12). Nedelsky illustrates her argument by citing a Supreme Court case (*Wyman v. James*, 1971) in which the Court ruled that a warrant was not required for a social worker to enter the home of a Ms. James, who was receiving AFDC, on the grounds that, by accepting AFDC payments, she had "declared her home life to be the state's business" (32). According to Nedelsky, the traditional model of rights as protection against intrusion is inadequate to deal with this kind of case, where there are "overlapping spheres of public and private interest" (32).

As I have already argued, agency rights include both welfare rights and option rights, and that welfare rights cannot be captured by the metaphor of a "wall" or "shield" around individuals. But what is ironic about Nedelsky's example is that Ms. James required just such protection—a barrier against an agent of the state intruding on her private space. Or, to put the matter more precisely, she asserted a claim to a right against unreasonable search in order to have a private space. The fact that there was an overlap of "public and private interest" does not in itself distinguish this case from the traditional model of rights as protection against intrusion. Many of the "classical" rights, including freedom of speech, assembly, and the press, not to mention due process of law, are intended to protect the individual against the state when individuals are acting politically—that is, "when they are *within* the legitimate sphere of collective power" in a fairly straightforward sense of that phrase.

All rights are relational, specifying (some of) the claims that people can make on each other. In many cases, we need rights as barriers against improper interference; in others, we need rights as powers, enabling us to act in the world; in still others, we need rights as security, providing us with basic goods and services necessary to exist as members of a particular community. There may be some rights that we need only because we conceive of ourselves as capable of self-direction, and see the exercise of those capacities as essential to the expression of our identities and the realization of our good. But in *no* case do we need, or even have a use for, rights as "isolated" individuals. Rights are by no means sufficient to address all the problems of difference, but their limitations in cases where the capacities of agency are at issue do not appear to undercut their centrality—or their inclusiveness—in other settings.

"Natural" Difference and Social Advantage

If the idea of agency is broadly inclusive, the institution of agency rights has often been criticized on the grounds that rights can function to translate "given" differences among people into social inequalities: "rights-discourse," the critique goes, is and has often been used "to protect the interests of the powerful" (Horwitz 1988), rather than protecting diversity. I have already considered the argument that agency rights foster inequality by protecting property, not only in the usual sense of land and various forms of wealth but also in the more general sense of control over the use of one's own body and skills, thereby enabling individuals to transform differential capacities into social advantages. In this section I will consider the more general criticism that the discourse of rights and the associated language of "equal protection" operate in such a way as to preserve historical patterns of stratification by giving them a semblance of legitimacy. In particular, rights-discourse focuses our attention on the ways in which different individuals are treated, rather than on the overall pattern of social outcomes as they bear on different groups.

Consider, for example, the issue of discrimination in hiring or in selecting candidates for places in educational programs. In these settings, different individuals will necessarily be treated differently: some will gain admission, valued jobs, or coveted promotions, and others will not. In the discourse of rights, differential treatment can be justified only if the criteria used to discriminate among individuals are logically related to the purposes of the practice in question, if these purposes are themselves legitimate, and if the application of these criteria identify genuine differences among the candidates. Thus, in admitting students into universities, the justification of differential treatment would require showing that at least three conditions are satisfied. First, the criteria for admission must be logically related to kinds of performances that will be required of matriculated students (such as academic ability, artistic or athletic aptitude, the ability to contribute to important student organizations or activities). Second, the purposes of the university must be legitimate; at a minimum, they must not involve systematic violations of the rights of others, or the perpetuation of injustice in some form. Third, the instruments (test scores, grades, portfolios, essays, and so forth) used to assess the degree to which students meet these criteria must be reasonably accurate and unbiased (in the sense that they predict future performances for all groups of candidates).

This is a perfectly familiar model, and for wide sections of our society it defines what is meant by just treatment in such contexts. It is the model that has historically been relied upon to rule out differential treatment based on race, ethnicity, religion, sex, sexual orientation, as well as discrimination on "particularized" grounds, such as favoring one's friends, relations, or members of one's fraternity. Ascriptive and particularized criteria, because they are by definition unrelated to an individual's performance or abilities, are not legitimate *criteria* for differential treatment. Of course, this judgment could be overridden if the purpose of the institution in question were to maintain a pattern of social subordination, but such a purpose is itself illegitimate, violating the ideal of equal rights enshrined in rights-discourse.

Sometimes ascriptive characteristics are correlated with the capabilities that contribute to the performance of a social role. For example, there are jobs (such as firefighting) that require a high degree of upper body strength, and women tend to have less upper body strength than men. It would not, however, be justifiable to discriminate against women for such jobs. Rather the relevant trait should be measured directly for each individual. In settings where it is impossible to get direct information about the job-related qualities of an individual, discrimination on ascriptive criteria may be "rational" for the organization concerned if (and only

173

if) the job-related characteristics are in fact related to these ascriptive qualities. Nonetheless, even in these cases such discrimination would not be justifiable within rights-discourse, because permitting it as a social practice will tend to create and perpetuate an unjust pattern of social subordination.

But it is easy to see how the model of equal treatment sketched above also functions to translate "given" differences among people into social advantages. If a certain aptitude or skill, such as fluency in standard English or the ability to write well, is a genuine qualification for a desired social position, and if our measures of the required quality are reasonably accurate, then those who possess the trait will be selected for the position. The model of equal treatment directly translates a "given" difference into a social advantage, and the model becomes a means of legitimating inequality.

In many cases the difference in qualifications among individuals is itself a result of social processes. To the extent that the distribution of traits required for desired positions is a result of a history of social subordination in which certain groups were systematically deprived of the opportunities to acquire them, and to the extent that occupying desirable positions enables one to provide one's children with the opportunities to acquire such positions in turn, then the model of equal treatment can function to maintain unjust patterns of subordination, not in spite of but because of its commitment to equal treatment. In the case of gender, to the extent that the social expectations of women and men differ, women may be disadvantaged in competing for certain positions. An obvious example in our society is that women are assigned principal responsibility for the care and nurturance of young children, but most of the "good" jobs in our society require people who can devote long, uninterrupted hours to their work on a consistent, day-to-day basis. Although formally neutral, this way of structuring work obviously disadvantages women in competing for these positions.

Whether patterns like these will occur depends on contestable empirical assumptions, and on social choices that are, at least in principle, alterable. In the reproduction of class inequalities, it is assumed that the opportunity to acquire the skills and abilities necessary to perform effectively in the "good" schools or jobs is largely confined to the groups who already possess them. To the extent that there is "fair equality of opportunity," the model of equal treatment will function not simply to reproduce patterns of social advantage, but will reflect "natural" differences among individuals no matter what their class background. Similarly, in the case of gender, there are many ways in which work might be restructured, and gender roles altered, to ameliorate these socially created disabilities. We could recognize that the bearing and raising of children is an activity of critical social importance, whose costs should be further socialized, in the form of more extensive provision for day care and services to care for children when they are ill, public policies providing for parental leave, and we could act to redefine the expectations of fatherhood to include more responsibilities for the direct care and nurturance of children. The provision of fair equality of opportunity and the restructuring of roles to remove arbitrary disadvantages are not only consistent with, but are required by, political liberalism's commitment to equal rights.

But, it might be charged, these possibilities hardly alter the basic situation: the practice of rights and equal treatment are still rights of inequality, even if they serve only to translate natural differences into social advantages. After all, what is so special about *natural* differences? As natural, they are merely differences; only social practices transform them into inequalities. The distinction between natural differences and differences rooted in social processes is of no particular moral or political significance, taken in itself. In itself, it is no more justifiable to transform natural differences into social advantages than to transform existing social differences into subsequent social advantages. Justifying differential outcomes involves answering three questions. In the first place, we must ask whether the position in question is itself justified. Is it necessary to construct social activities in such a way as to create this particular position or good—one that is in short supply, so that its possession will be a source of social advantage? A second, and closely related question, is whether the position or context might be restructured in such a way as to eliminate the disabilities that some face in their efforts to acquire the good in question. Finally, we must ask what other values, if any, would have to be forgone to make these changes.

Many of the criticisms of rights-discourse discussed in this chapter have focused on the second question. An obvious example is the structuring of certain jobs in such a way as to require people to be physically able in order to perform them. In many cases jobs could be structured so that they do not exclude the handicapped. Doing so may be as easy as installing ramps for wheelchairs, or redesigning the physical layout of an office. By changing the requirements of the job, we can prevent the translation of physical differences into social advantages. Similarly, altering the structure of work to accommodate childcare responsibilities could contribute to an equalization of the situations of men and women.

But there is a real limit to this strategy. While it may sometimes be possible, for example, to put the handicapped on a "plane of equality" (Sunstein 1990:64) with the able-bodied, this will only be true for those who are otherwise qualified for the positions in question. And even if the costs of childcare are significantly socialized, and even if men come to assume a fair share of responsibilities for the time-intensive aspects of raising children, childless people will be at a significant advantage vis-à-vis those with children, at least in positions where sustained individual performance can make its mark. Those who are willing, able, and free to invest their energy in work will tend to achieve more and advance faster.[7] However we fiddle with structures to overcome the disadvantages that some groups have faced, as long as we work within the framework of individual rights and equal treatment, in a world in which desired positions and social goods are relatively scarce, we can only alter the forms and distribution of disadvantage, not the fact.

Recognizing this, we can see that the critical questions are the first and the third: do we need to create institutions and practices that produce significant inequalities, and what would the costs be (in terms of other values) of reducing or eliminating them? Many have argued that we should abandon the concern with equal treatment and take equality of condition as the norm. In the case of gender, for example, MacKinnon has argued for a shift from a jurisprudence based on equal treatment or relevant differences to a direct concern with "sex equality." This shift would require (inter alia) that wages be based on the "comparable worth" of different jobs, that pornography be abolished, and that abortion not only be permitted but be freely available (1989: chaps. 10–13). Whatever the merit of these specific proposals, they too involve only a redistribution of social advantages and disadvantages. Comparable worth, for example, may ameliorate sex-based differences in wages, but only at the price of institutionalizing a new system of administered inequality, involving the creation of an elaborate structure of "difference" (in credentials, in seniority, in job characteristics) which would form the basis for entitlements to unequal rewards. Although MacKinnon seeks to

---

[7] This is one of the factors that makes gender inequalities in earnings so intractable. Given the practice of hypergamy, where women tend to marry men who are older and better educated than they are, it is often rational (at least if they expect the marriage to last) for a couple to invest in the man's career by the woman assuming more of the tasks of childcare and household management, leaving him free to concentrate on work. This is one of the reasons why the difference between the earnings of men and women who have never married is much smaller than the difference between married men and married women. (See, e.g., Fuchs 1988:58–60.)

substitute a "feminist" jurisprudence for the prevailing "liberal" jurisprudence, the implementation of her proposals would reproduce the very
kind of judgments of difference, and the translation of these judgments
into inequalities, which she finds objectionable.

Substituting a norm of equality for one of equal treatment involves
other difficulties as well. Even if we confine ourselves to a particular area
of social life, such as gender relations, the meaning of the term
"equality"—as opposed to equal treatment—is not self-evident. Sometimes, of course, inequalities are blatant, obvious, and patently unjust.
Amartya Sen has called attention to the fact that there are over 100 million "missing women" in the world. As a result of systematic patterns of
neglect and abuse, women and girls in much of Asia and Africa die at
higher rates than men. But, in North America, Europe, and Japan, where
"women suffer little discrimination in basic nutrition and health care,"
women have significantly lower death rates than men, and as a result
outnumber men in the overall population. Would a concern with sex
equality (with men and women occupying equal situations) as opposed to
a concern with equal treatment (with their being subject to the same rules
and entitled to the same opportunities) require that men receive relatively
more medical attention and health care than women in order to cancel
out the "biological advantages that women have over men in resisting
disease?" (Sen 1990c:61–66). On the face of it, such unequal treatment
would appear to be entailed by MacKinnon's demand for sex equality!

It is far from clear that we could organize society in such a way as to
eliminate all positions of social advantage, and even if we could, we
would have to ask what the costs of doing so would be. I will not attempt
to answer these questions here, for to do so would require at least another
book. But apart from the fact that no one has produced, either in theory
or in practice, an institutional design for a society in which all groups
enjoy equality of condition, there are important reasons for doubting its
possibility in a morally pluralist society. For in such a society, the concept
of "social advantage" will itself be controversial. What constitutes an
"advantage" will depend upon what is valued, and different individuals
and groups will value different things. To ensure that everyone enjoys the
same "social advantages" presumes that we can achieve agreement on
what constitutes a social advantage. Of course, there will certainly be
some agreement on these issues—particularly about what constitutes a
social disadvantage. Without that agreement, it would be impossible to
define a system of welfare rights and to institute programs to achieve
equality of opportunity. But in a morally pluralist world there will be
important differences among individuals and groups, and so judgments

about the relative positions of various groups may differ. As we have seen, even an attempt such as Rawls's to establish an "index of primary goods"—a measure based not on what people ultimately value, but on their command over goods that are broadly instrumental to their final ends—will be controversial. MacKinnon would ban pornography and make abortions publicly funded in order to help equalize the conditions of men and women. Needless to say, these proposals are rejected by large numbers of women who do not share MacKinnon's conception of what constitutes an "advantage" for women. Substantive equality requires a common measure of well-being or value, which is precisely what is lacking in a morally pluralist society. It is not surprising, then, that equal treatment has proven to be such a powerful moral ideal in pluralist societies. On the other hand, equal treatment translates differences among individuals into inequalities of conditions that can undermine the ideal of equal treatment itself by rendering the agency rights of some groups merely formal. This tension cannot be avoided in a theory—or practice—in which rights play a central role. Under some circumstances, it may become so severe that it calls into question the acceptability of the framework of agency rights itself, leading to a tragic conflict between opposed moral positions. But such severe conflict is by no means inevitable—although the politics of liberal democratic regimes will always involve a constant struggle to define and maintain a balance between the need for rights and the claims of equality.

Universality as a False Ideal

The basic idea behind my defense of agency rights is the need to provide a sphere of freedom in order to accommodate moral diversity. Democratic individuality, I have contended, is necessary to the creation of political community in a society characterized by moral pluralism. Many critics of traditional liberalism have argued, however, that individualism is corrosive of community because it undermines the bonds that tie individuals to the communities that constitute the fabric of social life. Due to its stress on individual rights, liberal theory and practice weaken the authority of "the vital communities standing between the individual and the state," leading to an erosion of the "neighborhood community, craft guild, church, . . . and the like" (Bowles and Gintis 1986:144). For these critics, "we must have legally sanctioned communities or groups that take socially recognized priority over individuals" if we are to overcome the "ravages of individualism" (Fox-Genovese 1991:78, 46).

From a different point of view, other critics fault individualism on the grounds that it denies plurality, that it represents a form of forced assimilation to a culture and set of practices that effectively prevents the expression of important cultural values. Because an individualist framework is committed to treating people equally as individuals, it is generally associated with an ideal of "neutrality," in which cultural, ethnic, or other characteristics differentiating different groups are ignored in formulating public policies, particularly in the definition of rights and responsibilities. Individualism permits people to form associations in order to express their shared identities, but it is hostile to the creation of "special rights" for particular cultural, ethnic, or other groups. People who share religious beliefs are free to organize their own churches or temples, but religious affiliation is not to count in the assignment of benefits or burdens in other spheres of social life. Similarly, people should be free to publish newspapers, to broadcast, or to set up schools in any language they wish, but no "special rights" should attach to groups simply on the basis of their language. Because it may be difficult for many identities to survive in the absence of special protection, an individualist framework may be said to promote an ideal of assimilation. Citing the "English-only" movement in the United States today and the treatment of "American Indians," Iris Young argues that "an assimilationist ideal amounts to genocide" (Young 1990:182).

It is certainly true that individualism undermines traditional forms of community by denying official sanction to the exercise of authority of traditional elites over other members of the groups in question. This has been an uneven and often halting process; for example, it is only in recent years that the rights of women and children have come to be recognized and enforced within the family, particularly against abusive husbands and fathers. Nonetheless, agency rights directly limit the exercise of traditional forms of authority by, for example, restricting the use of force against subordinates. Perhaps more important, they provide indirect checks by guaranteeing what Hirschman calls "exit"—the right to withdraw from groups or relationships. If I can leave a religious group or an employer, I can avoid the sanctions they otherwise might impose on me, and so my freedom limits their authority.[8]

Agency rights cannot secure a general right of "exit," since the specific rights necessary to withdraw from particular groups of relationships vary with the context. Moreover, "exit" can often be secured only with "posi-

---

[8] For exit to be effective I must actually be able to leave, and not merely free to leave. Oppression can exist even in a regime where rights are formally guaranteed, though having the liberty to leave is generally a necessary condition for overcoming oppression.

tive" state action. In some cases, it may be sufficient to have a general liberty of action to secure effective exit; as long as one is free to move from one area of the country to another, for example, one may be able to escape localized forms of authority. But in other cases, exit is possible only if there is an appropriate structure of legal rules. One may be unfree to quit one's job, for example, if contracts to work can be enforced and damages assessed against someone who resigns. Similarly, a society in which there is no civil marriage or divorce places enormous powers in the hands of religious authorities over a fundamental aspect of one's life, since abandoning one's religious affiliation could mean that one could not legally marry or get divorced. Thus, effective religious freedom requires the existence of an institution of civil marriage.

Democratic individuality is deeply committed to universality in holding that all individuals are of equal worth and are entitled to equal rights and equal treatment. But many critics would contend that universality is itself a false ideal. According to Pateman, for example, the effort to define principles or norms that transcend gender denies "political significance to womanhood" (1988:227). While she agrees that it is necessary for women to achieve "juridical freedom and equality," "women's equal standing must be accepted as an expression of the freedom of women *as women*, and not treated as an indication that women can be just like men" (231). Pateman therefore demands that we abandon the idea of a "unitary individual" in order "to open up space for two figures; one masculine, one feminine" (224). In a similar vein, Iris Young attacks universalist conceptions of citizenship on the grounds that the "impartial perspective" it presupposes "is a myth" (1989:257). While insisting on the universality of citizenship in the sense of "the inclusion and participation of everyone in public life" (273), she rejects "the ideal of a public realm of citizenship as expressing a general will, a point of view and interest that citizens have in common which transcends their differences" (252). This ideal, she argues, rests upon a conception of the public realm as a realm of universal reason, therefore excluding the emotions and the body, aspects of our being which particularize us. And this is followed by the exclusion of those groups, including women, who are associated with emotion and the body or nature, and their confinement to a private realm of particularity and feeling.

Many of these kinds of arguments arise from a concern with the ways in which supposedly universalist principles in reality represent a form of normalization. By specifying a particular set of traits as "normal," they repress legitimate and important differences among people, and those classified as "other" are denied full or equal citizenship. The problem with the ideal of universality, in this view, is its insensitivity to differences among people, which results in marginalization and repression. These considerations have led Seyla Benhabib to argue that we should replace "generalized discourses," in which we abstract from our differences to find shared interests, with discourse oriented to the "concrete other," in which we "view each and every rational being as an individual with a concrete history, identity, and affective-emotional constitution" (1986: 341). Such discourses, Benhabib argues, can establish a "community of needs and solidarity" in which we affirm not simply the abstract humanity of others but also their concrete individuality. Liberal discourse, issuing only in a "community of rights and entitlements," should be replaced by a "moral-transformative discourse" that can create a "politics of empowerment" which creates "friendship and solidarity" (352).[9]

There are obvious difficulties in imagining a form of political life in which each person is viewed and treated in terms of his or her concrete particularity, at least in a world such as ours where large numbers of people are affected by political decisions. For that reason, Nancy Fraser has argued that, if we wish to take the perspective of the concrete other in political contexts, we must do so from "the standpoint of the 'collective concrete other,' " a standpoint in which others "are encountered less as unique individuals than as members of groups or collectivities with culturally specific identities, solidarities and forms of life." Rather than responding to others in terms of universalist norms, "the most general ethical force of this orientation" holds that "we owe each other behavior such that each is confirmed as a being with specific collective identifications and solidarities" (1986:428).

The specific policies this calls for are not entirely clear, but it is certainly true that enforcing the authority of traditional or, more generally, "cultural" groups can contribute to their survival by making it costly for individuals to abandon them, and by strengthening the ties of members of the group to each other and the salience of one's identity as a member of the group.[10] Because these policies reinforce group identities and help to

---

[9] See chapter four, above.

[10] It should be clear that Fraser's concern with "the collective concrete other" can only apply to ascribed identities, such as race or gender. Individualists believe that people participate in different groups and experience different sources of identity and solidarity, and that each person to some degree participates in shaping his or her own identity by affirming particular aspects of his or her experiences and solidarities. Because I can't know what someone's "specific collective identification" is until I know that person, I can show respect only by responding to him or her in terms of universal norms. To do otherwise is to make a presumption about the person that negates his or her specific identity, which is not to respect that person. For a valuable discussion of this issue, see Spellman (1978).

constitute groups as collective entities, we might call them policies of "pluralist encapsulation." At an extreme, each individual's public standing would depend only upon his or her membership in a cultural, ethnic, or other ascribed group. Unlike traditional systems of hierarchical encapsulation, the status of these groups could at least in principle be equal, but there would be no social space outside of these groups. Pluralist encapsulation might be seen as an alternative to democratic individuality as a strategy for accommodating social pluralism.

The division of a culturally plural nation-state into separate, more homogeneous societies might be considered as an extreme example of pluralist encapsulation. Such a division is possible, and may even be desirable, when the groups are concentrated in particular territories, like the Inuit in Canada or the Slovenians in former Yugoslavia. The newly formed states, then, would each be in a position to promote their distinctive cultural identities. Given that many multicultural societies have resulted from conquest and the forcible incorporation of minority peoples, a strong case can be made for secession in many cases (see Buchanan 1991). But secession is hardly an adequate answer, if only because the resulting countries will often continue to be multicultural, and the problems of accommodating cultural pluralism will remain.

There are strong echoes of pluralist encapsulation in some contemporary avowals of multiculturalism which pass beyond the celebration of diversity to proposing policies that erect boundaries among groups in part by strengthening their authority over their members, and in part by formally assigning public status to individuals in terms of their ascribed group identities. For example, laws in Quebec that require the children of non–English-speaking parents to be educated in French are designed to enable French culture to survive by limiting the opportunities for French-speaking children, or the children of new immigrants, to acquire English. Similarly, the absence of civil marriage in Israel may strengthen Jewish identity by limiting intermarriage and increasing the powers of the religious courts (see Zucker 1973:108–21).

Pluralist encapsulation is sometimes motivated by the belief that a system in which there are common standards and norms for everyone inevitably disadvantages some groups. There can be no genuinely universal standards that all could accept and any "attempt to reduce all persons to the unity of a common measure constructs as deviant those whose attributes differ from the group-specific attributes implicitly presumed in the norm" (Young 1990:169). Moreover, "because there is no unsituated group-neutral point of view, the situation and experience of dominant groups tend to define the norms" that are put forward as universal (164). Thus, a politics of inclusion requires a certain degree of "group autonomy," with different norms applying to different groups.

Although Young does not endorse pluralist encapsulation, she does argue that citizenship should not be a universal but a differentiated status. The ideal of equal treatment should be replaced—or at least supplemented—with new structures of representation specific to "disadvantaged" groups, and with a set of "special" rights prescribing differential treatment for them. In Young's view, the groups to receive such treatment in America today would include "women, blacks, Native Americans, Chicanos, Puerto Ricans and other Spanish-speaking Americans, Asian Americans, gay men, lesbians, working-class people, poor people, old people, and mentally and physically disabled people" (1989:261). These groups would be provided "institutional mechanisms and public resources" that would, first, support the "self-organization of group members," enabling them to gain a sense of "collective empowerment"; second, they would enable the group to voice its analysis of social policies and to propose policy in a context in which "decision makers are obliged to show that they have taken these perspectives into consideration"; and, third, they would empower each group to veto "specific policies that affect [it] directly" (261–62).

There are obvious difficulties in imagining how different groups could all agree on the norms specifying differential treatment based on group membership. Any form of differential treatment would obviously advantage some groups relative to others. It is conceivable that the distribution of gains and losses in different areas might balance out to everyone's satisfaction; special rights accorded to one ethnic group or to women, for example, may be compensated by privileges accorded to other groups or to men, so that all parties were reasonably satisfied with the treatment they received. But in a dynamic society, maintaining such a balance would require constant adjustment, with innumerable opportunities for conflict and resentment.

Even if these issues could be resolved, pluralist encapsulation could not pass the dialogical tests demanded by political liberalism, since there is no space in such a society for identities that are not defined in terms of the "given" set of groups. Pluralist encapsulation requires significant exclusions. In a society where the ideal of inclusion is widely accepted—and it is only in such societies that pluralist as opposed to hierarchical encapsulation will be advocated—rigid ascriptive boundaries will already have been eroded. In saying this, I do not mean to invoke a naive version of modernization theory, according to which economic change brings in its wake a transformation of the sociocultural system from ascriptive and particularistic values to achievement and universalist orientations. The persistence of traditional identities has certainly falsified that expectation. But "traditional identities" are themselves transformed as a result of the social, economic, and intellectual changes that undermine the validity of models of hierarchical encapsulation and support concerns with equality and inclusion. Many people will find that their own experiences and identities cannot be accommodated in terms of traditional ascriptive groupings. This may result from intermarriage, from their having changed the occupations and ways of life associated with their groups of origin, or from their having accepted scientific or philosophical orientations incompatible with the belief-systems of traditional groups, and so forth. Growing up in a society where there is significant mobility over time, they will form identities that are not adequately expressed through their membership in particular ascriptive groups, and will therefore find a system of pluralist encapsulation oppressive, preventing them from living in accordance with their deepest self-understandings. Consider, for example, the Jew in Israel who wishes to marry someone in violation of Jewish law, or an immigrant family in Quebec who wish to raise their children to speak English.

The failure of pluralist encapsulation does not by itself vindicate liberal individualism, even in theory, let alone in its practice. It is easy to appreciate the sources of the concerns expressed by these arguments. Too often our history has been marked by pseudouniversalist principles, ones permitting everyone to act like white, Protestant men or, I should say, permitting everyone to act as white, Protestant men are supposed to act. But numerous examples of norms that are not genuinely universal do not show that the ideal of universality should itself be abandoned. Nor, in fact, are its critics able to consistently reject it. For example, Young insists that her proposal is not designed to "encourage the expression of narrow self-interest" on the part of the identified groups. Rather, she argues, the demands of these groups must be defended on the grounds "that justice requires" these demands be granted. This appeal to "justice," in Young's view, must be made to the citizenry as a whole (1989:263, 266).

The deep incoherence of Young's argument is revealed when we ask how the groups that are to be given special privileges are to be identified. Her response is to argue that "a public must be constituted to decide which groups deserve specific representation in decision-making procedures" (266). If the actions of that public are to be defensible, they will presumably have to strive to achieve a position of impartiality among the claims of various groups for special forms of representation and for special rights and privileges. Thus, far from rejecting the ideal of equal citizenship, Young's very conception of differentiated citizenship presupposes and rests upon it.

This concern with difference, then, should not lead us to reject the ideal of universality and universal citizenship. Rather it points to our all too common failings in realizing that ideal. By failing to attend to the actual life situations and needs of certain groups, by glossing over and ignoring important and legitimate differences, we come to frame principles and norms that reflect partial, not generalizable interests.

The commitment to universality will, in general, support a framework of democratic individuality, a regime in which agency rights are protected for all individuals equally. Nonetheless, the commitment to democratic individuality may itself require some deviations from the principles of equal rights and equal treatment based upon individuals' group membership. There are three cases that are of particular interest here.

The first case is the use of group-based rules designed to overcome the effects of past or current discrimination. Affirmative action and similar policies are often justified on these grounds. The second includes "consociational" regimes, which use group-based norms to define structures of political representation and policy-making. These are often employed in situations where groups are separated by major cultural differences. Even if there is no history of oppression in these cases, there may not be enough trust and mutual understanding to adopt a purely individualist framework if that would lead to the majority group monopolizing political power. Many of the smaller European democracies including Switzerland fit this model, which is particularly appropriate for sharply divided societies with large minority groups.[11] Third, group-based rules might be legitimately employed to enable cultural and other groups to sustain their ways of life. The individualist commitments of political liberalism require "permissive" policies that enable associations to form for educational, cultural, religious, and other purposes, without undue hardships. But a liberal state may wish to go further, not only permitting such associations to form but subsidizing them in various ways, including the provision of direct financial support. Liberal states might also grant certain collective or group rights to enable cultural groups to manage their own affairs so that they can sustain their identities in the face of pressures for assimilation.

---

[11] See Lijphart (1977) for an account of consociationalism.

We are obviously not faced with a choice between pluralist encapsulation and pure individualism. In all the cases above, a legal and moral framework that is essentially individualist in nature is supplemented by special group or corporate rights to address particular problems. In the first case, best typified by affirmative action and other policies of racial or gender preference, these measures are temporary, intended to make a purely individualist regime possible in the future. They do not pose deep, conceptual problems for political liberalism because these departures from equal rights are intended to make a regime of genuinely equal rights possible in the long run. There are, of course, very real questions to be raised about the efficacy of such measures—whether they will stigmatize their supposed beneficiaries in ways that will defeat their purpose; whether they will reinforce racial stereotypes and thinking, undermining the goal of a unified society; and whether they will cause other groups to mobilize to demand such measures, eventually entrenching a system of ethnic quotas in the assignment of social positions. For these reasons, affirmative action may be inadvisable under certain circumstances, but the issues involved are broadly empirical rather than normative or conceptual.

The second and third cases raise somewhat different problems because they envision a permanent qualification of the framework of liberal individualism. In each of these cases, the principle of equal rights is qualified by differential restrictions or privileges applying to people based on their ascribed group identity, and so they raise troubling questions for political liberalism. On the one hand, doctrinaire individualism can enforce a degree of homogeneity that undermines moral pluralism and the ability of individuals to express their identities. Religious groups, for example, should be free to discriminate in favor of coreligionists when it comes to hiring priests or ministers. On the other hand, permitting differential treatment of citizens based upon their membership in ascribed groups can be deeply unjust, even when its original intent was benign. These are the kinds of cases that often pose the tragic choices that political liberalism must confront.

Democratic individuality is self-undermining when it leads to a situation in which people are, in effect, deprived of important goods that are available to others because of their ascribed identities. In a culturally plural democratic society, it is easy to see how members of a minority group may effectively be deprived of political rights because they are always defeated in elections for public office, if members of the majority group only vote for candidates from their group. Similarly, as Kymlicka points out, the cultures of Native Americans are constantly threatened and are under pressure from English- and French-speaking populations. While Anglophone Canadians or Americans can take the survival of their cultures for granted, Native Americans must make sacrifices to sustain their cultural communities. In such cases effective equality of rights is denied: although the minority may have the same formal rights as others, its members are unable to attain the goods that these rights are intended to protect. In the case of the survival of a cultural community, the good in question is the very set of traditions, values, roles, and characters that form the "context of choice" within which individuals can make decisions about the goods and ideals they will pursue (Kymlicka 1989:165). In these kinds of situations, group rights are intended to secure the ends of democratic individuality itself.

Unfortunately, because the use of group rights tends to violate individual equality, this solution is far from perfect. Kymlicka and Young, for example, suggest that people should have a right to receive an education in their native language. Kymlicka denies that Native Americans are entitled to be educated in English (although he allows that they should be permitted to attend English-language schools at their own expense) (195). Young objects to programs (such as bilingual education) designed "to increase English proficiency to the point where native-language instruction is unnecessary" (1990:180). In both cases their concern is to sustain minority cultures. This is, in many ways, an admirable goal; language is obviously one of the most important cultural markers, and policies that disvalue a particular language and prevent people from becoming fully proficient in it show disrespect for its speakers. On the other hand, both Kymlicka and Young strongly object to the fact that Native Americans and Hispanics are significantly worse off than other citizens in terms of other social goods, including income, wealth, and access to valued social positions. Unfortunately, in this case the very policies intended to secure "the respect owed them as members of a cultural community" (Kymlicka, 195) will result in these groups not having fluency in English, which effectively precludes their achieving economic success in an English-speaking society. By providing differential treatment in order to achieve the goods available as a member of a minority community, we can make it more difficult for cultural minorities to achieve the goods available in the larger society.

There are no easy answers in this kind of situation. Assimilationist policies intended to provide opportunities to acquire the advantages of the majority culture may be so damaging to those exposed to them that

187

they are ineffective. Even when they are not, it may on balance be better to secure the goods available in the minority culture than to provide greater opportunities in the majority culture. It is certainly true that more could be done to ameliorate the plight of cultural minorities (as well as other disadvantaged groups in our society), easing the kind of dilemmas described above. But as the example of language policy makes clear, the dilemma cannot be entirely eliminated.

Quite apart from the conceptual dilemmas involved in creating group rights, we also must ask whether specific proposals for differential treatment would be efficacious in achieving their goals. These are largely instrumental and pragmatic questions requiring empirical investigation, and the appropriate answers may vary from case to case. One of the advantages of the account of the liberal strategy I am developing is that, because of its nonfoundationalist nature, it allows for departures from the strictures of formal equality and other principles which traditional liberal thought tends to take as absolute. But justifying such departures requires a careful analysis of how they are likely to function in particular circumstances.

In some areas we have begun to develop a considerable amount of knowledge about how such policies work, particularly differentiated structures of representation. As the study of consociational democracies has shown, there may well be circumstances in which differentiated forms of citizenship are necessary to realize even such minimal common goals as civil peace. Most recently, for example, we have heard calls for consociational solutions to the problem of overcoming apartheid in South Africa. But even a casual study of consociational regimes, and the operation of systems of special rights such as affirmative action policies in America and the practice of reserved seats in India, is enough to demonstrate that these policies are no panaceas. In fact, they often have the consequences of solidifying the power of irresponsible elites and driving deeper wedges between and within groups. A tradition of differentiated citizenship did not make Lebanon a place where the concrete other is affirmed and respected in all his or her uniqueness and difference.

In considering such arguments for differentiated citizenship, we must be alert to the ways in which the effort to identify and respond to differences among people may turn into a process of reification, leading to a false imputation of essentialist qualities to the members of some group, ignoring important variations within groups. This danger seems particularly acute in the kind of position advanced by Fraser, who requires that we "relate to people as members of collectivities or social groups with specific cultures, histories, social practices, values, habits, forms of life, vocabularies of self-interpretation and narrative traditions" (1986:428). By all means, let us be sensitive to difference. But the idea that groups are internally homogeneous in these ways, particularly such large and diverse groups as "lesbians, gays, blacks, Hispanics, other peoples of color and subordinated classes," let alone "women," is absurd. The range of differences within any of these groups on virtually any dimension of social importance is invariably greater than the differences between groups. In fast-changing societies such as ours, both individuals' affiliations and the nature and identity of particular groups will alter significantly in relatively short periods of time.[12] The task of articulating the principles that ought to govern relations within the group will be, I suggest, no less intractable than the task of doing the same for the larger society of which these groups are parts. And it will require, if it is not to be imposed on its members, the same effort to achieve a standpoint of impartiality, bracketing areas of disagreement in search of common values and common ends.

In our political and moral lives we must recognize and affirm both our commonalities and our differences.

[12] Notice that many of the groups in the above list did not self-consciously define themselves as groups with a distinct, publicly recognized identity even twenty years ago.

Democracy

INDIVIDUAL RIGHTS, I have been arguing, are necessary to accommodate moral pluralism and to make a discourse-based polity possible. But, as we have seen in the last three chapters, a rights-based system is not without its own antinomies, its own exclusions and evasions. By providing scope for individual action, rights may protect differences, but they also function to reproduce inequality. By guaranteeing equal treatment of individuals, a system in which rights have primacy may actually undermine valued forms of community. Intended to enable individuals to exercise direct control over different aspects of their lives, a rights-based system creates large areas of social life within which social processes unfold according to their inner logics, exempt from human control. Rights, as Marx insisted long ago, institutionalize a form of alienation, in which social forces come to have an "external" character vis-à-vis the individuals whose activities literally create them. Rather than expressing our purposes and ideals, our activities result in social forces that shape or even determine many important aspects of our lives. Many have suggested that we could escape these antinomies by instituting a form of radical democracy, in which citizens would collectively and self-consciously direct all the social processes that affect their lives.

Liberalism has often been viewed as the enemy of democracy. There are historical reasons for this, as many nineteenth-century liberals were fearful that the extension of the suffrage would undermine constitutional government and the institutions they considered necessary for economic prosperity. But there are deeper reasons as well, rooted in the fundamental liberal commitment to individualism and limited government. If there is to be a sphere of activity that is not subject to authoritative or political direction, then there are limits to what the "people" can democratically decide: liberal rights constrain democratic choice. In liberal-democratic regimes these limits are decided through democratic processes, thereby preserving their formally democratic character.[1] But, it might be argued, the tension remains: the criteria of democratic legitimacy are distinct from

---

[1] Assuming that judicial decision-making is ultimately subject to democratic control through the processes of constitutional amendment and the appointment of judges by elected officials. For a critique of judicial review, see (among others) Dahl (1989).

and at least potentially in conflict with those affirmed by liberalism. Where democracy envisions a politics of "collective self-determination," liberalism envisions a politics of individual autonomy.

Political liberalism affirms both individual autonomy and collective freedom, while acknowledging the tension between these ideals. Unlike libertarian and certain natural law- or natural rights–based accounts, it insists that the limits to collective authority must be collectively decided. But it also rejects extreme versions of the ideal of "democracy as collective freedom" partly on the grounds that it is ultimately incoherent, as suggested by the oxymoronic expression "collective *self*-determination." But it also rejects this ideal because of its inability, despite recent disclaimers, to accommodate differences among individuals and groups. The commitment to accommodating difference is at the heart of political liberalism.

COLLECTIVE FREEDOM AND
THE ACCOMMODATION OF DIFFERENCE

Collective freedom offers a vision of political life which conceives of politics not as a struggle over position, power, and wealth, but as a form of self-determination. In the *Laws* Plato complained "that no human being ever legislates anything, but that chances and accidents of every sort, occurring in all kinds of ways, legislate everything for us" (*Laws* 709a). Plato envisioned a form of political activity that would not leave our collective fate to chance, but would enable us to self-consciously direct our affairs in accordance with the aspirations and commitments we deliberately accept. At least as an ideal, the political sphere can be a realm of human freedom, one in which we use our energies and wit not simply to adapt to our fate but consciously to shape it.

Those who conceive of politics as a potential realm of freedom believe that it can differ from other spheres of social life where outcomes do not express a deliberate human choice. Much of social life consists of the unanticipated consequences of actions. For example, the purchase of automobiles by American families in the first half of this century profoundly affected the shape of American cities, not just in geographical but also in demographic, social, and economic terms. Another example is the dramatic increase in the birthrate in the United States in the years following World War II, which arguably caused the average age of marriage in the late 1960s to rise, thereby contributing to increased female labor force participation, to a new wave of feminist thinking and political action, and to major changes in the structure of the family.

191

Because we are natural beings, some of the things that condition our lives are the result of natural processes over which we have little or no control. In the early nineteenth century, for example, a volcanic eruption in what is today Indonesia caused the earth to cool, the corn crop in New England to fail, and led to an increase in the death rate (see Stommel and Stommel 1979). In other cases, the interaction between human activities and natural processes have produced dramatic but unintended results. Perhaps a precursor of what is happening today on a massive scale, the destruction of the ancient civilizations of Mohenjo Daro and Harrapa in the Indus River valley, in what is today Pakistan, may have resulted from agricultural practices that were destructive to the ecology of the region. But many of the forces that condition our lives are not "natural" but social; while we cannot avoid our dependence upon nature, many thinkers have argued that these social forces should not escape our control, should not shape our lives as if they were simply another part of the natural world, since they are only the products of our own activities. Through political action we may be able to take stock of these processes and subject them to deliberate human control.

In contrast to this view of political life, the dominant conception of politics in much of political science is reductive and naturalistic, conceiving of politics as just another sphere of social activity in which phenomena are determined by a concatenation of causal forces. For example, the structure of political institutions and patterns of policy output are often seen simply as the effects of various social conditions. Studies that explain the growth of democracy or patterns of social policy as the consequences of levels of industrialization or urbanization are examples. Following Plato, but without his lament, they assume that politics is like the rest of nature, and seek the general laws that would enable us to explain and predict its patterns. It is a vision of politics that is necessitated by what we might call a "scientistic" worldview, in which the only kind of explanation worth its salt is one that shows why things had to be the way they are. There is little scope for freedom in such a view.

But this is by no means the only possible understanding of politics. As long ago as the story of Joseph's interpreting Pharaoh's dream, the idea that the political sphere affords us an opportunity to direct our collective lives has also been available to us.[2] We may not be able to prevent the seven lean years from following the seven fat ones; but, through foresight,

---

[2] Indeed, the "naturalistic" understanding described above is quite recent; the competing understanding of politics in Joseph's day was one in which political activity, as Hocart has argued, involved the symbolic reproduction of a divine order. The Pharaoh was, first and foremost, a god.

we can control or at least ameliorate their effects on our society, by storing up surpluses to use in times of scarcity.

It would be odd to argue that the story of Joseph suggests a vision of politics as a realm of freedom. Even though the policy adopted was arguably in everyone's interests, the only actors in this drama were Joseph and the Pharaoh; the rest of the population was as passive in the face of the new order as they were with regard to the weather itself. Like a gentle rain at the time of the planting, they may have welcomed the policy (at least once they understood and recognized its results), but they did not in any way shape their lives through it. For politics to be a sphere of collective freedom, it must be a democratic politics, in which there is "direct participation in the collective decisions that shape individual lives. To be political is to be free and vice versa, because it is in the realm of politics that people unite to constitute a human world, to empower each other in order to jointly take control and responsibility for forces that might otherwise control them" (Euben 1990b:16).

It is easy to see the appeal of this conception of democracy. In part, I think, its appeal is due to often-exposed but persistent weaknesses in the dominant, individualist tradition of theory and practice in America. The preoccupation of this tradition with individual liberty and choice—a preoccupation that is strikingly exhibited in Nozick's work—rests on the fallacious belief that, if a condition results from the free choices of individuals, it is at least nonobjectionable, if not completely justified. If, for example, America spends more of its gross national product on dog food than on promoting artistic creation, or if some people amass great fortunes while others suffer grinding poverty, there is nothing more to be said so long as these are the results of our freely chosen actions. The fallaciousness of this as a general claim has long been recognized; as the example of Hobbes demonstrates, it was well understood at the very beginnings of individualist political theory. After all, the state of war results from freely chosen actions.

More positively, the contemporary appeal of the ideal of collective freedom rests on the way in which it promises to "moralize" the social world and render it transparent. The demand for the "moralization" of social conditions reflects the wish that our fates be meaningful, that our lives be explainable in terms of the purposes they serve or the values they realize. For example, social processes that decide individual outcomes through procedures that are acknowledged as fair, such as athletic contests or civil service examinations, answer to this need because they are seen as identifying and rewarding merit.

Collective freedom is closely related to the ideal of transparency, an ideal in which social order does not depend upon widespread ignorance of or delusion about the processes through which society is reproduced. Social orders that systematically foster illusion, whose existence depends upon their being opaque to their participants, appear to be incompatible with human freedom. The major practices and institutions of the society must be rationally grounded, and the members of the society must have some understanding of the justifications of these practices. Otherwise, their adherence to these practices could only be understood as some kind of habitual or conditioned behavior, and such behavior could hardly be said to be free. In a transparent society, individuals act with full understanding of what they do, and thus can will themselves in all that they do. A world that is transparent is one that is fully acceptable to its members.

The concepts of moralization and transparency reflect a worldview that emphasizes the conventionality of social relationships, practices, and structures, a worldview in which less and less is taken simply as "given," as "natural," or as ordained by the gods. Once we recognize that all relationships can be questioned and must be justified, we can insist that they express the judgments of the citizenry. Moralization and transparency go hand in hand with freedom.

An example of the way in which opacity undermines freedom is the cynical exploitation by politicians of the public outrage over increases in fuel prices and oil companies' profits, which resulted from the Iraqi invasion of Kuwait in 1990. Many people felt that the oil companies' actions were illegitimate because, by raising their prices, they took advantage of a crisis that we collectively faced. Even conservative politicians, including George Bush, felt called upon to protest this situation, demanding that the companies reduce their prices or that the government take action to control them. Of course, these demands were deeply problematic, since they could not be met without violating the functional imperatives of the market system through which oil is produced, refined, and distributed— as we saw during the gas lines and supply disruptions of the 1979 crisis. But to understand the necessity of the price increases requires a knowledge of the functioning of this system that many citizens do not possess. In this case we see several elements coming together: a perceived violation of our moral expectations due to the oil companies' alleged exploitation of a common crisis for self-enrichment; a call for political action to correct the situation by bringing about a conformity between social outcomes and citizens' moral beliefs; and a certain opacity of our social life for most of its members. It is the combination of these three elements that makes it possible for elites to cynically manipulate others by, for example, espousing policies that they know cannot be enacted. This is only one particular example of the way in which the opacity of social practices can contribute to domination by making it possible for citizens to be manipulated.[3]

As an ideal, a transparent society will be one in which all aspects of social life are self-consciously "willed" by its members, which means that there would have to be a high degree of unity in such a society. Where it does not spontaneously exist, unity is to be brought about through the practices and institutions of "strong democracy" (Barber 1984), which embody processes of deliberation in which citizens present their own views, and hear those of others, and come to modify their initial judgments and to discern a common good. Because such transformations can come about only through one's direct participation in political life, theorists of collective freedom from Rousseau to the present have seen "representative democracy" as a "contradiction in terms" (see, for example, Euben 1990b:102).

Individualist thinkers have often denied that collective freedom is a form of freedom at all, but this is too sweeping a condemnation. When there is a high degree of unity, when there is a genuinely common good whose attainment eludes the group as long as its members act individually, then collective freedom is a genuine form of freedom. It enables people to escape what might be called the tyranny of small choices—individual actions that aggregate to produce outcomes no one wants or would intend. It is obviously more problematic when citizens initially disagree among themselves regarding the collective ends they would like to see realized. But when unity results from citizens freely changing their judgments as a result of their deliberating with each other, there is a clear sense in which the "collective" processes enhance "self-determination." To the extent that individuals come to understand their needs and aspirations differently, to the extent that collective deliberation results in a kind of "learning," individuals are more fully self-determining. It is obvious that the capacity for self-determination is dependent upon social conditions, and at least on some occasions the required conditions may be processes of collective deliberation. As I argued in chapter four, this possibility expresses the moment of truth in the demand for moral-transformative discourse.

The difficulty, however, is that unity may not always be forthcoming.

---

[3] The ideal of transparency, however, is deeply problematic, for reasons brought out in the rest of this section. For a fuller discussion, see Moon (1987).

It is no surprise, then, that advocates of collective self-determination are drawn to Aristotelian forms of moral and political theory, insisting that the choices and beliefs of citizens can and should be set aside by reference to "the best or highest conception of human happiness" so that citizens can experience genuinely "satisfying lives."[4] But even if there were a "highest conception of human happiness," what reason is there to suppose that it could be discovered and universally embraced through democratic deliberation? Collective deliberation may fail to change people's judgments, or it may lead to changes but not to convergence. When there are differences in interests or ideals, so that even after a genuine and honest debate some continue to dissent, deliberative democracy begins to look less like collective freedom and more like—in John Stuart Mill's phrase—the rule of some by all the rest.

We are all familiar with the gymnastics that have been employed to get around this difficulty. In Rousseau's infamous discussion in chapters one and two of book four of the *Social Contract*, he imagines that citizens who had initially been opposed to the action adopted by the assembly would be glad that they were defeated. As Rousseau put it, "When the opinion contrary to mine prevails, that proves nothing except that I was mistaken, and what I thought to be the general will was not. If my private will had prevailed, I would have done something other than what I wanted. It is then that I would not have been free" (1978:111). Marx would have us believe that unity would not be a problem once the class divisions of bourgeois society were overcome, for they alone are responsible for setting people in opposition to each other. But the naïveté of this belief is evident in our world, rife with continuing national, religious, racial, and other conflicts. Neither the essentialist views of human nature on which Aristotle or Plato relied, nor the historicist constructions of Rousseau and Marx, are now credible. The dangers of the rule of some by all the rest cannot be put aside in the expectation that democratic deliberation will yield agreement. In the face of significant disagreement, "collective self-determination" can be, as its critics suggest, a disguise for repression if not tyranny.

---

[4] Sunstein 1991:9, 14, and passim. Sunstein actually speaks of "preferences," but this term is defined in terms of the choices that citizens make (note to p.7). In general, in this essay he assumes that the deliberative democracy produces "considered judgments" while he describes citizens as having only "preferences" (though he allows that they may sometimes rise to the level of having "judgments as well": 18). Little reason is offered for the belief that the actual political processes of the American (or other) political systems are likely to produce better judgments regarding "the best or highest conception of human happiness" than other social processes.

In sophisticated defenses of collective freedom, it is not assumed that participation will generally produce unity on substantive issues. Indeed, participation may, as Euben argues, lead us to see the ways in which we are different from each other: through political participation, we "confront those beyond the sphere of family or neighborhood" and so "encounter difference." But through that encounter, through the need to deliberate with others who are different, we develop the capacity "to think in public and as public beings, to make public claims and give reasons that appeal to shared predicament and tradition" (Euben 1990b:102). In this way, political activity creates people who are and see themselves as citizens, and so are united with each other in a public life that gives expression to, and preserves, their differences. Thus, as citizens we can experience ourselves as self-determining even in those situations where our own aspirations are thwarted, our own judgments rejected. On this view, democratic deliberation will not necessarily overcome our differences—our shared traditions and predicaments may not be more compelling than the experiences and ideals that divide us. Thus, a participatory politics can acknowledge the tragic aspect of political life, even while affirming the centrality of citizenship in the moral lives of its members.[5]

Although more attractive than unitary views, even this case for collective freedom ultimately rests upon the assumption that political participation has a privileged place among the ends of human life—to delegate the authority "to act for me or in my name" is, in Euben's telling phrase, "a renunciation of what is distinctively human about me" (1990b:102). Needless to say, this is a highly contentious view of the human good, no more capable of commanding agreement than other teleological views. While it avoids the fatal errors of such totalizing theorists as Rousseau or Marx, its privileging of the public life at best marginalizes, at worst suppresses, those for whom citizenship is a subordinate good.[6]

Many theorists of democracy as collective freedom have responded to the criticism that their positions do not show adequate respect for "difference" by arguing, in effect, that this critique begs the question at issue. Like many thoughtful defenders of collective self-determination, Sunstein admits that the "foreclosure of the preferences of the minority is unfortunate," but he goes on to argue that in such situations the "choice is between the considered judgments of the majority and the preferences (and perhaps judgments as well) of the minority." To prohibit the majority

---

[5] The tragic nature of politics is a major theme of Euben's work; see particularly his (1990a).

[6] In the next section of this chapter I will argue that the hopes for such citizenship cannot be realized by the kinds of institutions that can be constructed today.

"from vindicating its considered judgments" would eliminate "an important arena for democratic self-government."[7] In an obvious sense, the claim this argument makes is too strong, for "democratic self-government" is not constricted when the scope of political decisions is limited to a specific set of questions, and when an extensive sphere of liberty exists within which individuals can pursue their own ends, however much others might disapprove of their choices. So long as the boundaries of the political are politically decided, the "sovereignty of politics" is affirmed. But even if the situation is correctly described as one in which either a majority or a minority must prevail, and even if we agree that the majority should rule in these circumstances, it is hard to see how the suppression of the minority's values and aspirations—or even its mere preferences—can be described as "collective self-determination."[8] At least when the stakes are high, these are better described as situations of political tragedy, situations where the claims of opposed but genuine values clash.

PARADOXES OF COLLECTIVE FREEDOM

Even if we accept the privileging of political activity that collective freedom entails, this ideal is self-limiting in other important ways. In particular, the deliberative processes through which citizens collectively determine their affairs presuppose a set of rights which, although not immutable, limit the scope of political decision. Citizens must be guaranteed the rights to participate in political discourse, including the familiar rights of speech, press, assembly, thought, and so forth. And, as I argued in chapter four, they must also be guaranteed some degree of privacy. There must be a limit on the extent to which they can be required to reveal themselves to others and on the necessity to defend their basic values and commitments if their participation in political activity is not itself to be

[7] Sunstein 1991:18. There are numerous arguments directed toward similar conclusions. See, e.g., Barber (1984) and (1988) for defenses of the "sovereignty of politics" and the impossibility of imposing external constraints on the scope of political decision.

[8] I should note that Sunstein would impose potentially significant restrictions on the authority of the majority, including "rights" that are fundamental to deliberative democracy itself or to "autonomy or welfare"; he would also insist that "the collective judgment must not be objectionable on moral grounds" or "reflect a special weakness on the part of the majority" (19). Given the sweeping nature of these restrictions, the differences between Sunstein's position and the doctrine he attacks—what he calls "subjective welfarism"— appear to be quite minimal.

coercive. Radical democracy, if it is to retain its democratic character, must be a constitutional democracy. The politics of collective freedom, if it is to be a genuine form of freedom, must eschew the arbitrary use of power. Thus, the scope of political authority must be limited, and those who exercise power must be accountable for their actions.

Among the many advantages of representative democracy is its ability to incorporate the principles of limited power and accountability. By dividing the powers of government among different branches, and by making elected officials accountable to the electorate as a whole, representative government mediates the exercise of power. At least in principle, all officials must answer to others, explaining the reasons for which they have acted, and they must do so in a context in which the others have some degree of authority over them. Otherwise, their accountability would be merely formal.

It is true, of course, that citizens themselves must ultimately decide through the political process what limits to impose upon political authority, but at any point in time that process must itself respect certain limits. Thus, collective freedom is necessarily limited by respect for the individual liberties it presupposes.

But the necessity to respect certain limits on the processes of collective self-determination involves further difficulties. Providing social space for individuals to make important choices in certain areas of their lives in accordance with their own judgments, without being answerable to others for what they decide, is a major source of opacity in society. To the extent that individuals are free to make such choices and to act on them, significant areas of social life will exhibit an unplanned and uncontrolled process of development. Social outcomes will not reflect collective decisions reached on the basis of reasons that have been widely discussed and have become generally shared in the society. Rather they will reflect concatenations of individual choices; they will often be unintended, and may sometimes be undesired, leading to calls for collective action to correct them. Restrictions on the scope of collective decision necessarily limit the extent to which political activity can be the active shaping of our destinies rather than a process of adapting to our fate. If people are to have negative liberty—at least in areas that are of any real significance—much that occurs in social life will have to be by accident. Moreover, and perhaps more important, the existence of a significant private realm will affect the processes of public deliberation, for it will lead to and reinforce the plurality of experiences and diversity of interests that must be accommodated politically.

199

A commonly used example of this process is a market economy, but an equally, perhaps even more important example is cultural life, whose development and reproduction is not consciously planned in liberal societies. The processes of cultural reproduction, the self-understandings through which our aspirations are expressed and shaped (and also constrained), are not deliberately organized through democratic (or any other) means.

As many critics have pointed out, the (relative) autonomy of culture does not mean that the production and reproduction of cultural categories are independent of the major structures of social power in society. Indeed, a common complaint is that, insofar as cultural life is unplanned, it merely reproduces the values and serves the interests of the dominant groups in the society. These critics, ironically, see liberalism as insufficiently respectful of difference, as a totalizing discourse that shuts out alternative voices. Although there are many variations on this complaint, common themes include a view of liberalism as based upon an abstract conception of agency that prestructures the way in which issues can be defined in contemporary society. In Fraser's analysis, for example, this prestructuring of the "socio-cultural means of interpretation and communication" limits the vocabularies through which people can construct their identities and understand their needs. In liberal society, citizens are entitled to certain basic rights that are supposed to protect the exercise of their capacity for agency, in part by delimiting the sphere of public authority from private life. But, Fraser argues, what this actually means is that certain needs are "depoliticized" and patterns of inequality are rationalized. Although formally universal and egalitarian, liberalism delimits political space in such a way as to exclude certain voices. Far from respecting difference, then, liberalism merely represents a different form of exclusion (Fraser 1989b: chaps. 6–8).

These kinds of considerations have led to a call for explicit control over the processes of cultural reproduction—a staple of both conservative and radical critiques of liberal society. George Will is united with Bowles and Gintis in the view that politics (broadly understood to include much that is not specifically governmental) must play a tutelary role in deliberately shaping the preferences and ideals of citizens.[9] Arguing from the incontrovertible fact that, as social beings, our values and preferences are a result of social processes, they insist that democratic control should

[9] See Bowles and Gintis 1986:194, where they approvingly cite George Will, noting the similarity between his position and theirs in this regard.

be exercised over "the conditions under which members of a community come to have the preferences" they have (Bowles and Gintis 1986: 182–83).

Similarly, Fraser argues that the "socio-cultural means of interpretation and communication" are dominated by privileged groups in our society, and other groups—women, people of color, the poor—often find themselves unable to articulate their needs within the dominant vocabularies. The very structures of discourse, she argues, are not neutral, and tend to either repress or distort the experiences of subordinated groups, or lead to the marginalization and exclusion of their voices from public arenas. She calls for subordinate groups to "contest this situation and organize to win a greater measure of collective control over the means of interpretation and communication," in the hopes of realizing "collective self-determination."[10]

These accounts are continuous with the "educative" (Fay 1987:85–116) view of politics that has historically been associated with the ideal of collective freedom. If we are to collectively determine the conditions of our lives, and if these conditions are powerfully affected by the dispositions and aspirations of members of society, then political life must itself shape these dispositions and aspirations. Even "a democratic government should sometimes take private preferences as an object of regulation and control" (Sunstein 1991:13). If "politics is a partnership in virtue,"[11] as Aristotle argued, then it must not only afford opportunities for the development of citizens' virtue, but it must be designed to actively encourage that end. It is in this context that we must understand Plato's objections to poetry or Rousseau's objections to the theater.

In general, educative views of politics are elitist. It is not the society as a whole that educates itself, but specially qualified agents who educate others—a Platonic philosopher-king, or a Leninist vanguard party. In these cases, there is a definite subject (the political elite) and a definite object (the unenlightened masses), with the former shaping the latter. Even Rousseau, celebrated as a theorist of democratic collective freedom, does not really offer a theory of democratic self-education, as a consideration of the role of the legislator demonstrates.[12]

"Democratic self-education" has something of a paradoxical ring to it, for one cannot self-consciously determine for oneself what one will be-

[10] Fraser 1986:425–26. The phrase "collective self-determination" is found in her (1989a:313).

[11] The phrase is quoted in Euben 1990b:102.

[12] See my discussion in chapter four, above.

201

lieve. Beliefs impress themselves upon us because of the weight of the evidence that comes with them. We may often deceive ourselves, of course, and our beliefs certainly respond to other needs, but it is essential to this process that we *not* be aware of these influences. Whether we are being rational (which can, I would hasten to add, include giving appropriate weight to emotional and aesthetic considerations) or are deceiving ourselves, we don't *choose* what to believe.

There is a further source of paradox in the idea of collectively determining our own beliefs and aspirations, one that is analogous to the fallacy that Popper (1964) saw in what he called historicism. In choosing something, we select an object from a larger set that is in some sense given. We may, and often do, choose the sets from which we will choose, as when we have primary elections to select the candidates for the general election. But in the case of beliefs, including moral beliefs and values, emotional dispositions, qualities of character, and the like, the set of possible systems of belief is not in any sense given but always open to change through discovery and criticism. This is an inherently dynamic process, and since we cannot anticipate the "growth" or, if you prefer, the alteration of knowledge—for to do so would suppose that we already know what we will only later come to know—we cannot determine the direction that it will take. That is, no doubt, why most programs that have actually been designed to implement the ideal of self-consciously controlling the beliefs and aspirations of society inevitably lead not so much to a deliberate shaping of the culture but to its ossification. Even so, as James Scott (1990) has argued, and as the experience of Eastern Europe under state socialism powerfully suggests, these programs fail as ordinary people reach their own conclusions on the basis of their own experiences.

Neither Fraser nor Bowles and Gintis, however, would accept the kind of "unitary" understanding of political life that characterizes these earlier forms of an educative politics. They reject traditional notions of collective freedom, including a unitary view of the political or general will, according to which only a single pattern would be valid for the whole society. Thus they reject traditional, totalizing conceptions of politics with their potential for repression. This rejection is based at least in part on their affirmation of difference, and they call for and affirm decentralized, self-determining local communities of various sorts.

So far as I know, no one has worked out anything like a precise account of how this ideal is supposed to work. Recognizing the possibly repressive consequences of an exclusive emphasis on popular sovereignty, Bowles and Gintis include a commitment to "liberty" as part of their understanding of democracy, where liberty is defined in essentially liberal terms as "an extensive range of social life over which individuals have the freedom . . . to act . . . as they see fit without social impediment" (1986:4). But they do not offer any account of how we can have collective control over the formation of individual identities—of our preferences and aspirations—without sacrificing liberty. If there is a sphere in which people are free to act and to think without answering to others, if there is to be no authoritative regulation of what people read, communicate, think, or say—and Bowles and Gintis insist on these freedoms—then how can we exercise control over the consequences of these unregulated activities, so that only people with certain kinds of identities and characters are produced by the society? Further, if collective control is to proceed through small, decentralized communities, if we reject the unitary view of Rousseau, then do we not sacrifice the ability to shape our social world as a whole? Don't we already have a plurality of communities and organizations shaping the identities and aspirations of their members, none exercising anything like full control because everyone participates in many different communities?

It is possible that I have misunderstood these accounts, attributing to them what we might call a "strong program" of democratic self-education, according to which we would collectively control our specific "preferences," to use Bowles and Gintis's term, or the "socio-cultural means of interpretation and communication" to use Fraser's term. Perhaps, however, what is advocated is only a "weak program," in which the aim is to shape the broad dispositions of the citizenry by appropriately designing the institutions and practices of the society. There is nothing paradoxical about the weak program, but there is nothing unique about it either. Nor, I might add, does it embody a degree of "collective freedom" that is significantly different from that achieved in liberal societies already. Thus, John Stuart Mill advocated a regime of free expression and nonpaternalism in part on the grounds that it would tend to produce strong characters with a sense of their own individuality, and he called for the equality of women partly on the grounds that it would lead to a more widespread and deeper commitment to human equality and mutual respect in the society. Similarly, George Kateb has argued persuasively that representative democracy is "morally distinctive" in part because it "signifies a radical chastening of political authority," and so gives rise to "a pervasive skepticism toward authority," both on the part of ordinary citizens and those who occupy political office (1981:358). In Kateb's view, this extends not only to governmental institutions but to all relations of life, as individuals come to see themselves as autonomous and reject paternalism in other settings as well (363). The encouragement of conflict and the limited scope of collective decision encourages the development of a tolerance for differences and a distance from the self enabling democratic individuals to experience a kind of "impersonal individuality" (Kateb 1984: 344) forming the basis for "democratic connectedness" and "mutual acceptance" with others (1990:552). The weak program recognizes and affirms the powerful cultural and psychological effects of political institutions, but that recognition falls far short of a deliberate, self-conscious effort to direct the processes of cultural reproduction.

There is, then, a deep tension between the idea that individuals can be empowered to control their lives by being able to affect collective conditions through democratic participation, and the idea that they may be empowered to control their lives by directly determining certain aspects of their situations by their own free, unaccountable choices. But this does not mean that the more we enable people to control their lives collectively by extending the range of matters over which collective decisions may be made, the less scope there is for individual liberty. Nor is it true that the more we allow free, individual choices, the less scope there is for collective freedom. In many ways, democratic self-determination and individual liberty are mutually reinforcing. But they limit and constrain each other as well. Political liberalism represents an effort to effect a balance between the claims of collective freedom and its own self-limiting conditions.

DEMOCRATIC INSTITUTIONS

The limits of collective freedom examined above are conceptual, resting on the way in which it privileges a life of political participation, or on the incoherences in the idea of collective self-determination itself. But there is a further set of difficulties in implementing the ideal of collective freedom. The most obvious problem is creating the institutions or procedures through which "preferences" would be transformed, leading to convergence on a common good. Typically, advocates of this ideal argue for some version of "strong democracy," involving intense citizen participation in formulating and deciding public policy. Political activity could not be effective in shaping citizens' judgments and volitions unless it played a major part in each citizen's life—comparable in the time and energy it requires to their other major commitments, including vocation, family, and religious affiliation. If politics is to create a strong sense of citizenship and solidarity, if it is to be central to the identities of participants, then its role in their lives cannot be peripheral. That is why republican citizenship tends to be exclusive, as it makes such strenuous demands on people—demands that not everyone can satisfy.[13]

Designing institutions that will generate the required levels of participation is a difficult problem. Calls for participation are often little more than rhetorical devices, but in some cases theorists have offered provocative proposals to be implemented in existing circumstances, including the democratization of nongovernmental institutions, particularly business firms, and the formation of neighborhood assemblies or "citizen juries" to discuss and evaluate areas of public policies. Many of these proposals are fully consonant with the values of political liberalism and could significantly add to the vitality of public life in contemporary democracies by increasing the range of voices that are heard in political settings. Unfortunately, there are severe limits to these proposals, limits rooted in apparently unalterable conditions of our lives today.

These limits derive from three critical sources: the complexity of political issues; the scarcity of time and attention; and the scale of political decision. The classical ideal of democracy as collective freedom supposes a world in which politics will not itself be part of the division of labor, where all citizens can participate more or less equally and effectively in deciding public issues. This vision seems increasingly utopian as the complexity of public issues grows. Even full-time, professional politicians have become specialists in different areas of public policy, and decide how to act in other areas by, for example, following the lead of those who have specialized in the area and whom they trust, or their political party. The need for such specialization is even more pronounced for ordinary citizens, whose time and attention is necessarily more scarce than that of people for whom political life is a full-time occupation. It is no accident that the polis was founded on slavery, and that Rousseau's ideal was a society in which the development of the arts and sciences and the division of labor and trade were dramatically restricted. Finally, the scale of political life in the modern world means that the critical decisions must be made through nonparticipatory processes; realistically, our choice is between representative democracy, in which decision-makers are held responsible for their actions, and systems of unaccountable power. Even a dramatic increase in citizen participation, then, must take place against a

[13] See the discussion of republican citizenship in chapter seven.

background in which representative institutions would continue to play the central roles in formulating and deciding public policies. As many theorists of participatory democracy have acknowledged,[14] we must evaluate proposals to increase participation at least in part in terms of their effects on the structures of representative government.

Many of the reforms that have been proposed by advocates of strong democracy would have the effect of strengthening representative institutions. But others, such as the weekly citizen assemblies and the enlarged role for referenda and initiatives that Barber (1984) has proposed, could weaken parties, representative institutions, accountability, and ultimately democracy itself.

There are relatively few citizens who are prepared to spend the kind of time and energy in political activity that strong democracy requires. Even if we suppose that public willingness to participate would increase dramatically—by a hundredfold—we would not have enough to sustain these institutions. Of course, there will always be some who have the time and energy for politics, who will go to the meetings and discuss the issues, who will vote in the referenda, who will carry out initiative drives, who will take advantage of the opportunities these structures will provide. But if their activities are not carried out in a genuinely public context, there is every reason to believe that these structures will be used to advance partial interests rather than creating citizens and contributing to our capacity to direct our common life. Much of the political science literature suggests that this happened with many of the Progressive reforms in America, and with the national referenda in Switzerland. When referenda are held in special elections, they usually have such low turnout that relatively small numbers of voters can control the outcome. Thus, referenda can become yet another means through which sectional interests can subvert broader structures of public accountability and control, such as political parties and legislatures.[15]

Strong democrats hope that participation will breed participation, and that the opportunity to shape our collective lives and an ethos of political action and citizenship would overcome these difficulties. But this is doubtful. Barber (1984) focuses much of his attention on local-level politics—the only area in which direct citizen involvement could make much difference to the perceptions and experiences of citizens. At the national level we might listen to debates and get to vote on more issues of public

[14] See, e.g., Pateman 1970.
[15] For a critique of "referendum democracy," see Sartori 1987:115–20.

policy directly, but there is no way that one's voice will be heard, nor one's influence felt, for all but a tiny few. But it is at the national level where the great issues of the day are decided, and it is at the national level where most political attention and energy on the part of citizens are directed. Citizens often know more about national politics—the issues, the identities of leaders, the positions of different leaders and parties—than they do about state or local politics. And they are far more likely to participate through voting, campaign activity, making monetary contributions, and so forth at the national level. Participatory democrats have long seen local politics as the school of citizenship, but truancy is so high that very little learning takes place.

One response to this situation would be to enhance the value of local experience, in order to make it more attractive to citizens, so that they will spend more time in local political activity, thereby developing a commitment to political life and attending more to politics at all levels. There have been many experiments in this direction, but the results have not been encouraging. All too often newly created structures have been captured by small groups of activists who used them for purposes that ran counter to the ends of many of the people whom the program was to benefit. This was notably true of many of the community action programs created during the 1960s, and many of the experiments in school decentralization. It is possible, of course, that we have lacked patience, that we should have waited longer for the learning and self-correcting mechanisms of participatory democracy to take hold. Participatory democrats have rightly stressed the role of political action as a form of civic education; perhaps these abuses would have been corrected over time. But there is little evidence that such learning was taking place, or that it would have begun had the programs continued.

Any measure to extend participation provides opportunities that will be of greater interest to some than to others. Activists—those who have the interests and resources (including most especially time) to devote to political activity—will be in a position to dominate the new institutions and to use them to advance their own ideals and interests, as they are prepared to expend resources that others are not (which may amount to little more than staying at meetings when others get tired and go home). Representative institutions are designed to hold activists accountable through elections. In a well-designed representative system, with relatively little expenditure of effort, ordinary citizens can reject those whose policies or performance they find unsatisfactory. But when participatory structures displace representative institutions, the only way in which activists can be checked may be "the high-cost control of co-participation" (Elster 1986:122). This can lead to the worst possible result, in which the high costs of participation lead to an effective weakening not only of democracy but of responsible government as well.

Measures to increase participation, even when they are effective, may also undercut representative democracy by creating a "segmented and fragmented citizenship" (Hernes 1988:203). With the decentralization and fragmentation of authority necessary to make participation possible, there can be problems of coordination among various institutions and processes, and the ability of any agency to make significant decisions can be compromised. Rather than providing for effective participation, the process of devolution may involve "a loss of power on all parts, and certainly on the part of (electorally based) political institutions" (207). To the extent that this occurs, the effort to broaden democracy may have the paradoxical effect of weakening it.

Some would welcome reforms that would undermine representative democracy. Arendt, for example, acknowledges that the "council system" she envisions is "aristocratic" and would "spell the end of the general suffrage as we understand it today," because only those who care deeply about politics would participate. Since the elite is a self-chosen elite, she feels that the exclusion of others would not be invidious and would even protect "one of the most important negative liberties"—"freedom from politics"(1965:284). Similarly, Burnheim (1985) has proposed the abolition of representative democracy by replacing general-purpose representative institutions with specialized "committees" that are statistically representative of those affected by the decisions they are empowered to make. Obviously, such schemes could hardly be justified in the name of collective freedom; Arendt's is deliberately exclusive, and Burnheim is hostile to any conception of sovereignty, to the kind of overall authority necessary to the notion of collective self-determination.

It is hard to see how either of these proposals, or any scheme that does not make authority accountable to those who are subject to it, could be justified through discourse. Arendt's proposal, in particular, rests on the dubious assumption that those who devote themselves to political life represent an "elite" who "care for more than their private happiness and are concerned about the state of the world." These qualities entitle them to "a right to be heard in the conduct of the business of the republic" (1965:284). Obviously, one might question the equation of political interest and activity with virtue, since there are many motives that lead to political activity, and the costs of participation are not equal for everyone. More significantly, however, one might reject the notion that only those who are willing to devote substantial time and effort to public affairs have an exclusive right to a voice in public life. There are many different conceptions of the human good: privileging the life of public involvement is only one of these conceptions, and it has not commanded unanimous support among reflective people.

Burnheim's "demarchy" is in many ways compatible with political liberalism; its difficulty, oddly enough, is that it does not make adequate allowance for the moment of truth in the arguments for collective freedom. He envisions an essentially anarchistic society, with different functional activities governed through juries of citizens who volunteer for the task, and who are chosen by lot in such a way as to statistically "represent" those affected by their decisions. But how are we to determine what constitutes a functional area? And how are we to determine who is "affected" by particular decisions? In what way can we monitor the activities of these disparate organizations, assessing the necessarily unintended consequences of their separate activities, and take action to redress outcomes when they are undesirable? Although in modern societies there is considerable scope for the kind of scheme Burnheim recommends—in general, for increasing the use of selection by "lot"[16]—it cannot be the sole structure of authority.

Political liberalism embraces the fundamental republican ideal of a "jurisgenerative politics"—of a political order in which "laws and rights [are] both the free creations of citizens and, at the same time, the normative givens that constitute and underwrite a political process capable of creating constitutive law" (Michelman 1988:1505). It is, therefore, deeply sympathetic to the claims of strong democracy and collective self-determination. But, acknowledging the inevitability of disagreement, it rejects versions of republicanism that are premised upon a commitment to the centrality of citizenship among the ends of human life because such visions exclude a large and important range of voices and human experiences. Moreover, recognizing the constraints we face—constraints of complexity, scarcity, and scale—it is also committed to representative institutions as a practical necessity. To the extent that self-rule is possible, it can only be through representative processes, which preclude the ideal of a politics of such intense involvement that it shapes citizens' identities

---

[16] For an interesting suggestion, one intended to strengthen representative institutions by providing alternative sources of information and analysis of public issues, see Dahl's proposal (1989:338–40) for panels of randomly chosen citizens which would be charged with investigating and debating public issues.

and transforms their beliefs and values.[17] There is much that can be done to enhance the processes of public discourse and increase the effectiveness of representative democracy, including measures to increase the scope of citizen participation. What is critical is that such measures be evaluated in terms of their contribution to public discourse and representative democracy, and that we not lose sight of both the value of, and the limits to, collective freedom.

[17] Except in unusual and critical circumstances (see, in this connection, Ackerman 1991 for his distinction between constitutional and ordinary politics). I do not wish to suggest that republican conceptions of citizenship are necessarily committed to participatory democracy. For a defense of representative institutions in a broadly republican context, see Schwartz 1988.

Conclusion: Consensuality—and Nonconsensuality

"THE FARTHEST I WOULD GO," Foucault has said, "is to say that perhaps one must not be for consensuality, but one must be against nonconsensuality." To be for consensuality would be to "grant that it is indeed under its governance that the phenomenon has to be organized" (Foucault 1984:379). In this brief interview Foucault does not tell us what is problematic about taking consensus as a regulatory ideal, nor how we can be against nonconsensuality without being for consensuality. In this book I have tried to explore and sometimes even to answer these questions. I have been concerned with the ways in which consensuality as a regulative ideal can turn into nonconsensuality as a political reality (or, to put it somewhat more precisely, how nonconsensuality can be rationalized by an appeal to consensuality). There are many different versions of this story; the one that I have been interested in presupposes a morally pluralist society—a society in which there are significant differences in the fundamental moral commitments and beliefs of different individuals and groups. Although the problem of nonconsensuality exists in all societies, it is exacerbated by moral and cultural pluralism. In pluralist societies, the problem of nonconsensuality cannot be avoided, though it can perhaps be minimized. I have argued that minimizing nonconsensuality requires that we adopt what I have called "political liberalism." Political liberalism is a variant of traditional consensus theories of legitimation, but one that does not share their faith in supposing that nonconsensuality can be overcome.

FROM CONSENSUS TO NONCONSENSUALITY

Of course, no "actually existing" politics is based upon consensus in the sense of full and free agreement with all the laws, policies, and actions of the collectivity. But Foucault questions whether consensus should even be taken as a regulative ideal, irrespective of whether it is or even could be fully realized. The real difficulty with consensuality does not involve its realizability, but its apparently circular, even paradoxical nature. The problem arises when we ask what consensuality requires, for any understanding of consensus must specify the conditions that must be satisfied if

211

consent is to be genuine. But any account of the conditions necessary for genuine consent to occur will prestructure political discourse, barring certain needs and perspectives, and certain participants, and it will do so in a way that cannot itself be tested by reference to the ideal of consensuality.

We do not have to look very hard to remind ourselves of how these moves are made. Locke, for example, insists that no one can be "subjected to the Political Power of another, without his own *Consent*" (1970:348), but it turns out that one "consents" by "travelling freely on the Highway" (366). Similarly, Kant (notoriously) attributes to each citizen the "*freedom* to obey no law other than that to which he has given his consent," but immediately goes on to distinguish between "active" and "passive" citizens, noting that the latter "are all mere auxiliaries to the commonwealth, for they have to receive orders or protection from other individuals" and have no right "to influence or organize the state itself" (1970:139–40). Kant goes on to qualify the consent of even the active citizens, insisting that "it is our duty to consider the law as just, even if the people is at present in such a position or attitude of mind that it would probably refuse its consent if it were consulted," so long as "it is at least *possible* that a people could agree to it" (79). Needless to say, such expansive notions of "consent" leave a great deal of room for what we ordinarily regard as nonconsensuality, which will be manifested in the use of coercion to enforce laws and decisions to which the people involved have supposedly "consented."

The more recent accounts of consensuality that I have examined, including both contractarian and discourse-based theories, are much less expansive than Locke's or Kant's, but they are also—and necessarily—burdened with the possibility of nonconsensuality. Because such accounts "prestructure" what we might call "political space," they run the risk of excluding certain voices, and so generating a false consensus. But how serious is the danger of a false consensus? And does that danger require a different kind of politics, perhaps a politics of resistance, which responds to the dangers of consensuality by withholding assent to any structures of authority? These questions will occupy the next two sections of this chapter.

FALSE CONSENSUS

Political liberalism, like all conceptions of a consensus-based politics, seeks to avoid the danger of false consensus by ensuring that individuals are able to develop and exercise the capacities for agency, for these capacities are necessary if someone is to "consent" to social arrangements. I have argued that exercising the capacities of agency requires a set of agency rights and certain institutional arrangements, notably representative democracy, markets, an extensive sphere of action for voluntary associations. (These institutions are not exhaustive; socialization practices that enable children to develop a strong sense of self-esteem and self-worth are also required, and other practices may also be necessary as well.) But, it goes without saying, these conditions are not sufficient: even if the major institutional structure of the society is adequate, there will be many individual failings and pathologies, and there will be some who lack the mental capacities required even for minimal levels of agency.

Some critics of modern society go farther, arguing that liberal-democratic institutions do not secure the conditions for meaningful consent because most people are thoroughly conditioned to play their parts in the social order. Their doing so willingly merely shows that they are, in Don Herzog's phrase, "happy slaves." Huxley's *Brave New World* offers an image of a society in which consent to social arrangements is deliberately manufactured, and some critics regard that work as an allegory for liberal society, both in theory and practice. Liberal critics of liberal societies characteristically view this allegory in individualistic terms. They see conformity, consumerism, and an educational system that fosters careerism.[1] Their main concern is to actualize individual freedom, and to ward off the manifold threats to it in modern society. Like Herzog, they tend to view the crucial issue to be the capacities of the individual to follow the Socratic adage, to grasp the ways in which one's choices may have been constrained by forces outside of one's understanding and control. For them, the solution is to enlighten individuals in order to enable them to recover their autonomy.

Socialist critics—using the term broadly—naturally tend to see the issue in collectivist terms, as they seek to explain why less privileged groups or classes fail to utilize the opportunities for oppositional activity provided by liberal-democratic societies. Viewing many of Mill's and Herzog's examples as marginal or even frivolous, they focus their attention on structured processes of domination that reproduce themselves partially through the systematic indoctrination of disadvantaged groups. "Slave" is a social category, not in the first instance an individual condition; thus, to diagnose its etiology and prescribe a cure, such critics attend

---

[1] Thus, John Stuart Mill inveighs against the social conformity of middle-class society, fearing the loss of creative forms of individual self-assertion, and Don Herzog worries about socializing one's children to hold certain religious convictions (1989:240–43).

to the structures of social relationships that constitute and create it—particularly, to the actions and resources of the dominant class.

There are many variants of the collectivist story, but the main outlines are fairly common: the dispossessed are rendered acquiescent through processes that systematically strip them not only of the capacity to understand the ways in which their dissatisfactions result from the operation of the "system" itself but also of the ability to imagine any alternatives to it. The disadvantaged become resigned to their lot, falsely believing that there is no alternative, and so they come to articulate their demands (when they are not so demoralized as to lose the capacity to make demands) only within the terms allowed by the system itself. Workers, to take the classic example, develop only trade-union consciousness, struggling for higher wages and better working conditions, and fail to develop socialist consciousness.[2] Even in their conflict with capitalists, they act in ways that sustain the capitalist system by confining their demands to goods that the system can at least in principle deliver. When the ruling ideology is fully hegemonic, the subordinate class defines itself only in the terms provided by the oppressors, fully endorsing the hierarchy that produces its own subordination.

As a general account of the stability of hierarchical systems, this account is deeply problematic. As James Scott has persuasively argued, subordinate groups have always been able to imagine alternatives to the present regime, including "a total reversal of the existing distribution of status and rewards," and a set of utopian beliefs that constitute "a more or less systematic negation of an existing pattern of exploitation and status degradation as it is experienced by subordinate groups" (1990:80, 81). Indeed, considering the historical experiences of revolt and rebellion in highly stratified caste and slave societies, where the means of control and coercion are securely monopolized by the dominant group, Scott argues that what requires explanation is the unwillingness of subordinate groups to resign themselves to conditions that appear, from an external perspective, to have been genuinely inevitable.

Nor does ideological incorporation entail a necessary reduction in social conflict. All legitimating ideologies claim that the different classes or status-groups in a particular society serve morally important ends. But this means that any ideology will necessarily provide opportunities for "internal" criticisms that show that particular individuals or groups fail to discharge their responsibilities. More radically, Scott argues, although

---

[2] Lenin's "What Is to Be Done?" may be the *locus classicus* of this kind of analysis, though most recent formulations are inspired by Gramsci (see Gramsci 1971).

legitimating ideologies or myths often provide terms of discourse that are common between dominant and subordinate groups, their "interpretations follow wildly divergent paths in accordance with vital interests" (100). Because each group can construe supposedly shared terms or concepts in accordance with its own interests and needs, ostensibly common ideologies can serve to frame conflict, rather than muting it. Scott's rich descriptions and analyses of the various "arts of resistance," the "hidden transcripts" through which subordinate groups in different cultures have articulated their own visions and resistance to oppression, provide compelling evidence against the existence of "happy slaves."

AGONISTIC DEMOCRACY

Scott's work suggests that the dangers of a false consensus are easily exaggerated. Nevertheless, taking consensuality as a regulative principle may prestructure political and social life in ways that can seriously disadvantage some visions of the human good, and in extreme cases can even silence certain voices. As we have seen, this issue is not simply one of reaching agreement on social norms, but the ways in which organizing political life using consensuality as a regulatory principle can itself involve a kind of imposition. As I argued in chapter four, this is particularly true if we interpret consensuality using a model of unconstrained discourse, a model that makes potentially unlimited demands for self-disclosure, demands that will be coercive for those who hold certain conceptions of privacy and personal integrity. But, as I have argued throughout the last several chapters, even the more restrictive model of generalized discourse is subject to this objection insofar as it prestructures the language of public discourse, thereby running the risk of preventing certain experiences from being articulated, certain voices from being heard. I have examined some of the particular objections to political liberalism in chapters six through nine, but—in the nature of the case—only those objections that have found a voice could be examined. And even in those cases, not all the objections could be satisfactorily answered. Since even a politics of consensuality may give rise to its own patterns of exclusion, perhaps we should consider a radically different form of politics—a politics of agonistic democratic struggle.

William Connolly has recently advanced an account of agonistic democracy, an account that shares many of the concerns of political liberalism as presented here. In particular, Connolly insists that there is no predesign of human material to fit a particular order, and so he concludes

215

that "every form of social completion and enablement also contains sub-jugations and cruelties within it" (1991:94). He also recognizes that the "human animal is essentially incomplete without social form; and a com-mon language, institutional setting, traditions, and political forum for enunciating public purposes provide the indispensable means through which human beings acquire the identity and commonalities essential to life" (94). We thus face a genuine *paradox* of difference: social order is absolutely necessary for us, but any social order is also repressive.

Although his diagnosis shares much with political liberalism, Connolly rejects the liberal strategy of discovering shared principles on the basis of which public life can be organized, while providing for significant social space within which individuals and groups can pursue their distinctive ways of life. Rather than accommodating moral pluralism by privatizing areas of social life, Connolly would politicize our contrasting ideals and identities. Because every identity is partial, because "life exceeds identity" (170), and because any given feature of one's identity—one's nationality, gender, sexual orientation, work—is contingent, we must come to resist "the demand to *ethicize* or universalize [our] entrenched contingencies on the grounds that they flow from a true identity," a demand that "is a recipe for the repression of difference" (174). Thus, Connolly calls upon us not merely to tolerate difference but to acknowledge and respect our antagonists because they represent forms or modalities of being that we do not need to deny to affirm our own identities. Nonetheless, because any identity is necessarily partial, because identity presupposes differ-ence, those who are different will also be antagonists, against whom we will struggle even while we respect them.

The politicization of identities is necessary, in Connolly's view, in large part because the liberal strategy of privatization is no longer viable. The interdependencies of late-modern society are too great, and the forces of normalization, surveillance, and disciplinary controls too pervasive, to accommodate difference by depoliticizing social spaces, thereby permit-ting individuals the liberty to pursue their own ideals and to express their distinct identities (see, e.g., 188). Moreover, the centrality of agency to the liberal strategy implicitly "endorses a theory of an unambiguous, in-trinsic identity" and a "commitment to a strong theory of rationality" (163), both of which underlie forms of normalizing practice and a politics of resentment fueled by the need to find culpable agents to whom respon-sibility for evil can be imputed.

Thus, agonistic democracy abandons *both* the liberal vision of individ-ual freedom and the ideal of collective freedom in its communitarian or socialist variants. From this diagnosis, Connolly prescribes what might be called a politics of doubleness, one that "is simultaneously a medium through which common purposes are crystallized and the consummate means by which their transcription into musical harmonies is exposed, contested, disturbed, and unsettled" (94).

In some ways agonistic democracy differs more in tone than in substance from political liberalism. Like the latter, it requires a system of "rights to life, a significant degree of personal self-governance, freedom of expression, and full citizenship in representative government," rights designed to "cultivate care for the diversity of life" (213). Similarly, political liberalism is akin to agonistic democracy in that it acknowledges the impossibility of neutrality. Both recognize that the need to secure welfare rights, to define the legal structures necessary to the functioning of social institutions such as the family, and to draw the boundaries between public and private, requires that political judgments be made regarding the goods and identities that will be publicly promoted, and those that will be disadvantaged or even suppressed. Inevitably, then, both political liberalism and agonistic democracy agree that at least certain aspects of our identities will be politicized.

But if politicization is inevitable, it must also be limited. If one of our aims is to secure space for difference, then we need to be alert to the ways in which agonal struggle can be replaced by coexistence, ways in which we can design public policies to avoid the necessity to make choices among the identities to which citizens are committed. The liberal strategy is designed to replace the conflict between opposed ideals with a tolerance of difference, a tolerance that can and does grow into an appreciation of diversity and an enriched cultural life. For that reason, it resists politicization, rather than embracing it.

Political liberalism is also reluctant to embrace the full politicization of identities because to do so implies a very much greater role for politics than political liberalism thinks possible. The conditions of modern life impose limits on the kinds of institutions that can be created and on the capacity to shape the social order through politics. As I argued in chapter nine, it is impossible to overcome all the sources of opacity in social life; important parts of culture and social structure will be decisively shaped by factors over which no one exercises effective control, and in ways that social actors do not understand, or at least do not understand at the time. Even political interventions designed to avoid undesirable outcomes will have unintended consequences and will in some ways contribute to social opacity. To the extent that the commitment to politicization of identities

217

represents an extension of the areas of social life subject to political control, it fails to acknowledge the limits of political action.[3]

Because political liberalism recognizes the limits of political action and the inevitable opacity of social life, it also acknowledges limits to social and individual responsibility. Liberalism has been criticized for its commitment to agency, and thus to understanding persons as in some way capable of directing and controlling their actions, for this conception of the self is tied to a conception of personal responsibility which can and has led to failures of imagination and sympathy. Sometimes we blame those who cannot make it on the market, or who commit crimes against others, and we use their failings to wrap ourselves in a smug superiority that is as self-deceived as it is undeserved. But even if political liberalism sometimes lends itself to an uncritical belief in personal responsibility, it does not hold that all suffering is the result of human agency, nor that we—any "we"—could have the ability to arrange our collective lives in such a way as to create those, and only those, outcomes that accord with our will.

Agonistic democracy celebrates struggle, but often these struggles are tragic. The political activities Connolly describes—using such benign terms as contesting, disturbing, or unsettling—are often confrontations in which people face each other across a gulf of hostility and incomprehension. Such conflicts involve real human suffering. True, the institutionalization of any ideal may cause suffering to those whose experiences and needs it does not adequately express, but the suffering and cruelty involved in the conflicts among different ideals must also be acknowledged.

Part of the appeal of agonistic democracy is the fear that the implicit exclusions of a consensual politics will pass unnoticed, that we must "unsettle" certain practices because their "injuries, cruelties, subjugations, concealment, and restrictions" are "*worthy* of opposition and contestation" (93; emphasis added). If they are worthy of opposition, they should be opposed, even if the society has so successfully "naturalized" them that the victims do not feel their own oppression. But how are we to determine which restrictions are "worthy" of opposition? What criteria should we employ to make this determination, and how can we justify the restrictions involved in employing any particular set of criteria? Or are we to say that *all* restrictions ought to be opposed?

---

[3] The extension of political control is a particular issue for Connolly's agonistic democracy, for it would require a major increase in collective consumption and redistribution of income. The policies necessary to achieve these ends would intensify the disciplinary controls and pressures for normalization that Connolly identifies as endemic to liberal society.

Political liberalism, like the politics of resistance, acknowledges the possibility that any form of political order may be, and may be experienced as, repressive by some of its members. It can grant, as Connolly argues, that "humans are not predesigned," that "they do not fit neatly into any particular social form," and that in any social order some human capacities and potentialities will be repressed. But it does not follow that it is necessary that these repressed potentialities "find a political voice" (93). Any social order—certainly any defensible one—will limit our ability to act on our capacity for cruelty or our capacity to be indifferent to the suffering of others. It need not do so in a way that denies scope for self-assertion, but any enforcement of rules requiring regard for others will, from time to time, frustrate some of the drives of many of us. But the mere fact that some drive, some need, is repressed is not sufficient to establish the "paradoxical" nature of political life, for we may all agree that certain drives, certain desires, ought to be repressed, even while we strive to remain open to the possibility that our judgments in this regard are mistaken. Even if there are no "true identities," there may be true evils, and not all repression of those evils "does violence to those to whom it is applied" (12). By acknowledging its own contingency, political liberalism seeks to maintain an openness to the possibilities it implicitly denies, without losing sight of its own affirmative commitments.

LIVING WITH AMBIVALENCE

Political liberalism represents a response to moral pluralism, to a world in which there is systematic disagreement about the ends and significance of human life. Political liberals seek to forge political community by discovering norms and values that all can accept, and that can be used to regulate our common affairs. These commonalities can be found, if at all, through a strategy of political discourse, in which we attempt to "bracket" our differences by abstracting from our particular identities and ends in search of mutually acceptable principles. Because the bases of agreement are limited, political liberalism endorses only a limited state, leaving wide areas of social life to be regulated through the nonpolitical or at least nonauthoritative processes of civil society. And because individuals must be able to exercise the basic capacities for agency presupposed by the notion of "free agreement" itself, political liberalism requires a system of rights that protects these capacities.

But unlike standard liberal theories, political liberalism recognizes the

219

contingency of its own constructions. It acknowledges that the particular
principles that come to be accepted are historically situated. Even when
different groups and individuals accept "common" principles, they may
do so for different reasons, and so may disagree about their meanings and
how they should be applied in particular cases. It recognizes that our
shared principles may come into conflict with values that are not shared,
and that the former may not always carry greater weight than the latter.
Any formulation of common principles, particularly of the basic rights
and structures of society, may disadvantage or even silence certain voices,
denying them the means to articulate their own needs and experience.
Political liberalism acknowledges that no model of an "ideal speech situation" or "initial bargaining position" can provide an ultimate court of
appeal for questions of justice. For any such model at least tacitly rests on
some specification of human needs and capacities, which can itself be
challenged through discourse—a challenge that can call into question
even the most fundamental presuppositions of the framework of discourse itself. Political liberalism, then, acknowledges the possibility of
tragic conflict, the possibility that no conception of justice may prove
adequate even in principle to eliminate the experience of imposition and
injustice in social life.

Learning to live with ambivalence, to recognize the contingencies of
one's own identities, to abandon the quest for self-certainty, to recognize
that even one's most cherished principles may be experienced as unjustly
repressive—in many ways political liberalism may strike one as a philosophy of middle age, one that can appeal only to those who have lost the
will and the imagination to pursue a purer and brighter vision. It is true
that political liberalism is, in part, a response to an age that has witnessed
mind- and spirit-numbing brutality on a humanly unimaginable scale,
motivated at least in part in the name of such pure and bright visions. And
some of those visions *were* pure and bright, attracting many of the most
thoughtful and sensitive men and women of the time. But only moral and
political innocents—or fools—could look at the history of the last one
hundred years and simply dismiss the idea that our political and moral
lives are fraught with ambiguity and ambivalence, and that we must learn
to live with this condition.

Political liberalism is not merely a reaction to the violence and evil of
our time, for it also offers a vision of its own. It rests upon a deep commitment to mutuality, and to respect for others. This commitment requires
that we come to have enough self-acceptance, enough self-confidence,
that we can affirm the value of our ideals without demanding that others

conform to them, without having to impose ourselves and our ends on others. To fully accept plurality, one must overcome the need to have others validate our aspirations and identities by adopting them for themselves. Having accepted plurality, we can go beyond a narrowly circumscribed toleration of difference to become enriched by the wonderful plentitude of human possibilities and projects, free of the need to grade, to rank, to enclose each culture or way of life in a grid defined by our own need for "truth." And we are enriched even when we find ourselves contesting others, seeking space to fulfill our own aims. Political liberalism is not just another harmonian vision. Rather it aims to show us how we can contest with, and appreciate, each other, once we have sufficient strength that we no longer have the need to dominate.

References

Ackerman, Bruce. 1980. *Social Justice in the Liberal State*. New Haven, Conn.: Yale University Press.

———. 1989. "Why Dialogue?" *Journal of Philosophy* 86: 5–22.

———. 1991. *We the People*. Vol. 1, *Foundations*. Cambridge: Harvard University Press.

Adler, Mortimer. 1958. *The Idea of Freedom*. 2 vols. Garden City, N.Y.: Doubleday.

Anderson, Benedict. 1983. *Imagined Communities*. London: Verso.

Anscombe, G. E. M. 1963. *Intention*. 2d ed. Oxford: Basil Blackwell.

Arendt, Hannah. 1965. *On Revolution*. New York: Viking.

Aristotle. 1941. *The Basic Works of Aristotle*. Edited by Richard McKeon. New York: Random House.

Arneson, Richard. 1990. "Is Work Special?" *American Political Science Review* 84: 1127–48.

Ashe, Geoffrey. 1968. *Gandhi*. London: Heinemann.

Baier, Annette. 1987. "The Need for More than Justice." In Hanen and Nielsen.

Barber, Benjamin. 1984. *Strong Democracy*. Berkeley: University of California Press.

———. 1988. *The Conquest of Politics*. Princeton: Princeton University Press.

Barry, Brian. 1989. *A Treatise on Social Justice*. Vol. 1, *Theories of Justice*. Berkeley: University of California Press.

Bellamy, Edward. 1982 [1888]. *Looking Backwards*. New York: Random House.

Benhabib, Seyla. 1986. *Critique, Norm, and Utopia*. New York: Columbia University Press.

———. 1987. "The Generalized and the Concrete Other." In Benhabib and Cornell.

———. 1989. "Liberal Dialogue versus a Critical Theory of Discursive Legitimation." In Rosenblum.

Benhabib, Seyla, and Drucilla Cornell, eds. 1987. *Feminism as Critique*. Minneapolis: University of Minnesota Press.

Benn, Stanley. 1988. *A Theory of Freedom*. Cambridge: Cambridge University Press.

Bentham, Jeremy. 1948 [1823]. *An Introduction to the Principles of Morals and Legislation*. Edited by R. Harrison. Oxford: Basil Blackwell.

Berlin, Isaiah. 1969. *Four Essays on Liberty*. New York: Oxford University Press.

———. 1972. "The Originality of Machiavelli." In Berlin, *Against the Current*. New York: Viking, 1980.

Bondurant, Joan V. 1965. *The Conquest of Violence*. Rev. ed. Berkeley: University of California Press.

Bowles, Samuel, and Herbert Gintis. 1986. *Democracy and Capitalism*. New York: Basic Books.

Buchanan, Allen. 1991. *Secession*. Boulder, Colo.: Westview Press.

Burnheim, John. 1985. *Is Democracy Possible?* Berkeley: University of California Press.

Christensen, Anna. 1980. "Disqualifications from Unemployment Benefits: A Critical Study in Swedish Social Security Law." *Scandinavian Studies in Law*: 155–74.

———. 1984. *Wage Labour as Social Order and Ideology*. Sweden: Secretariat for Futures Studies.

Cohen, Gerald A. 1986a. "Self-Ownership, World-Ownership, and Equality." In Frank Lucash, ed., *Justice and Equality Here and Now*. Ithaca, N.Y.: Cornell University Press.

———. 1986b. "Self-Ownership, World-Ownership, and Equality: Part II." *Social Philosophy and Policy* 3: 77–96.

———. 1989. "On the Currency of Egalitarian Justice." *Ethics* 99: 906–44.

Cohen, Joshua. 1986. "Reflections on Rousseau: Autonomy and Democracy." *Philosophy and Public Affairs* 15: 275–97.

Collini, Stefan. 1979. *Liberalism and Sociology*. Cambridge: Cambridge University Press.

Connolly, William. 1991. *Identity\Difference*. Ithaca, N.Y.: Cornell University Press.

Cover, Robert. 1986. "Violence and the Word." *Yale Law Journal* 95: 1601–29.

Dahl, Robert. 1989. *Democracy and Its Critics*. New Haven, Conn.: Yale University Press.

Des Pres, Terence. 1976. *The Survivor*. New York: Oxford University Press.

Doppelt, Gerald. 1988. "Rawls' Kantian Ideal and the Viability of Modern Liberalism." *Inquiry* 31: 413–50.

Douglass, R. Bruce, G. Mara, and H. Richardson, eds. 1990. *Liberalism and the Good*. New York: Routledge.

Dumont, Louis. 1980. *Homo Hierarchicus: The Caste System and Its Implications*. 2d ed. Chicago: University of Chicago Press.

Durkheim, Emile. 1984 [1902]. *The Division of Labor in Society*. Translated by W. D. Halls. New York: Free Press.

Dworkin, Ronald. 1981. "What Is Equality?" *Philosophy and Public Affairs* 10: 185–246 and 283–345.

Ellwood, David. 1988. *Poor Support*. New York: Basic Books.

Elster, Jon. 1986. "Self-Realization in Work and Politics." *Social Philosophy and Policy* 3: 97–126.

———. 1988. "Is There (or Should There Be) a Right to Work?" In Gutmann.

Esping-Anderson, Gosta. 1990. *Three Worlds of Welfare Capitalism*. Princeton: Princeton University Press.

Euben, J. Peter. 1990a. *The Tragedy of Political Theory*. Princeton: Princeton University Press.

———. 1990b. "Democracy in America." *Tikkun* 5.

Fay, Brian. 1987. *Critical Social Science*. Oxford: Polity Press.

Feinberg, Joel. 1970. "The Nature and Value of Rights." *Journal of Value Inquiry* 4: 243–57.

———. 1988. *Harmless Wrong-doing*. Vol. 4 of *The Moral Limits of the Criminal Law*. Oxford: Oxford University Press.

Fingarette, Herbert. 1978. "The Meaning of Law in the Book of Job." *Hastings Law Journal* 29: 1581–1617.

Flathman, Richard. 1987. *The Philosophy and Politics of Freedom*. Chicago: University of Chicago Press.

Foucault, Michel. 1984. *The Foucault Reader*. Edited by Paul Rabinow. New York: Pantheon.

Fox-Genovese, Elizabeth. 1991. *Feminism Without Illusions*. Chapel Hill: University of North Carolina Press.

Frankfurt, Harry. 1988. "Equality as a Moral Ideal." In Frankfurt, *The Importance of What We Care About*. Cambridge: Cambridge University Press.

Fraser, Nancy. 1986. "Toward a Discourse Ethic of Solidarity." *Praxis International* 5: 425–29.

———. 1989a. "Talking About Needs," *Ethics* 99: 291–313.

———. 1989b. *Unruly Practices*. Minneapolis: University of Minnesota Press.

Friedman, Lawrence M. 1990. *The Republic of Choice*. Cambridge: Harvard University Press.

Friedman, Marilyn. 1987. "Beyond Caring: The De-Moralization of Gender." In Hanen and Nielsen.

Frohock, Fred M. 1992. *Vocabularies of Healing*. Chicago: University of Chicago Press.

Fuchs, Victor R. 1988. *Women's Quest for Economic Equality*. Cambridge: Harvard University Press.

Galston, William. 1991. *Liberal Purposes*. Cambridge: Cambridge University Press.

Gandhi, Mohandas. 1940. *An Autobiography, or The Story of My Experiments with Truth*. 2d ed. Ahmedabad: Navajivan Press.

Gaus, Gerald F. 1990. *Value and Justification*. Cambridge: Cambridge University Press.

Gauthier, David. 1986. *Morals by Agreement*. Oxford: Oxford University Press.

———. 1988. "Morality, Rational Choice, and Semantic Representation: A Reply to My Critics." *Social Philosophy and Policy* 5: 173–221.

Gilligan, Carol. 1987. *In a Different Voice*. Cambridge: Harvard University Press.

Ginsburg, Faye. 1989. *Contested Lives*. Berkeley: University of California Press.

Glendon, Mary Ann. 1991. *Rights Talk*. Cambridge: Harvard University Press.

Golding, Martin. 1984. "The Primacy of Welfare Rights." *Social Philosophy and Policy* 1: 119–36.

———. 1986. "Towards a Theory of Human Rights," *The Monist* 52: 521–49.

Gramsci, Antonio. 1971. *Prison Notebooks*. Edited and translated by Q. Hoare and G. Smith. New York: International Publishers.

Green, T. H. 1967 [1882]. *Lectures on the Principles of Political Obligation*. Ann Arbor: University of Michigan Press.

Gutmann, Amy, ed. 1988. *Democracy and the Welfare State*. Princeton: Princeton University Press.

Habermas, Jürgen. 1971. *Knowledge and Human Interests*. Boston: Beacon Press.

Hanen, Marsha, and Kai Nielsen, eds. 1987. *Science, Morality and Feminist Theory*. Calgary: University of Calgary Press.

Hayek, Friedrich. 1976. *Law, Legislation, and Liberty*. Vol. 2, *The Mirage of Social Justice*. Chicago: University of Chicago Press.

Hegel, G. W. F. 1952 [1821]. *The Philosophy of Right*. Oxford: Oxford University Press.

Held, Virginia. 1987. "Non-contractual Society." In Hanen and Nielsen.

Hernes, Helga M. 1988. "Scandinavian Citizenship." *Acta Sociologica* 31: 199–216.

Herzog, Don. 1987. "As Many as Six Impossible Things Before Breakfast." *California Law Review* 75: 609–30.

———. 1989. *Happy Slaves*. Chicago: University of Chicago Press.

Hobbes, Thomas. 1909 [1651]. *Leviathan*. Edited by W. G. Pogson Smith. Oxford: Oxford University Press. Pagination in the text is to the edition of 1651.

Hocart, Arthur M. 1970 [1936]. *Kings and Councillors*. Chicago: University of Chicago Press.

Holmes, Stephen. 1988. "Liberal Guilt." In Moon 1988a.

———. 1989. "The Permanent Structure of Antiliberal Thought." In Rosenblum.

Horne, Thomas. 1988. "Welfare Rights as Property Rights." In Moon 1988a.

———. 1990. *Property Rights and Poverty*. Chapel Hill: University of North Carolina Press.

Horwitz, Morton J. 1988. "Rights." *Harvard Civil Rights–Civil Liberties Law Review* 23: 393–406.

Kant, Immanuel. 1970. *Kant's Political Writings*. Edited by H. Reiss. Cambridge: Cambridge University Press.

Kateb, George. 1981. "The Moral Distinctiveness of Representative Democracy." *Ethics* 91: 357–74.

———. 1984. "Democratic Individuality and the Claims of Politics." *Political Theory* 12: 331–60.

———. 1990. "Walt Whitman and the Culture of Democracy." *Political Theory* 18: 545–71.

Kohn, Hans. 1965. *Nationalism*. Rev. ed. Princeton: Van Nostrand.

Kymlicka, Will. 1989. *Liberalism, Community, and Culture*. Oxford: Oxford University Press.

Larmore, Charles. 1987. *Patterns of Moral Complexity*. Cambridge: Cambridge University Press.

Lijphart, Arend. 1977. *Democracy in Plural Societies*. New Haven, Conn.: Yale University Press.

Lindblom, Charles. 1977. *Politics and Markets*. New York: Basic Books.

Locke, John. 1955 [1689]. *A Letter Concerning Toleration*. 2d ed. Indianapolis, Ind.: Bobbs-Merrill.

———. 1970 [1690]. *Two Treaties of Government*. 2d ed. Edited by Peter Laslett. Cambridge: Cambridge University Press.

Lomanksy, Loren E. 1987. *Persons, Rights, and the Moral Community*. Oxford: Oxford University Press.

Luker, Kristin. 1984. *Abortion and the Politics of Motherhood*. Berkeley. University of California Press.

MacIntyre, A. 1981. *After Virtue*. Notre Dame, Ind.: University of Notre Dame Press.

———. 1988. *Whose Justice? Which Rationality?* Notre Dame, Ind.: University of Notre Dame Press.

MacKinnon, Catharine. 1989. *Toward a Feminist Theory of the State*. Cambridge: Harvard University Press.

McClure, Kirstie. 1990. "Difference, Diversity, and the Limits of Toleration." *Political Theory* 18: 361–91.

Marshall, T. H. 1977. "Citizenship and Social Class." In Marshall, *Class, Citizenship, and Social Development*. Chicago: University of Chicago Press.

Mason, Mary Ann. 1988. *The Equality Trap*. New York: Simon and Schuster.

Mead, George Herbert. 1964. *On Social Psychology*. Chicago: University of Chicago Press.

Mead, Lawrence. 1992. *The New Politics of Poverty*. New York: Basic Books.

Michelman, Frank. 1988. "Law's Republic." *Yale Law Journal* 97: 1493–1537.

Mill, John Stuart. 1951 [1859, 1861]. *Utilitarianism, Liberty, and Representative Government*. New York: Dutton.

Miller, David. 1990. *Market, State and Community*. Oxford: Oxford University Press.

Minow, Martha. 1990. *Making All the Difference*. Ithaca, N.Y.: Cornell University Press.

Moon, J. Donald. 1977. "Values and Political Theory." *Journal of Politics* 39: 877–903.

———. 1987. "Political Science and Political Choice: Opacity, Freedom, and Knowledge." In Terence Ball, ed., *Tradition, Interpretation, and Science*. Albany: State University of New York Press.

———, ed. 1988a. *Responsibility, Rights and Welfare*. Boulder, Colo.: Westview Press.

Moon, J. Donald. 1988b. "The Moral Basis of the Democratic Welfare State." In Gutmann.

Morris, Herbert. 1976. "Persons and Punishment." In Morris, *On Guilt and Innocence*. Berkeley: University of California Press.

Nedelsky, Jennifer. 1989. "Reconceiving Autonomy." *Yale Journal of Law and Feminism* 1: 7–36.

Nietzsche, Friedrich. 1967 [1887]. *On the Genealogy of Morals*. Edited by W. Kaufman; translated by W. Kaufman and R. J. Hollingdale. New York: Random House.

Nove, Alex. 1983. *The Economics of Feasible Socialism*. London: Allen and Unwin.

Nozick, Robert. 1974. *Anarchy, State, and Utopia*. New York: Basic Books.

Nussbaum, Martha. 1986. *The Fragility of Goodness*. Cambridge: Cambridge University Press.

———. 1988a. "Nature, Function, and Capability." *Oxford Studies in Ancient Philosophy*. suppl. vol. 1. Oxford: Oxford University Press.

———. 1988b. "Non-Relative Virtues." In *Midwest Studies in Philosophy* 13, edited by Peter French et al. Notre Dame, Ind.: Notre Dame University Press.

———. 1990a. "Aristotelian Social Democracy." In Douglass, Mara, and Richardson.

———. 1990b. "Plato on Commensurability and Desire." In Nussbaum, *Love's Knowledge*. Oxford: Oxford University Press.

———. 1992. "Human Functioning and Social Justice." *Political Theory* 20: 202–46.

Nussbaum, Martha, and A. Sen. 1988. "Internal Criticism and Indian Rationalist Traditions." In *Relativism*, edited by M. Krausz. Notre Dame, Ind.: University of Notre Dame Press.

Okin, Susan M. 1987. "Justice and Gender." *Philosophy and Public Affairs* 16: 42–72.

———. 1989a. *Justice, Gender and the Family*. New York: Basic Books.

———. 1989b. "Reason and Feeling in Thinking about Justice." *Ethics* 99: 229–49.

Olsson, Sven E. 1990. *Social Policy and Welfare State in Sweden*. Lund: Arkiv forlag.

O'Neill, Onora. 1985. "Between Consenting Adults." *Philosophy and Public Affairs* 14: 252–77.

———. 1986. *Faces of Hunger*. London: Allen and Unwin.

———. 1988. "Ethical Reasoning and Ideological Pluralism." *Ethics* 98: 705–22.

———. 1989. *Constructions of Reason*. Cambridge: Cambridge University Press.

Pateman, Carole. 1970. *Participation and Democratic Theory*. Cambridge: Cambridge University Press.

———. 1983. "Feminist Critiques of the Public/Private Dichotomy." In S. I. Benn and G. F. Gaus, eds., *Public and Private in Social Life*. New York: St. Martin's.

228

———. 1988. *The Sexual Contract*. Stanford, Calif.: Stanford University Press.

Phelps-Brown, H. 1988. *Egalitarianism and the Generation of Inequality*. Oxford: Oxford University Press.

Pitkin, Hannah. 1984. *Fortune Is a Woman*. Berkeley: University of California Press.

Plamenatz, John. 1963. *Man and Society*. 2 vols. New York: McGraw-Hill.

———. 1975. *Karl Marx's Philosophy of Man*. Oxford: Oxford University Press.

Plato. 1961. *The Collected Dialogues of Plato*. Edited by Edith Hamilton and Huntington Cairns. New York: Pantheon.

Polanyi, Karl. 1957. *The Great Transformation*. Boston: Beacon Press.

Polsky, Andrew. 1991. *The Rise of the Therapeutic State*. Princeton: Princeton University Press.

Popper, Karl R. 1964. *The Poverty of Historicism*. New York: Harper and Row.

Putnam, Hilary. 1987. *The Many Faces of Realism*. LaSalle, Ill.: Open Court.

Radin, Margaret. 1986. "Residential Rent Control." *Philosophy and Public Affairs* 15: 350–80.

———. 1987. "Market-Inalienability." *Harvard Law Review* 100: 1849–1937.

Rajchman, John. 1985. *Michel Foucault: The Freedom of Philosophy*. New York: Columbia University Press.

Rajchman, John, and Cornell West, eds. 1985. *Post-Analytic Philosophy*. New York: Columbia University Press.

Rand, Ayn. 1964. *The Virtue of Selfishness*. New York: Penguin.

———. 1968. *The Fountainhead*. New York: Random House.

Rawls, John. 1971. *A Theory of Justice*. Cambridge: Harvard University Press.

———. 1980. "Kantian Constructivism in Moral Theory: The Dewey Lectures." *Journal of Philosophy* 77: 515–72.

———. 1982. "Social Unity and Primary Goods." In Sen and Williams.

———. 1985. "Justice as Fairness: Political—Not Metaphysical." *Philosophy and Public Affairs* 14: 223–51.

———. 1987. "The Idea of an Overlapping Consensus." *Oxford Journal of Legal Studies* 7: 1–25.

———. 1988. "The Priority of the Right and Ideas of the Good." *Philosophy and Public Affairs* 17: 251–76.

Raz, Joseph. 1986. *The Morality of Freedom*. Oxford: Oxford University Press.

———. 1990. "Facing Diversity." *Philosophy and Public Affairs* 19: 3–46.

Rorty, Richard. 1985. "Solidarity or Objectivity." In Rajchman and West.

———. 1989. *Contingency, Irony, and Solidarity*. Cambridge: Cambridge University Press.

Rosenberg, Morris. 1979. *Conceiving the Self*. New York: Basic Books.

Rosenblum, Nancy, ed. 1989. *Liberalism and the Moral Life*. Cambridge: Harvard University Press.

Rousseau, Jean Jacques. 1978 [1762]. *On the Social Contract*. Translated by Roger and Judith Masters. New York: St. Martin's Press.

Rousseau, Jean Jacques. 1986 [1751 and 1755]. *The First and Second Discourses*. Translated and edited by Victor Gourevitch. New York: Harper and Row.

Ruddick, Sara. 1987. "Remarks on the Sexual Politics of Reason." In Eva Kittay and Diana Meyers, eds., *Women and Moral Theory*. Savage, Md.: Rowman and Littlefield.

———. 1989. *Maternal Thinking*. Boston: Beacon Press.

Sachs, David. 1981. "How to Distinguish Self-Respect from Self-Esteem." *Philosophy and Public Affairs* 10: 346–60.

Sandel, Michael. 1982. *Liberalism and the Limits of Justice*. Cambridge: Cambridge University Press.

———, ed. 1984. *Liberalism and Its Critics*. New York: New York University Press.

———, ed. 1984. "Introduction." In *Liberalism and Its Critics*. New York: New York University Press.

Sartori, Giovanni. 1987. *The Theory of Democracy Revisited*. Chatham, N.J.: Chatham House.

Schwartz, Nancy. 1988. *The Blue Guitar*. Chicago: University of Chicago Press.

Scott, James C. 1990. *Domination and the Arts of Resistance*. New Haven, Conn.: Yale University Press.

Sen, Amartya. 1980. "Equality of What?" *Tanner Lectures on Human Values*.

———. 1985. "Well-being, Agency, and Freedom: The Dewey Lectures 1984." *Journal of Philosophy* 82.

———. 1990a. "Justice: Means versus Freedoms." *Philosophy and Public Affairs* 19.

———. 1990b. "Individual Freedom as a Social Commitment." *New York Review of Books* (June 14): 49–54.

———. 1990c. "More Than 100 Million Women Are Missing." *New York Review of Books* (December 20).

Sen, Amartya, and Bernard Williams, eds. 1982. *Utilitarianism and Beyond*. Cambridge: Cambridge University Press.

Shklar, Judith. 1984. *Ordinary Vices*. Cambridge: Harvard University Press.

Simon, William. 1985. "The Invention and Reinvention of Welfare Rights." *Maryland Law Review* 44: 1–37.

———. 1986. "Rights and Redistribution in the Welfare System." *Stanford Law Review* 38: 1433–1516.

Singer, Peter. 1991. "On Being Silenced in Germany." *New York Review of Books* 38 (August 15): 36–42.

Skinner, B. F. 1953. *Science and Human Behavior*. New York: Free Press.

———. 1971. *Beyond Freedom and Dignity*. New York: Vintage Books.

Spellman, Elizabeth V. 1978. "On Treating Persons as Persons." *Ethics* 88: 150–61.

Stearns, Carol Z., and Peter Stearns. 1986. *Anger*. Chicago: University of Chicago Press.

Stommel, Henry, and Elizabeth Stommel. 1979. "The Year Without a Summer." *Scientific American* 240: 176–86.

Sullivan, Andrew. 1989. "The Case for Gay Marriage." *The New Republic* 3893: 20–22.

Sunstein, Cass R. 1990. *After the Rights Revolution*. Cambridge: Harvard University Press.

———. 1991. "Preferences and Politics." *Philosophy and Public Affairs* 20: 3–34.

Taylor, Charles. 1985. "The Diversity of Goods." In *Philosophical Papers*, vol 2. *Philosophy and the Human Sciences*. Cambridge: Cambridge University Press.

Thurow, Lester. 1981. *The Zero-sum Society*. New York: Penguin.

Tribe, Laurence. 1990. *Abortion: The Clash of Absolutes*. New York: Norton.

Viroli, Maurizio. 1988. *Jean-Jacques Rousseau and the 'Well-ordered' Society*. Cambridge: Cambridge University Press.

Von Wright, Georg. 1971. *Explanation and Understanding*. Ithaca, N.Y.: Cornell University Press.

Walzer, Michael. 1983. *Spheres of Justice*. New York: Basic Books.

———. 1989–90. "A Critique of Philosophical Conversation." *Philosophical Forum* 21: 182–96.

Weizman, Lenore. 1985. *The Divorce Revolution*. New York: Free Press.

White, Stephen. 1988. *The Recent Work of Jürgen Habermas*. Cambridge: Cambridge University Press.

Williams, Bernard. 1981. *Moral Luck*. Cambridge: Cambridge University Press.

———. 1985. *Ethics and the Limits of Philosophy*. Cambridge: Harvard University Press.

Winch, Peter. 1965–66. "Can a Good Man Be Harmed?" Reprinted in his *Ethics and Action*. London: Routledge and Kegan Paul, 1972.

Wollheim, Richard. 1984. *The Thread of a Life*. Cambridge: Harvard University Press.

Young, Iris. 1987. "Impartiality and the Civic Public." In Benhabib and Cornell.

———. 1989. "Polity and Group Difference: A Critique of the Ideal of Universal Citizenship." *Ethics* 99: 250–74.

———. 1990. *Justice and the Politics of Difference*. Princeton: Princeton University Press.

Zucker, Norman L. 1973. *The Coming Crisis in Israel*. Cambridge: MIT Press.

Index

abortion, 71, 78–80, 94–95, 101
Ackerman, Bruce, 63, 75–78, 90, 93, 210
affirmative action, 185, 188
agency, 39, 48, 72, 113–15, 142, 200; agency and disability, 165
agency rights, 40–42, 108–112, 116, 147, 163, 178–79; and unintended consequences, 117, 165
anger, 159
Apel, Karl-Otto, 87
Arendt, Hannah, 148
Aristotle, 13, 29, 146
Aristotelian strategy, 26–28, 34
autonomy, 64, 82, 92–95, 171

Baier, Annette, 153–54
Barber, Benjamin, 195, 206
Bellamy, Edward 127
Benhabib, Seyla, 75, 87–97, 181
Benn, Stanley, 93
Bentham, Jeremy, 46–47, 165
Berlin, Isaiah, 24
Bowles, Samuel and Herbert Gintis, 178, 200–203
Bowers v. Hardwick, 6
Burnheim, John, 208–9

care vs. justice, 153–62
Christensen, Anna 137–39
citizenship, 14, 70, 146–49, 180, 183, 196, 208
Cohen, Joshua, 82–83
collective freedom/collective self-determination, 191–98, 201, 204, 216
concrete other, 89, 94–95, 160
conception of the self, 9, 45–51, 52–53, 55, 63–64, 74, 115
Connolly, William, 215–19
consensus, 211; false consensus, 212–15
consent, 80–84, 114–15, 156, 164, 212; circularity of consent, 82, 84, 95–97, 164, 211

consociationalism, 185, 188
contractarianism, 38, 42, 45, 74
Cover, Robert, 7

Dahl, Robert, 190
deliberation, 195
democratic individuality, 180, 182, 185–87
democratic self-education, 201–3
democracy, 99, 118, 190–210; participatory democracy, 90, 95, 148, 204–6
dependence, 132, 142
difference, 163, 185, 202, 216; "natural" differences, 172–78; real vs. social interpretation, 169
discourse, 74, 109, 112, 144, 164, 212; generalized discourse, 97, 156–57, 170; unconstrained discourse 87–95
discourse ethics, 87–88
discrimination, 167, 172–73, 185
Doppelt, Gerald, 52–56
Durkheim, E., 10, 15

Ellwood, David, 135
Elster, Jon, 137, 208
equal respect, 60, 147, 153
equal social worth, 69
equal treatment, 147, 163, 167, 176, 178
equality, 16; juridical, 68
Esping-Anderson, Gosta, 141
Euben, Peter, 20, 193, 195
"exit," 179–80

false universality, 149–62
family law, 64–66
Fay, Brian, 201
Feinberg, Joel, 64, 111–12
Foucault, Michel, 211
Fox-Genovese, Elizabeth, 178
Fraser, Nancy, 181, 188, 200–203
freedom, 81–83

233